the digital photographer's
notebook

A Pro's Guide to Adobe Photoshop CS3, Lightroom, and Bridge

bring back
the sky
and clouds

black and white conversion

color balance

location photography

card 07

KEVIN AMES

THE DIGITAL PHOTOGRAPHER'S NOTEBOOK

A Pro's Guide to Adobe Photoshop CS3, Lightroom, and Bridge

KEVIN AMES

Peachpit
Press

The Digital Photographer's Notebook:
A Pro's Guide to Adobe Photoshop CS3,
Lightroom, and Bridge
Kevin Ames

Peachpit Press
1249 Eighth Street
Berkeley, CA 94710
510/524-2178
510/524-2221 (fax)

Find us on the Web at www.peachpit.com
To report errors, please send a note to
errata@peachpit.com

Peachpit Press is a division of Pearson Education

ACQUISITIONS EDITOR
Nancy Ruenzel

EDITOR
Ted Waitt

PRODUCTION EDITOR
Hilal Sala

PROOFREADER
Dustin Hannum

INTERIOR DESIGN
Mimi Heft

COMPOSITOR
Kim Scott, Bumpy Design

INDEXER
James Minkin

COVER DESIGN
Aren Howell

COVER IMAGES
Kevin Ames

ISBN-13 978-0-321-35841-7

ISBN-10 0-321-35841-4

9 8 7 6 5 4 3 2 1

Printed and bound in the United States of America

Dedication

Once more...
for Little Bear
and David Chapman

Acknowledgments

Thanking everyone who has contributed directly or tangentially to the creation of a book is, for me, one of the best things about being an author and one of the most daunting—which, no doubt, explains why it is one of the last parts of a book I write. The thing I love about a book's acknowledgments is that they are the publishing world's credit roll to all who have made the work possible. And, as in movies, they are often overlooked by readers intent on getting into the first chapter. There are so many wonderful people who have, in ways large and small, made a difference in my life and, therefore, become a part of this book. Please take a couple of minutes to read about some of the people who have helped make this a book a reality.

First, I want to thank Scott Kelby who, during lunch at the PEI Digital Conference in March of 2002, asked me to write a feature on digital asset management for *Photoshop User*. That led to my writing a regular column—"The Digital Photographer's Notebook"—and was the genesis of the book you now hold in your hands.

For her amazing support, wisdom, love, and friendship, I once again thank Starr Moore. And again, I could not have done this without you.

To David Chapman, manager of Pro Photo Resources here in Atlanta, thank you for your continued conversations on workflow, digital photography, life, and all of the great work you do for the photographic community.

At the National Association of Photoshop Professionals, my heartfelt thanks go to my editors past and present, Chris Main, Barbara Thompson, Mike Mackenzie, and Isaac Stolzenbach. Also Kathy Siler, Dave Moser, Larry Becker, Felix Nelson, Melinda Gotelli, Dave Cross, Matt Kloskowski, and Corey Baker, as well as the entire staff who publish the magazine and produce Photoshop World, especially Julie Stephenson and Barbie Taylor.

At Peachpit Press, huge kudos go to Ted Waitt, my editor for the *Notebook*. Ted is engaging, generous, and at times sadistically delighted to ask the incisive question that causes massive rewrites and results in a far superior book. Also to publisher Nancy Ruenzel and senior editor Pam Pfiffner.

In my mind, the most wonderful contribution digital has made to photography is that photographers are now sharing ideas, techniques, and even clients. Those who have shared with me from the early days are Jim DiVitale and Eddie Tapp. Thanks, guys.

I am privileged to share ideas with many talented, gifted instructors and friends...Ben Willmore, Katrin Eismann, Bert Monroy, Julieanne Kost, Peter Bauer, Jack Davis, Joe Glyda, Taz Tally, Terry White, Deke McClelland, Terry White, Vincent Versace, Jeff Schewe, and Michael Ninness. Special extra thanks to Michael for helping with the original organization of the book.

Thanks, too, to members of the photographic and digital imaging industry, especially Linda Collins, Gary Burns, David Burns, Thann Clark of Software Cinema, Diane Moore, Scott Rawlings, Peter Dietrich, Wes Maggio and "Techman Joe" Sliger of Wacom Technologies, Janice Wendt, Josh Haftel, Ed Sanchez, and Tony Corbel of nik software. Thanks, too, to Tony for making my author's portrait.

Special thanks and industrial-strength kudos to Thomas Knoll, John Nack, Addy Roff, Russell Williams, Scott Beyer, Tom Hogarty, and George Jardine for answering myriad questions and to the entire Photoshop and Lightroom teams at Adobe Systems for constantly improving the tools we have and creating the new ones that make photography the rewarding profession it has become.

There are many wonderful restaurants in Atlanta. Three of them have been involved in my book writing from the beginning. Thanks to Everybody's Pizza in Virginia Highlands for great pizza and cold Stella, and for always asking, "How's the *Notebook* coming along?"; to Aurora Coffee for the brew that keeps creativity flowing; and to Stephen, Shera, and the staff at Java Jive on Ponce for breakfasts well worth the wait and for being the best place to review proofs of this book. When you find yourself in my city, these places are truly worth a visit.

For wisdom and guidance through the years, as well as friendship, camaraderie, and that oh-so-vital encouragement, my thanks goes to Kevin Hyde, Traci Jordan, Dave Cruickshanks, and Victoria Wojciechowski.

In memoriam...thanks to all of the photographers who have left us...including my mother, Janette Guthmann Ames, Dean Collins, Richard Avedon, Helmut Newton, and Eddie Adams. We are all richer for their images and inspiration.

To Bruce Fraser for his quiet inspiration and encouraging words over many years.

The most important thank you is always the last one. It is to you, gentle reader, for spending your time with *The Digital Photographer's Notebook*. I look forward to hearing what you think of it. My email address is kevin@amesphoto.com.

About the Author

Kevin Ames is president of Ames Photographic Illustration, Inc., a studio that specializes in commercial photography, retouching, and post-production services. Based in Atlanta, Kevin's clients include Westin Hotels, AT&T, and Coca-Cola.

A professional photographer for over thirty years, Kevin made the transition to the digital age in 1993. Equally masterful behind the camera and in front of the monitor, Kevin is a highly sought after trainer for both the photographic and the digital arts. His assignments, workshops, and seminars have taken him to art schools and conferences around the world.

The Digital Photographer's Notebook is Kevin's fourth book. He has been writing the column of the same name for *Photoshop User* magazine since 2002. His previous books include *Digital SLR Photography with Photoshop CS2 for Dummies* and *The Art of Photographing Women* (for both Photoshop CS and Photoshop CS2). He also creates online training and DVDs for Software Cinema.

Find Kevin on the web at amesphoto.com.

Contents

PART 1　ACQUISITION: FROM

PART 2　MANAGEMENT: FROM

Introduction

THE LAST TEN YEARS span both centuries and millenniums. It is completely appropriate that during this time of transition, photography has grown from it roots in film emulsions developed chemically to electronic capture and digital image processing. In less than a generation, the world of digital—zeros and ones—has moved photographic possibilities that were merely dreams in the eighties and early nineties to being almost commonplace.

Change is the herald, a clarion call of opportunity. The possibilities are truly astounding. A photographic project can be shot, edited, retouched, and uploaded to a server for delivery in hours instead of the weeks it took with traditional or even hybrid film/digital methods. Photographers today face the daunting and always rewarding task of embracing the promise and challenges of ever-evolving digital tools for creating their imagery.

One of photography's major challenges today is the intangibility of a freshly captured digital negative. At that moment, it is in a most delicate, vulnerable state. It is nothing more than zeros and ones stored on the volatile magnetic media of either a memory card or hard drive.

The Digital Photographer's Notebook is and isn't a compilation of my columns of the same name published in *Photoshop User*. The magazine columns are snapshots of the state of the art of digital photography, combined with my thinking on how to use it at the time of their writing. This book restates the issues, updates the thought processes, and presents them in light of the latest and newest tools: Adobe Photoshop CS3 and Adobe Photoshop Lightroom. Longtime readers of the magazine will see familiar subject matter recast in the latest digital techniques. New readers will benefit from an organized presentation of topics that is not possible in magazines.

The first section of *The Digital Photographer's Notebook* is concerned with making photographs: shooting on location or in the studio, inspiration, and lighting.

Next up is getting the digital negatives from volatile media in the camera or computer into secure archives so they can be easily found and accessed for further work in Photoshop.

The third section shows how to enhance photographs for color and exposure. It goes on to build web galleries to share them with the world over the Internet. It explains, step by step, how to create self-running PDF presentations that are small enough to email, as well as large, bold, custom proof sheets.

The last section is photography and Photoshop—dealing with the "what-ifs" of creativity, black-and-white conversions, shooting for post-production in Photoshop, some more lighting (this time without lights), and some I-use-these-all-the-time retouching techniques.

Photography is the true subject of *The Digital Photographer's Notebook*. Everything I do in Photoshop begins in the camera. I do not believe that anything can be "fixed" in Photoshop any more than it could be "fixed" in the darkroom. Digital post-production is about enhancement and efficiency. I move into Photoshop only when it is more effective time-wise than it is at the camera. Keep in mind that the techniques and problem solving in Photoshop shown in the *Notebook* are done as enhancements that are either impossible or impractical to do with the camera.

Photography means *light writing*. Photoshop means *light working*. Bend light as much as you can at the camera. Then—and only then—hone it in post. Most important of all, keep shooting.

Kevin Ames
July 20, 2007
Atlanta, Georgia

PART ONE

Acquisition:
From Capture to Computer

The digital photograph begins in the camera and migrates to the computer faster than is imaginable…

CHAPTER 1

Out in Africa

IT'S AUGUST, 2001. Saroni, a Maasai warrior, and I walk across the border into Tanzania. We climb a hill to watch the sun setting on Mount Kilimanjaro. An eagle flies into our view from the right, sweeping across Kili, then around us, and finally lands behind us in the top of a tree (**Figure 1.1**). It watches us in its kingdom. Saroni and I sit enjoying the solitude. Africa is a very powerful, spiritual place. In the quietly fading light, we stand up and take turns making photographs of each other with the mountain. The sun sets. Darkness surrounds us, and stars light our way back to camp.

FIGURE 1.1

FIGURE 1.2

FIGURE 1.3

I boot up my Apple PowerBook and insert the Microdrive holding the RAW files of the afternoon's shoot. Images of acacia trees (also called yellow fever trees due to the distinctive color of their bark), impala, Saroni, and, of course, Kilimanjaro appear on the screen (**Figure 1.2**). Saroni's photograph of me holding his spear and walking stick is a favorite (**Figure 1.3**), then the shot of Saroni with his spear in front of Kili jumps off the screen and reaches out to me. The day is a brilliant success for capturing just this one image (**Figure 1.4**).

I marvel at how something I shot a couple of hours ago and a hundred kilometers from the nearest photo lab is now displayed in full color and high resolution on my Mac. Scrolling through the photographs I am in awe of how so much has changed so quickly in the world of photography and how little things have changed here in Amboseli. Change is good and not good, all at the same time.

I have been out in Africa for almost three weeks.

I stay in my tent because night belongs to the wild animals. As long as I am there they leave me alone. Elephants, lions, and leopards wander among our tents throughout the night. The night is quiet of the sounds of man. No radio, television, traffic, or airplanes disturb the stillness. The stillness is natural and yet not silent: Wind rustles the leaves, insects buzz, birds chirp, and animals call out. Falling into sleep, my mind goes back to all the preparation for a digital photographic safari and then to the first game drive into the Maasai Mara....

Digital Safari

Trip planning started eight months earlier, in January, 2001. On top of all the things one does to prepare for an African safari—getting vaccinations, buying special clothing, and the like—I faced the

FIGURE 1.4

daunting challenge of taking brand-new digital technology into a land with practically no electricity. From the beginning, it was clear that the cigarette lighter sockets in the Land Cruisers would be kept busy charging batteries for the video cameras belonging to my safari mates. I had to come up with an electric generator small and safe enough to take on an airliner and that could recharge the camera batteries and the PowerBook.

Kenya sits on the equator, and the sun is always high in the sky, making it perfect for solar power. Two notebook-sized 12-volt solar panels provided all the power necessary to recharge the camera batteries, the PowerBook, and its spare battery. I set the camera batteries and PowerBook in a camp chair and covered them with a towel to shield them from the sun and provide cooling air

FIGURE 1.5

FIGURE 1.6

circulation (**Figure 1.5**). The computer's hard drive stored the RAW digital files. I downloaded files to my two 1-gigabyte IBM Microdrives several times a day. One drive would be busy passing off files while I shot with the other.

The first afternoon in Kenya finds the seven of us transferring our equipment from our Boskovic Beechcraft Super Kingair plane on an airstrip in the Maasai Mara into two custom-built Toyota Land Cruisers driven by our guides, Verity Williams and her daughter Julie. Verity is the first woman to become a director of Kenya's oldest tour company, Ker & Downey Safaris. The first stop is our camp, where we drop our bags in our tents. Then, a little after 5:00 p.m. we embark on our first game drive.

We have ridden no more than fifteen minutes from our camp when Verity pulls over. I am seated in the back seat on the passenger side. She hands me a sandbag and has me roll up my window halfway. "May I suggest that you put this sandbag over the edge of the glass and rest your lens on it?" she says. "Make your game photographs this way. Your view is closer to their eye level. You won't be looking down on the top of their heads." I follow her "suggestion," having realized early on when Verity asks if she can make a suggestion, it is pretty much a commandment from on high.

She plays a tape of baboon calls, and magically a young lion raises his head out of the grass. My safari mates all stand on their seats with their heads and cameras sticking out of the openings in the tops of the trucks and begin shooting and videotaping furiously. I line up the lion in the viewfinder and, sure enough, he stares me right in the eye (**Figure 1.6**). Lots of lions and elephants—this fellow was less than six feet from me (**Figure 1.7**)—and 212 frames later, it is dark. We go back to camp for dinner, drinks, conversation, and sleep.

My sleep is sound, full of peace, contentment, and rest.

I rouse to the call of one of the crew. "Jambo, jambo, your coffee." I wish my alarm clock in Atlanta were as wise in matters of wake-up calls! This morning's coffee finds me considering the tracks and spoor made and left during the night. The size of elephant droppings is a wonder to behold, although not much of one to smell.

Today is my last full day in eastern Africa.

There will be no game drive. Instead, I spend the day in the compound—the *enkang*—photographing Maasai women making beaded jewelry and the young warriors standing by huts the women have made of cow dung.

In the evening, we attend a ceremony during which the teenaged men from several

FIGURE 1.7

enkangs perform the ritual *Ipid* jumping dance, a courting ritual to impress girls dressed in flowing robes and beautiful beads. The occasion takes place on top of a hill just before sunset. Three of us sit in camp chairs. Our driver has also provided a table, fresh popcorn, and cold Tusker beers. The dance begins. Mt. Kilimanjaro is the background. The scene is truly surreal. It's like watching a movie, though with no projector, screen, or speakers. The theatre is Africa herself. The dancers chant, clap, and jump as the sun dips below the horizon, the last rays of light touching Kilimanjaro's glacier. I shoot and shoot, almost filling up my last two gigabytes of space. Afterward, we walk back to camp in the gathering darkness. My time out in Africa is over.

Red dust and RAW files

Kenya is a very dusty place. The ultrafine red particles are everywhere, especially in the Land Cruisers. Their open roofs and half-shut windows resulted in our being covered daily with a fine patina of the powdery dust. The cameras were covered, too. One of my main concerns during the safari was dust getting onto the chip and my having no way to clean it. The Kodak DCS 760 has a filter in front of the mirror cage that kept the sensor dust free. I also worried that the Microdrives would fail due to dust getting inside them. To this day, remnants of that red dust are embedded in the camera and lens grips, and I can't clean them out. The Microdrives still work even though they aren't used often anymore. They are testimony to the quality of the technology at the time.

Fortunately, everything worked flawlessly. Even the 1.3 lens magnification of the 6.1-megapixel sensor worked to my benefit by making my lenses that much longer and bringing the game even closer. The four Nikkor lenses in my kit were the 17-35mm f2.8, 24-120mm f4.5/5.6, a 500mm f/8 mirror telephoto, and an 80-200mm f2.8 with a Nikon 2x teleconverter to make it cover 160-400mm.

I came back to the States with thirty gigabytes of RAW files—3,728 image files, to be exact. They fill forty-five CDs. I review this library of work periodically and pull up images that didn't strike me the first time. As my vision grows, I find new things that I didn't see before. I see things that my subconscious saw and urged me to photograph so I could discover them at a later time.

Better with time

I wrote the preceding words in 2001, many generations past in digital time. My digital photography safari became a reality when Kodak lowered the price of its premier digital cameras by $20,000. At the time, for only $8,000, the best portable digital single lens reflex (DSLR) camera available was the Kodak-Nikon DCS 760. It was built on Nikon's storied F5 body, captured 6.1-megapixel files, and held two Microdrives. The state of the art for laptops then was the Macintosh PowerBook G3. It had a twenty-gigabyte hard drive, a built-in PC card slot, and two bays that could be filled with batteries.

Now that same $8,000 (less, if you adjust for inflation) buys Canon's 1Ds MarkII, a professional-quality full-frame digital camera with almost three times the resolution of the one whose images you see on these pages. Canon is now and has been my camera of choice for quite some time now. Cameras with a resolution of 6.1 megapixels today are considered entry level. They cost less than an eighth of the price of the 760, have lower noise and higher ISOs, and can do time exposures.

In terms of storage, four-gigabyte Microdrives are now available. Today's CompactFlash cards can hold up to eight gigabytes.

The laptop computers available now have larger screens and astoundingly faster processors. The standard hard drive is now 100 gigabytes (rather than 20 gigabytes) with 200-gigabyte hard drives available. Laptops have built-in DVD burners. And the batteries? Now there's room for only one battery. Oh, well; you can't have everything.

Another thing that's better is also kind of mind-blowing: Digital negatives, like good red wines, get better with age. Yep. The longer you have them, the better they become, because the camera manufacturers and software companies keep improving RAW conversion (see the sidebar "What Is RAW Conversion?"). I can get more from a six-year-old RAW file today in Adobe Camera Raw 4 than I could when I shot it. And I can do it inside Photoshop CS3 (Adobe Bridge CS3, actually) instead of having to use Kodak's software (**Figures 1.8** and **1.9**). The RAW converter that came with my Kodak camera could darken the sky by two stops. Camera Raw 4 in Photoshop CS3 allows up to a four-stop exposure reduction as seen in the series of the dancers in Figure 1.9. And that's not even mentioning highlight recovery and fill-light settings. Life keeps getting better!

What a wonderful difference from the old days of photography when traditional film began degrading in quality immediately (albeit slowly) after processing. Now my (and your) digital negatives improve over time. I'll drink to that!

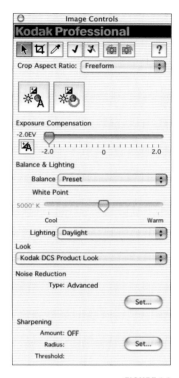

FIGURE 1.8

FIGURE 1.9

WHAT IS RAW CONVERSION?

I'll be referring to *RAW* many times in this book. It's an important development in digital photography. Why? Most RAW files from today's DSLR cameras hold around seven times more information than their JPEG counterparts. The extra data allows the photographer to push or pull the exposure, change the color temperature, and much more when making a Photoshop-editable file in Camera Raw. This process is called *converting* the RAW file.

The big benefit is that RAW converters don't actually convert anything. They make copies based on the settings you control. RAW files aren't changed; they're truly digital negatives. For more specifics on RAW files and the Adobe Camera Raw converter for Photoshop, see Chapter 11.

How to Make White Skies Blue

One of the iconic images of eastern Africa is Maasai warriors performing the ritual jumping dance called the Ipid. As I mentioned earlier, the evening of my last night in that most magical of places found me in the front row, literally, watching this ceremony in a camp chair with a can of Tusker beer and a bowl of fresh, hot, buttered popcorn on the table next to me. The sun was setting, bathing the warriors in warm directional light. Mount Kilimanjaro was in the distant background to my left. Clouds broke the blue sky.

My camera was glued to my eye. I metered to assure proper exposure of the warriors. The ensuing ten minutes were filled with the chants of these agile dancers. My shutter fired again and again and again. Then it was over. Darkness fell, and we walked with the warriors back to camp, surrounded by starlight. The photographs are wondrous. Really. Take my word for it. Except, of course, all the skies are completely blown out. In order to get the exposure on the dancers right, I had to sacrifice the sky behind them. If it had been a commercial shoot, I would have had the budget and logistics to get banks of fill lights and power to balance the dancers with the sky. Of course, this wasn't a commercial job.

Still, it's a nice series of photos. Oh, for goodness sake, would you *listen* to me? Sheesh! I mean, can you say "rationalization"? (Yet haven't we all said, "If only...," about one of our photographs?) I want my blue sky back! Yes, this could be the beginning of a photo tantrum. Then again, maybe there's hope.

Let's see if this situation is as bad as it seems. The Info palette shows the story. Each of the RGB values reads 255. That means pure white—no detail at all. None. White sky. Finished. Done. Game over (**Figure 1.10**).

If I'd been shooting in the JPEG format, it truly would have been "game over." Thanks to capturing in RAW, though, the sky is there. The dynamic range of the file is so large that the monitor just can't display it. RAW files are valuable because they record *all* the data the chip sees when light strikes it and in a significantly higher depth than the 8 bits used in Photoshop. The data is hidden; all I have to do is bring it out and put it together. Here's how:

STEP ONE

Go to my website, www.amesphoto.com/learning, click on the cover of *The Digital Photographer's Notebook* and register with code DPN8414. (The registration helps protect my copyrights.) Be sure to add learning@ amesphoto.com to your email's address book so the activation link email gets through. Once active you can download the files. Downloading the files means that I can keep you updated if changes to the files or more current information develops (as long as you opt in to receive email from me). Open the folder with the samples for this chapter in Adobe Bridge by double-clicking it in the Folders pane. Highlight 1814-3711.dcr, and open it in Adobe Camera Raw 4 (ACR 4) by pressing Command (PC: Ctrl) + R. (Double-clicking the file works too, only then Camera Raw opens in Photoshop CS3 instead of in Bridge. Get in the habit of working in Bridge and saving Photoshop for the heavy lifting. I'll explain all that later.)

STEP TWO

Click the Exposure slider and drag it to the left until it reads –2.00. This is similar to reducing the exposure two stops at the camera. The sky is back, thanks to all the data captured in the RAW file. See how much data is really

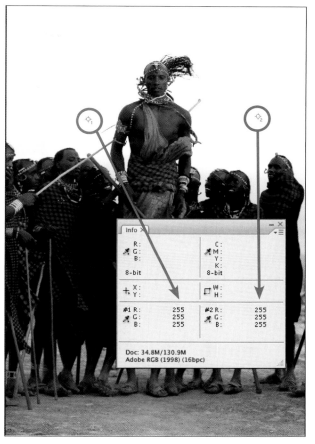

FIGURE 1.10

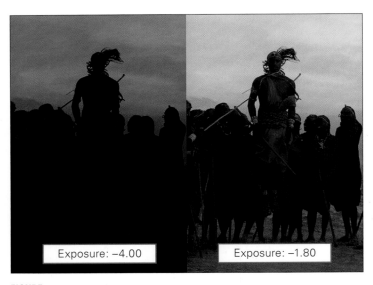

Exposure: −4.00   Exposure: −1.80

FIGURE 1.11

there by moving the Exposure slider all the way to −4.00. The sky is really dark now—too dark to make the photograph believable.

The settings I like and want you to use are Exposure: −1.80, Shadows: 0, Brightness: 39, and Contrast: −23. Leave Saturation set to 0. Click the Workflow Options box. Set Space: Adobe RGB (1998), Depth: 16 Bits/Channel, Size: 2008 by 3032 (6.1 MP), and Resolution: 300 pixels per inch. Click Open. The photograph of the Maasai with the sky opens in Photoshop (**Figure 1.11**).

STEP THREE

Go back to Bridge. 1814-3711.dcr is still highlighted. Press Command (PC: Ctrl) + R to open it again in Camera Raw. Set Exposure: −0.05, Shadows: 0, Brightness: 31, Contrast: +41, and Saturation: 0. Click Open.

STEP FOUR

Choose the Move tool from the toolbox by pressing the V key. Click the bright version of 1814-3711.dcr, and begin dragging it onto the dark version. Press the Shift key and release the mouse to drop the image in perfect register with the dark one. Name the bright layer Transition.

STEP FIVE

Duplicate Transition by pressing Command (PC: Ctrl) + J. Name the layer Normal. Hide Normal by clicking off its Eye icon. Highlight Transition. The layer stack looks like **Figure 1.12**.

FIGURE 1.12

SIZE MATTERS, SO DOES BRIGHTNESS

Subjects, in this case the backlit Maasai warriors, appear smaller due to light wrapping around them. They're slightly bigger in the version where the sky is darker. For this reason, a conventional mask won't work in combining the light version over the darker one. It will leave a dark halo around the transition from light to dark. This is also why ACR 4's Fill Light slider leaves a dark halo.

STEP SIX

Double-click in the blank area to the right of the Transition layer. Doing so opens the Layer Styles dialog box. At the bottom of the Blending Options is the Blend If section. Look for a white highlight slider on the top scale named This Layer. The slider has a line down the middle: Hold down the Option (PC: Alt) key and drag the left half of the slider to the left until it reads 104 (**Figure 1.13**). The darker sky on the layer below blends through the white of the sky. The jumping dancer's hair has detail in it now. Some of the detail, particularly in the highlights, looks dull. The Normal layer will fix that.

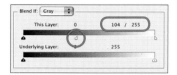

FIGURE 1.13

STEP SEVEN

Press L on the keyboard to choose the Lasso tool. Draw a selection through the heads of the warriors all the way around them, and include the entire foreground (**Figure 1.14**). Feather the selection 10 pixels (Command [PC: Ctrl] + Option [PC: Alt] + D).

NOTE FOR MAC USERS

If this keyboard shortcut doesn't work, it's because the command is assigned to OS X keyboard short-cuts. Here's the fix: Launch System Preferences from the Apple menu. Choose Keyboard and Mouse. Scroll down to Dock, Expose, and Dashboard, and uncheck Hide and Show the Dock. That's the keyboard shortcut Photoshop uses to feather a selection. If you don't want to change your system keyboard, choose Select > Modify > Feather.

FIGURE 1.14

FIGURE 1.15

STEP EIGHT

Highlight Normal. Click the Add Layer Mask icon at the bottom of the Layers palette. The sky is black, and the rest of the foreground determined by the selection is white (**Figure 1.15**). The dancers, their faces, and the hillside in front of them brighten. Areas where the highlight ought to be shining are dull.

FIGURE 1.16

FIGURE 1.17

USING THE TRANSITION LAYER

The smaller size of the warriors caused by the blown-out sky is blended with the darker sky layer below it, thereby revealing the darker sky, bringing back detail in the hair, and transitioning from the underexposed skin tone to the lighter ones. Look at **Figure 1.16**: The highlights that have been blended with their darker counterparts on the Background layer become transparent (as denoted by the checkerboard pattern). Painting white on the layer mask on Normal in Step Nine reveals the properly exposed highlights that were lost to the transparency. See for yourself: Hide and then show the Normal layer, and watch the highlights pop.

STEP NINE

Get a soft-edged brush of about 5 pixels at 100% Opacity. Set the foreground color to white. Zoom in to 200% by pressing Command (PC: Ctrl) + Option (PC: Alt) + 0, and then Command (PC: Ctrl) + +. Carefully paint over the forehead of the dancer to bring back the highlight. Paint over his beads and around the headpiece and his beaded necklaces. Paint over the rest of the bracelets he's wearing. Do the same for the jewelry worn by the other warriors and their teeth and headpieces. If you overpaint, tap the X key to exchange black for white. Brush over your error. Tap X again, and continue painting on the layer mask. White in the mask of the Normal layer shows what's on that layer—in this case, the normally exposed Maasai. The black area hides the white sky on Normal, allowing the darker version on the Background layer to show through.

STEP TEN

Hold down Command (PC: Ctrl) + Option (PC: Alt) + Shift and then press the E key. Doing so makes a copy of the visible layers on a new layer. Name it Final. Save your work, and rejoice in the power of Photoshop and Adobe Camera Raw—together with your skill in front of the computer, they made burned-out white skies blue again (**Figure 1.17**). Say Hallelujah! Your work here is done.

CHAPTER 2

Bridgework

MANAGING DIGITAL FILES from camera to computer used to be an awkward process. To copy image files from Compact-Flash (CF) or other media cards to your computer, you used either Windows Explorer, the Mac Finder, Bridge 1.0, or Photo Mechanic with minimal previews. Renaming those files meant manually retyping names in the Finder or using Bridge's Batch Rename command from the Tools menu. Bridge is a standalone application for browsing, sorting, renaming, and enhancing images, as well as adding metadata, that comes with Photoshop CS3. It's amazingly versatile. I often use it without ever launching Photoshop.

Batch Rename offers three choices: "Rename in same folder," "Move to other folder," or "Copy to other folder." The first renames the files on the CF card—a really *bad* idea. CF cards hate being treated like hard drives—so much, in fact, that they will often corrupt themselves by scrambling their File Allocation Tables out of spite. (A corrupt FAT renders a drive or card unreadable.) The second option copies the files to a designated folder on your computer and then sends the files on the CF card to the trash. Yet another truly bad idea. Bridge's third choice is a step in the right direction, allowing files to be copied from the memory card to a folder on the computer's hard drive.

Adobe Bridge CS3 has an even better answer for safe, efficient digital negative management from the memory card to the computer—Adobe Photo Downloader. Adobe Photo Downloader bridges (pun totally intended) the gap between a digital camera or a memory card and the computer by allowing files to be copied to multiple destinations and renamed, and to have basic metadata added (a copyright notice inside each and every photograph is a very good thing) all at once! It even hands off to Bridge with a window already set to the primary destination folder and—this has to be magic—the photographs appear in their full-color glory.

Back to the future…

Digital photography keeps getting better. Cameras improve. So does software. (Thank you Adobe!) And workflow keeps streamlining, becoming more automatic, easier, and less time consuming.

Notebooks, or journals, are a linear journey through time. Updating "The Digital Photographer's Notebook" columns from *Photoshop User* magazine (some were written when I was using Photoshop 7) for the CS3 version presented a challenge of temporal continuity. In order to share what I'd felt and experienced at the time the images were made, I wanted to keep as much of the original flavor of the photographs and written descriptions as possible.

Suspend your disbelief just a little, then imagine, if you will, that together we step into the WABAC Machine and have Mr. Peabody and Sherman send us back in time to the summer of 2005. Of course, the technology that accompanies us has changed: now we have Intel Core 2 Duo computers loaded with Photoshop CS3.

On Assignment

One weekend in 2005 found me on assignment at Atlanta's twelfth annual Music Midtown Festival to cover the WUPA-TV/96 Rock stage (**Figure 2.1**). The crowd was immense. People pushed to get as close to the stage as they could, so special access was required for making effective photographs. Press passes were given to credentialed photographers so we could shoot the first three songs from a

FIGURE 2.2

FIGURE 2.1

twenty-foot-wide area in front of the stage. I shot between 120 and 180 RAW files during those three songs. Heaven knew I was going to be happy if ten or so shots of each band were truly good.

After the third song, the cadre of photographers, myself included, dutifully left the pit and headed to the next assignment. My destination was the TV station's recreational vehicle to download images from the three 1-gigabyte CF cards I filled during the shoot. I connected a pair of Lexar stackable card readers to my MacBook Pro and loaded the cards into them with Adobe Bridge CS3 already running (**Figure 2.2**).

This is how I manage digital negatives using Adobe Photo Downloader, which comes with Bridge CS3.

STEP ONE

Before importing photographs from memory cards, there is some setup in Bridge's Preferences that will add some functionality. Press Command (PC: Ctrl) + K to open Bridge's Preferences, then click General. In the Behavior section, check the box next to When a Camera is Connected, Launch Adobe

Photo Downloader (**Figure 2.3**). The downloader will launch automatically when either a camera is connected or a card is inserted in a reader attached to your computer.

FIGURE 2.3

STEP TWO

Insert a card in the reader. The Photo Downloader launches. Click on the Advanced Dialog button in the lower left corner. The Source shows how many files are on the card, the size of the download, and the date the images were shot. The preview area is populated with thumbnails of each photograph. An initial edit can be done at this time by unchecking the box at the lower right corner of each image, though I recommend against that (see the "Save 'Em All!" sidebar).

STEP THREE

The Save Options section sets the primary import destination. Spin down the Advanced Options disclosure triangle to designate a place to save a copy of the digital files. My digital negatives are

SAVE 'EM ALL!

The temptation to edit your images at import is great, almost as big as cherry pie à la mode.... It's huge, I tell you. *Resist!* There are places to edit and this just isn't one of them. Get in the habit of importing and saving everything you shoot. Okay, maybe delete the out-of-focus ones of your feet, shot because the shutter went off accidentally as you were looking and pointing at the screen, jumping up and down and screeching, "Oh, Oh-Oh, OH, OH, OH!" (This is known as "chimping.") We all do this—even if we are silent and calm on the outside—when our inner child is hopping and screeching in our heads upon discovering a great shot we made. The only outward sign of our self-satisfaction is a wry grin...and that image of your feet.

From experience, I know that the decisions made in an initial edit are going to change. As I revisit my photography, I see things I truly love that I didn't particularly like the first time around. We change as we grow. Keep all of your options available. Save everything!

Recently, I was helping a friend do some portrait retouching. I needed some extra hair from an image right before or after the one I was working with. Unfortunately, all of the "outtakes" had been discarded. Without those extra files, I couldn't do a great job on the retouch. Hair is really tough (read impossible) to draw in Photoshop—unless you're Bert Monroy, who I am most definitely not!

stored on a RAID as well as backed up to a couple of DVDs—one is kept in the studio, the other is stored in a secure location offsite. The copy made in this step is a temporary backup that gets erased once the DVDs are made. Check Open Adobe Bridge to be ready to begin rating the shoot right away.

STEP FOUR

Rename the files in a meaningful way. The drop-down menu offers lots of choices that mostly include the date. Since the camera imprints each photograph with the date it was made, use Custom and enter a brief description. (You can change this after I share my thoughts on naming conventions for folders and digital negatives in Chapter 7.) Check Preserve Current Filename in XMP. This setting writes the original file name into an XMP "sidecar" file. If a file becomes corrupt, having the original name the camera assigned to the image is useful in finding it on the backup copy.

RAID: REDUNDANT ARRAY OF INEXPENSIVE DRIVES

RAIDs are groups of hard drives configured to do different jobs. One is speed, the other is redundancy. The speed version is called striping (RAID 0). Each drive writes part of the data, handing the next drive another part, and so on. Striped RAIDs are considerably faster than an individual hard drive. The downside: If one drive fails, all of the data is lost.

Mirroring (copying for redundancy) in its simplest form (RAID 1) copies the data onto two drives at once, so each backs up the other. It's safe, though it takes two drives to store what can fit on just one.

Another form of mirroring (RAID 5) distributes the data across four drives of equal size (**Figure 2.4**). The equivalent of three drives stores the data, while the fourth drive contains parity information. When (not if) a drive in a RAID 5 configuration fails, it is replaced and the other three rebuild the information. RAID 5 is safe and efficient. Four 500-gigabyte drives configured for RAID 5 end up yielding about 1.4 terabytes of storage.

FIGURE 2.4

THE NAME GAME

It's tempting to name every file with all the information you imagine ever needing in order to find it again. Think about a filename like joanjett-musicmidtown6122005atlantageorgia.0563.dcr: That would do it for just about any search for our come-back '80s rock star (**Figure 2.5**). There has to be an easier way! And, of course, there is.

The simplest method is to assign an event or job number to each image. I keep a spreadsheet that I use as a journal for my projects. This journal lists a job number, a description, and any other information I may want to remember. I can search the spreadsheet to find the job number and then search in a cataloging program like Adobe Photoshop Lightroom, Extensis Portfolio, or Microsoft's Expression Media (née iView MediaPro 3) to locate the images. For this example, the Music Midtown job number is 2211. Here is what follows the job number.

Dash or underscore. The dash or underscore after the job number is important for finding the file later. A job journal logically starts at 0001. So, if we aren't using a dash or underscore, the twenty-fifth image of the first project is 0001025.nef. A computer search of 0001 returns every image for project 0001 and the first image of every job after that, because the computer finds everything that has 01 in its name. A dash or underscore between the project or job number and the image number isolates the two like this: 0001-001.nef or 0001_001.nef. Telling the computer to find everything that begins with 0001- or 0001_ returns all the images for just that project. The Adobe Photo Downloader uses an underscore to separate the job number from the image sequence number.

Folder name. The next step to easy file finding is to put extra information in the folder name. The three days of the Midtown Music Festival photography featured several bands, from Joan Jett to Def Leppard to Tom Petty to the Killers (**Figures 2.6–2.9**).

I'll add the name of each band to the metadata (see Chapter 6) before I archive the digital negative. My name for the folder of this day's work looks like this: 2211-01 Music Midtown.

FIGURE 2.5

FIGURE 2.6

FIGURE 2.7

FIGURE 2.8

FIGURE 2.9

Parsed, it works this way:

  Job number: 2211-
  Disc number: 01
  Description: Music Midtown

When the folder is cataloged, or imported into Adobe Lightroom, the software picks up the job number and disc number and makes keywords of *Music*, *Midtown*. It also looks in the metadata for more keywords and descriptions. In this case, I will add *Joan*, *Jett*, and *UPN* to the description field in the Metadata tab in Bridge (or to the caption in Lightroom). If I can remember anything

about the project—even the singer's first name—a search on it will find the photographs. Naming folders properly and adding good metadata to files go a long way toward helping you quickly find them years after they were taken.

Note that at the time I shot what turned out to be Atlanta's last Music Midtown, DVDs weren't universal. Files were placed in folders holding between 650 and 680 megabytes of RAW files. Each folder was burned to a CD—so I had seven CDs for a three-day shoot that today would easily fit on two DVDs.

STEP FIVE

Apply metadata to the digital negative. For now, choose Basic Metadata. Chapter 6 shows how to make a template that can be used in this section's menu. It also covers in detail the methods of adding the metadata mentioned in "The Name Game" sidebar. Fill in the Author box with your name. The Copyright field gets the copyright symbol, the year, and your name.

© ON MAC AND WINDOWS

Accessing the copyright symbol is easy. Press Option + G on the Mac. For Windows, hold down the Alt key then type 0169 on the number pad. It won't work with numbers on the keyboard. Oh, make sure the Num Lock key is down.

FIGURE 2.10

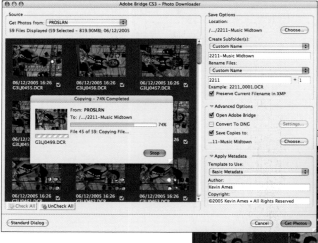

STEP SIX

Click Get Photos. The Photo Downloader does the heavy lifting while showing you a preview of the files being copied (**Figure 2.10**). When copying is complete, Photo Downloader thoughtfully opens a Bridge window to the primary import folder (**Figure 2.11**).

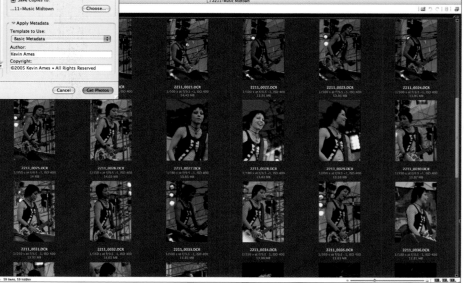

FIGURE 2.11

STEP SEVEN

You probably won't have this problem with your photos; on mine it seems that somehow the color balance in the camera was set to tungsten. (How in the world could that have happened, Kevin?) So they are ever so slightly blue. Alright, they are through and through blue. I should have checked the white balance on the camera before I shot. So sue me. (Had this been shot on film, most likely I would have been sued....)

Fortunately, the digital negatives are all RAW, so there's a fix. Press Command (PC: Ctrl) + A (Edit > Select All) to highlight all of the true-blue photographs of Joan and the Blackhearts. Press Command (PC: Ctrl) + R (File > Open in Camera Raw...) to open all of them in Adobe Camera Raw 4 (ACR 4). Next, press Command (PC: Ctrl) + A to highlight all of the thumbnails in the Filmstrip (by the way, seeing as this is digital, wouldn't "Thumbstrip" make more sense?) or click the Select All button in the upper left corner. Click the White Balance menu and choose Daylight (**Figure 2.12**). The blue disappears and all is once again good and golden, or at least natural. Best of all, the lawyers have to find another target.

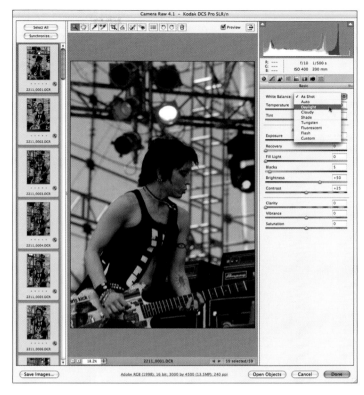

FIGURE 2.12

The digital negatives are now on two hard drives, awaiting a bit more metadata, some enhancements, and permanent archiving. That comes later. The next chapter is about how to shoot directly into Bridge without any memory cards at all.

CHAPTER 3

Shooting Tethered: Instant Gratification

THE ABSOLUTE HOTTEST, coolest (insert whichever temperature turns you on), and all-around best part of making photographs digitally is the instant gratification of seeing the image just shot—right now. Thanks to Reed Hoffman for the portrait of me in my studio (**Figure 3.1**).

FIGURE 3.1

Digital capture offers the photographer many choices when it comes to checking results during the shoot. The most common is the LCD monitor on the back of the camera itself. While this is useful for checking that an image has been recorded, the amount of information is not as helpful as it could be—especially when shooting RAW files. The preview is a JPEG, after all. Another and much more accurate way to get high-quality feedback is to pull the memory card out of the camera and open up the images in Bridge, then check the files in Adobe Camera Raw. This works well enough, although it is a bit slow.

MEMORY CARD ALERT!

A word of warning—if you access your images from the memory card, make sure that the Use Centralized Cache preference is selected (Command [PC: Ctrl] + K, then choose Advanced) so that Bridge CS2 (if you're working in CS2) will not write any cache files to the memory card. For Bridge CS3, deselect the Automatically Export Caches To Folders When Possible checkbox (**Figure 3.2**). Memory cards are quite finicky and don't like to be written to by computers, which can actually corrupt the card.

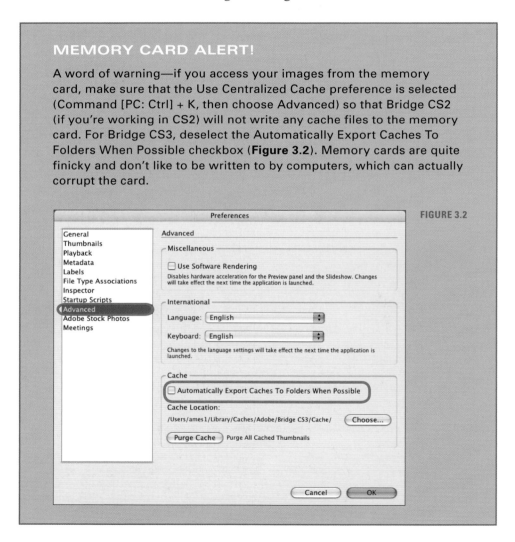

FIGURE 3.2

Into the Computer

The hands-down hottest and coolest (yes, that's both temps at once), totally superlative choice for getting maximum feedback on the fly is to shoot your digital SLR right into your computer. This is called shooting tethered. It works with either a desktop or tower in the studio or a laptop in the field.

Flashback to photography's future...

Back in the day of yester-century—you remember: around eight short years ago—when digital capture was in its infancy, the only way to capture big files was to connect the camera to a computer with a cable. The capture would transfer from camera to computer, which would process the file into its particular flavor of RAW for even more processing later in the manufacturer's converter. Lots of information was available, including the ability to see the photograph on a big screen at a 100% view. Clients (used to seeing Polaroid proofs then waiting for film) would ask, "When can I see the finals?" It was so much fun to point at the monitor and say, "How about right now?" We could even open it in Photoshop, too. Life was very good indeed. Now, the tools in Bridge allow us to fine-tune the white balance; adjust the exposure, brightness, contrast, clarity, and vibrance; use the Loupe tool to check sharpness; and so much more.

...and its past

Fast forward to the new millennium—the holy grail became making digital shooting just like film (that was supposed to be a good thing). Photographers went ape shooting a lot of stuff to memory cards and checking the results on the camera's screen. When they loved what they saw, they did their chimping dance. I told you: They went ape. Chimping is now standard practice, though usually without the jumping and hollering. Few photographers realize it is possible to tether their DSLR to a computer. Fewer still understand that tethering is a wonderful way to remain in the moment as photographs are made.

> ### SOFTWARE FOR TETHERING
>
> Canon and Fuji DSLR cameras come with tethering software. Nikons use Nikon Camera Control Pro ($79.95). There are other packages available that provide tethering functionality, including Capture One from Phase One ($499.00 from www.phaseone.com) and Bibble Pro from Bibble Labs ($129.95 from www.bibblelabs.com). Capture One supports and controls Canon digital SLRs. Bibble Pro tethers Canon, Nikon, and Kodak DSLR cameras, providing file transfer support without camera controls.

The setup

The threefold beauty of tethering allows the camera to shoot into the computer's hard drive (providing more storage room for images than even the largest memory card) to see the photographs as they pop up in Bridge, and to fine-tune them for exposure and white balance in Adobe Camera Raw. Best of all, it's really easy to set up.

FIGURE 3.3

STEP ONE

Create a folder named Capture on the desktop of your computer. Set up the capture software according to the instructions provided by the manufacturer. Browse in the capture software to the Capture folder and choose it. It's interesting and useful to note that software written by the camera manufacturers will often allow you to set the shutter speed, ISO, and aperture of the camera from the computer. Some, like Canon's EOS Capture, even allow you to shoot the camera from the computer as well (**Figure 3.3**).

STEP TWO

Launch Adobe Bridge CS3 from Photoshop CS3 by clicking on the Go to Bridge icon in the Options bar (**Figure 3.4**). Choose the same Capture folder you created in Step One from Bridge's Folders pane.

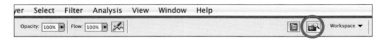

FIGURE 3.4

STEP THREE

Click on the Thumbnails View icon next to the size slider at the bottom of the Bridge window, or choose View > As Thumbnails. Move the Thumbnail size slider all the way to the right to display them as big as possible.

STEP FOUR

I strongly recommend starting each new lighting setup by shooting a reference like the GretagMacbeth ColorChecker Gray Scale balance card. The thumbnail will appear in Bridge. Click on it, then press Command (PC: Ctrl) + R to open the file in Camera Raw. Choose the 100% zoom level to check the focus by viewing the actual pixels (**Figure 3.5**). Fine-tune the white balance and adjust the exposure, brightness, contrast, and saturation in Camera Raw. (For more on setting the correct exposure in Adobe Camera Raw, see Chapter 13.)

FIGURE 3.5

STEP FIVE

Set the adjustments as the default setting for the rest of the shoot by choosing Save New Camera Raw Defaults from the Basic tab's flyout menu (**Figure 3.6**). Now all the settings are applied to your photographs as they are captured, saving a huge amount of time!

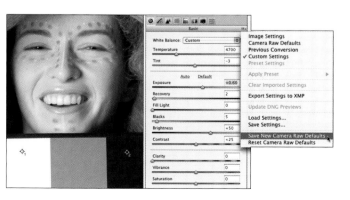

FIGURE 3.6

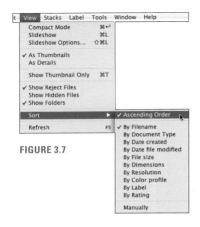

FIGURE 3.7

STEP SIX

By default, Bridge displays the lowest image number first and then populates the screen with the higher numbers. In order to view the latest image, you have to scroll down constantly. Here's the fix. Go to View > Sort and uncheck Ascending Order (**Figure 3.7**). Bridge now displays the most recent photograph in the upper left corner of the light box.

In the studio

I always shoot tethered when I am in the studio. I have a computer on a rolling cart with a large monitor so I can check my work as I shoot. Art directors and clients love seeing the images appear as the camera fires. They know when the shoot is over that I have captured exactly the image they want. Shooting tethered gives on-the-fly feedback, as in this project for Toni & Guy Salons (**Figure 3.8**).

FIGURE 3.8

CHECKING FOCUS

One of the great new tools in Bridge is the Loupe. It works in the Preview pane. Select several thumbnails in the Content pane. They display side by side in the Preview pane. Move your mouse over an image. The cursor acts as a magnifying glass. Click on an area that you want to see larger and the Loupe appears with a 100% (actual pixels) view. Each image displayed in the Preview pane can have its own Loupe. Click in the image to add a Loupe. Click the pointed corner of the Loupe then drag to move it (**Figure 3.9**). I prefer moving it this way, although the tool can be dragged by clicking anywhere inside it, as well. When the Loupe nears an edge it will automatically rotate around the pointed corner to give a full view. Click outside the Loupe to dismiss it.

Hit the + sign to increase the magnification. Tapping the – key reduces the magnification. Press the Command (PC: Ctrl) key then tap either + or – to increase or decrease magnification on all of the visible Loupes. Be aware that an image examined at 200% is going to look a bit fuzzy. Avoid the mistake of eliminating an image from the shoot for this reason by checking the magnification of the Loupe next to the image name at the bottom of the photograph. The active Preview's image name is highlighted.

When you find a photograph that just isn't sharp, Command-click (PC: Ctrl-click) it in the Content pane and it will disappear from the Preview pane. The Loupe, in combination with the Content and Preview panes, is a powerful editing tool. During the shoot, it can't be beat for ensuring that each image is tack sharp.

FIGURE 3.9

FIGURE 3.10

On location

Tethering works with a laptop on location, too. Shooting landscapes or building exteriors is an exercise in patience as you wait for the light to get "just right." The feedback on the laptop assures me that the photograph is exposed properly with the right white balance. An added bonus is that if the software can control the camera, too, then the laptop becomes a remote release (**Figure 3.10**).

Now you know tethering can be done, how cool (and hot) it really is, and how to set up Bridge CS3 and Camera Raw 4 to take advantage of it. The feedback you get will make your photographs better because you'll see things you missed in the viewfinder. So dig into the box your DSLR came in and find the disc of tethering software, load it up, and get into the world of maximum photographic feedback.

Lightroom for tethering

Lightroom is Adobe's new kid on the block, a tool created just for photographers that imports, catalogs, and exports digital photographs as slideshows, websites, or prints.

It's important to know that Lightroom, Bridge CS3, and Photoshop CS3 play very well together. Lightroom and Bridge do many of the same things: renaming, adding metadata, enhancing, sorting, and rating photographs to name a few. They differ in that Lightroom is a database while Bridge is a file browser. Lightroom catalogs and maintains thumbnails of photographs along with their metadata in a database that can be searched even if the source files are not available. Bridge can't do this; it always has to see the source files.

Since importing photography is one of Lightroom's primary jobs, asking it to shoot tethered makes a lot of sense. Lightroom is easy to use in a tethered workflow. It interacts well with Bridge and has the added advantage of cataloging digital photographs as they are created (as we'll see with the image in **Figure 3.11**). This makes finding them later a snap.

FIGURE 3.11

Setting up Lightroom

STEP ONE

Make sure that the Capture folder created for Bridge earlier in this chapter is empty. Lightroom cannot work with a populated Capture folder.

Open Lightroom and choose File > Auto Import > Enable Auto Import.

STEP TWO

Once again, go to File > Auto Import and this time choose Auto Import Settings…. Set the Capture folder as the Watched Folder. Lightroom monitors this folder and anything that is added to it is moved to the chosen Destination. Here's where Lightroom really helps in a workflow. As the files are moved, Lightroom renames them and adds metadata. (For more on renaming, see "The Name Game" sidebar in Chapter 2. Then get the complete details in Chapter 7.) Under the File Naming section, click the menu button named Filename (the default setting) and choose Edit… to open the Filename Template Editor. The token Filename is highlighted. Remove it by pressing the Delete (PC: Backspace) key. Click the Insert button in the Custom Text section. Click after the Custom Text token in the Example section just under the Preset menu at the top of the dialog. Type a dash (-) or an underscore (_). Click the Sequence # (1) menu under Numbering and choose Sequence # (0001). This sets a four-digit counter for the image number. Finally, click the Preset menu, choose Save Current Settings as New Preset… and name it Project Number-Image Number. Click Create. The Preset will be available any time this catalog is open (**Figure 3.12**).

FIGURE 3.12

STEP THREE

Custom color and exposure corrections can be added to each file during their import into Lightroom. Here I included a GretagMacbeth ColorChecker chart and used it to white balance the photograph as well as to fine-tune the exposure. How to make those corrections is covered in Chapter 13. Create a Develop preset for the shoot in Lightroom's Develop module by clicking the + sign in the header of the Presets pane. The New Develop Preset dialog box opens. Check the controls you want included. Name the preset; I use the project number. Click Create to save the preset (**Figure 3.13**). It will appear in the Presets pane.

FIGURE 3.13

STEP FOUR

Choose the new preset for the Develop Settings in the Auto Import Settings. When the project is finished, I'll delete it by highlighting it then clicking the – sign.

STEP FIVE

All of the basic metadata containing the photographer's name, contact information, copyright notice, and usage rights is added to each image's metadata as Lightroom imports it. Choose the appropriate metadata template from the drop-down menu. Chapter 6 explains metadata in detail and gives step-by-step guidance in creating templates for use in Bridge and Lightroom. Choose the template that contains your basic name, contact info, copyright, and usage. Click OK. Now every photograph made moves from the camera to the watched folder, Capture; Lightroom imports it to the folder specified in the Copy To section (**Figure 3.14**).

FIGURE 3.14

PRESETTING ACR 4 FOR LIGHTROOM

Lightroom honors the current Camera Raw default. Open the file in Camera Raw in Bridge, then follow the steps in Chapter 13 to color balance and refine the exposure. Choose Save New Camera Raw Defaults from the Basic tab's flyout menu (**Figure 3.15**). As Lightroom imports digital photographs, it applies the new settings.

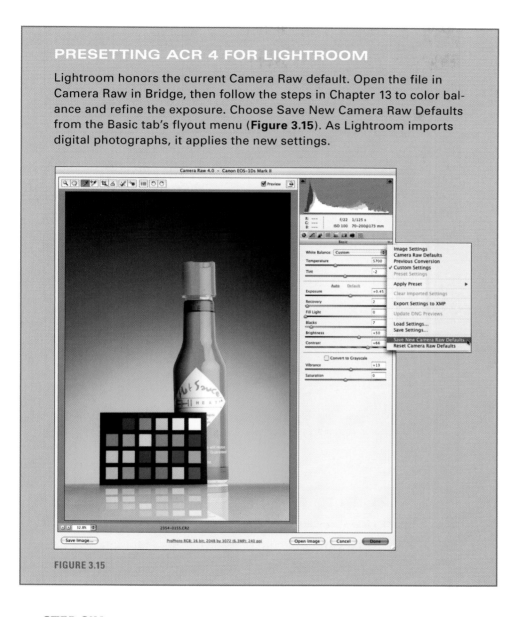

FIGURE 3.15

STEP SIX

Click on the Library module or press G for the Grid. In a product shoot like this one, the UPC number of each item is as important as its name. It is very useful to the designers and product managers who receive the photographs to have it as part of the metadata. After a product or group has been finished, click on the first thumbnail in the series then spin down the Metadata panel. Show the IPTC core pane. In the Caption field, add the product name, its UPC code, and any other pertinent info such as the company's catalog number. Choose Metadata > Copy Metadata from the menu. The Copy Metadata dialog appears. The keyboard shortcut is Command (PC: Ctrl) + Option (PC: Alt) + Shift + C. Click Check None, then check Caption. Highlight the rest of the images in the series by Shift-clicking the last one. Choose Metadata > Paste Metadata or press Command (PC: Ctrl) + Option (PC: Alt) + Shift + V. All of the shots of the same product now have the product name and UPC code in the caption (**Figure 3.16**).

Lightroom is a great tool for digital photographers who want less fuss behind the monitor so they can get back to the camera. The *Notebook* explores Lightroom's features throughout the rest of the book and specifically in Chapters 9 and 12.

FIGURE 3.16

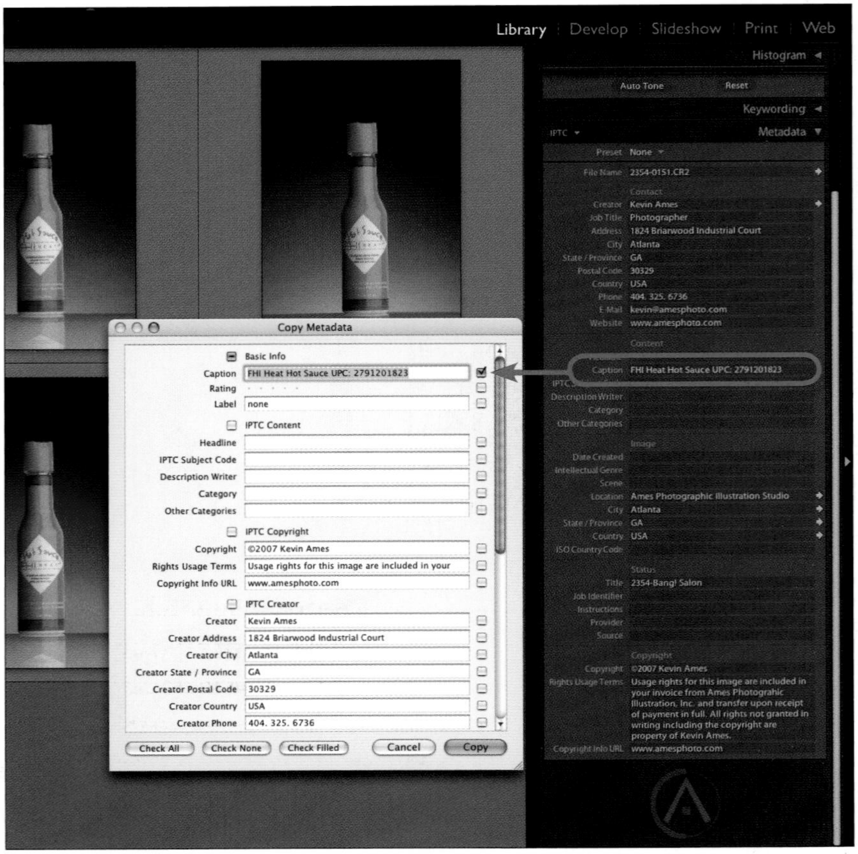

CHAPTER 4

Light Right!

PHOTOGRAPHY HAS UNDERGONE an earth-shattering sea change in its transition from film to digital. At the same time, the foundation of photography—light—remains the same. Photography literally means "light writing," which means that photographers are light writers. The ability to bend light to our vision is what makes us photographers. After all, anyone can buy a high-quality digital camera. Very few can light a subject well. You might say light writers light right.

Eye versus Camera

It all starts with how our brain sees light—and how the camera records it. Adding to the complexity is that what your camera records may not be possible to reproduce on the printed page. Here's how it breaks down.

The range of light on a bright sunny day is too wide to capture detail in both the shadows and highlights with a camera, whether digital or film-based. This fact doesn't seem to jibe with how the brain handles visual processing. When we look at a scene that has too wide a range, the brain looks first at the brightest areas. It remembers the details in the highlights and midtones, then it tells the pupils to widen to see what's in the shadows. The brain combines the two images—the lightest and the darkest—in real time, allowing us to think we see a wider range of brightness than we really do. In other words, the brain is doing Photoshop on the fly. Who knew?

Digital cameras can record a wider range of brightness than film can. That's good. The problem is that printers can't begin to reproduce the brightness range of film, much less that of digital. There is a range of brightness of light that can be printed that will give detail in the highlights and shadows at the same time. A good inkjet printer can hold detail if the image has RGB numbers of around 25 to 40 in the shadows and a range of 242 to 249 or so in the highlights. Printing from Lightroom works the same, except the RGB values are presented as percentages. From 7% to 95% will provide a brightness range of reproducible shadow and highlight detail. Your printer, ink, and paper combination will also affect the results. Newer printers can extend that range on glossy or luster papers. Fine art papers, matte, watercolor, or canvas have smaller ranges between highlight and shadow detail. If the RGB number reads lower or higher when sampled, detail must be sacrificed in either the shadows or the highlights. Digital cameras today have sophisticated built-in software to help with setting exposures that return fairly consistent quality images. The algorithms tell the camera which end of the brightness range to favor and which to discard. The usual bias is to keep detail in the highlights and let the shadows go dark. It's a good compromise for point-and-shoot situations.

LIGHTROOM NUMBERS

Lightroom's engineers (along with about half a million beta testers) took a fresh look at everything digital photographers do. Then they asked, "Does this really make sense?" One of the items that didn't make sense was how Red, Green, and Blue values are displayed. Lightroom shows RGB data as percentages. So 0% is black and 100% is white. Photoshop and Bridge show 0 as black and 255 as white. Photographers used to the 0–255 system can be confused by Lightroom's percentages. A workaround is to multiply the percentage reading in Lightroom by 2.56 to convert to the familiar 0-255 scale. So 97.3% in Lightroom is 249 RGB. And 25 in the RGB world is not quite 10% in Lightroom speak. Graphics in *The Digital Photographer's Notebook* will show both numbers where appropriate.

In **Figure 4.1**, Photoshop and Camera Raw RGB numbers are shown across the top. The equivalent Lightroom values are at the bottom. There are twenty-one steps in this grayscale between complete black and paper white. How many can you count? For comparison, a continuous tone grayscale runs through the middle of the step wedges.

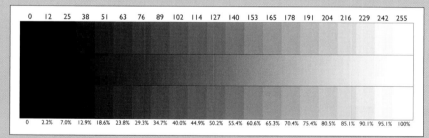

| 0 | 12 | 25 | 38 | 51 | 63 | 76 | 89 | 102 | 114 | 127 | 140 | 153 | 165 | 178 | 191 | 204 | 216 | 229 | 242 | 255 |

| 0 | 2.2% | 7.0% | 12.9% | 18.6% | 23.8% | 29.3% | 34.7% | 40.0% | 44.9% | 50.2% | 55.4% | 60.6% | 65.3% | 70.4% | 75.4% | 80.5% | 85.1% | 90.1% | 95.1% | 100% |

FIGURE 4.1

Specular highlights—catchlights in the eyes, or sun glinting off a chrome bumper—are reflections of the source of light. They have no detail and don't count when considering the tones for printing. When printed they appear as paper white.

The photographer's job is to use light to control (and often compress) the brightness range so both subtle shadows and highlights shine through. Lighting starts with exposure.

Exposure and metering

Exposure, or the amount of light that hits your camera's sensor, reveals the *diffused value* or true tone of the subject. That's simple to say and a bit trickier to do, especially with a digital camera. There are two methods of reading light to determine exposure. One measures light after it has already lit the subject, bounced off, and is on its way to the camera. The other measures the light before it hits the subject. The first method is *reflected* metering. It interprets the amount of light that has already illuminated the subject. The second is called *incident* metering because it measures light before it reaches the subject. Let's look at each in turn.

Reflected metering

Reflected meters are the kind that are built into cameras. This type of meter sets a default exposure that returns a middle gray value, or RGB numbers of around 127 (Lightroom: 50.2%). If your camera's meter reads a white value, the meter tells the camera to underexpose the scene by 2⅔ stops so that it yields the desired middle gray. Pointing the meter at a black value results in a two-stop overexposure so that it once again results in middle gray (**Figure 4.2**). Reflected meters return an exposure value equal to 12.5% gray on any value they read.

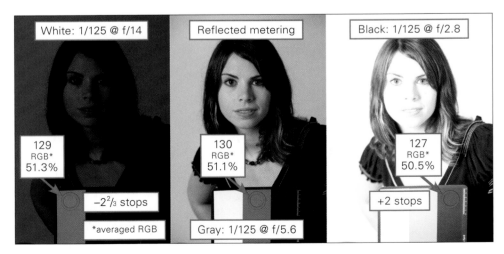

FIGURE 4.2

Look at the average RGB numbers for the three separate exposures shown in Figure 4.2. Each average is taken from white, gray, and black areas in the scene. The results of the separate exposures for the three swatches are: white: 129 (LR: 51.3%); gray: 130 (LR: 51.1%); and black: 127 (LR: 50.5%). The only exposure that can be called useful is that made by reading the gray patch. To make accurate reflected-meter readings, it's common for photographers to carry a neutral gray card or the GretagMacbeth ColorChecker Gray Scale balance card, shown here. If a card is not available, worn asphalt and green grass can do the trick as both are close to 12.5% gray.

FIGURE 4.3

Incident metering

Incident meters—separate handheld devices not built into the camera—are the most effective meters for setting proper exposure because they measure the light falling on a subject. Unlike reflected meters, they are not affected by the tonality of the subject. Incident meters are held at the subject's position (**Figure 4.3**). The dome receiving the light is aimed at the source of light. The reading is then set on the camera. This exposure setting is the *diffused value*. Once the exposure readings are entered in the camera, everything else in lighting is subjective and done at the photographer's whim for the desired effect.

Contrast

Contrast is the difference between highlights and shadows. When the contrast range is greater than four f/stops from darkest to lightest, the result will be out of the range most printers can handle. Usually the result is solid black shadows (**Figure 4.4**). The shadow area in the photograph of model Marie Friemann shows a reading well below the 25–40 minimum RGB range that's required to show detail. This example is a high-contrast photograph. The difference between the lightest and darkest areas is well beyond a reproducible four stops. The shadows are blocked up so much as to be black.

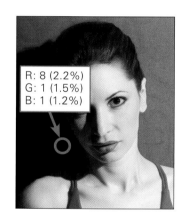

FIGURE 4.4

Lowering contrast

Adding light to the shadows lowers contrast. My assistant, Holly Jones, holds a reflector panel that bounces light from the source back into the shadows at

FIGURE 4.5

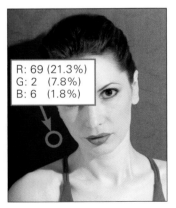

R: 69 (21.3%)
G: 2 (7.8%)
B: 6 (1.8%)

FIGURE 4.6

Marie's right (**Figure 4.5**). As a result, detail within the shadows is revealed (**Figure 4.6**). The Red channel now reads 69 (LR: 21.3%). Her hair, forehead, cheek, ear, and the texture in the shadow area of the background are revealed. The exposure remains the same, as no more light is coming from the source.

One of the reasons photographers love the light in the latest part of the afternoon, just before the sun dips below the horizon, is its directionality, warm color, and lower contrast. The shadows are filled in by the open sky.

Quantity or Quality?

Light is confusing. Consider this question: "As a subject gets closer to a light, does the light become harsher or softer?" Think about this for a minute. Imagine you are in a room at night with a single table lamp across the room providing illumination. Hold up your hand. Walk toward the light. Does the amount of light falling on your hand increase? Yep. Sure does. So the closer you move to the light, it gets brighter and harsher. Right? Well, half right, anyway. It does get brighter. It also becomes softer. And we humans, thanks to the way our brains work, universally confuse brightness with harshness. We mix up the quality of light with the quantity we see.

Shadow edge transition

Imagine you are walking away from the light. Hold one finger over the other palm of your hand. It casts a shadow. Look at the edge of the shadow. It sharply outlines the shape of your finger (**Figure 4.7**). The edge marks the transition from highlight to the shadow. If the shadow has a sharp edge, the light is harsh. Now think of shadows cast on a sunny day. They are very defined. The earlier photographs of Marie as seen in Figures 4.4 and 4.6 are made with harsh light. The edges of the shadows cast by her nose and chin are very sharp.

Now pretend you are walking toward the lamp. As you get closer, notice the edge of the shadow cast by your finger on your palm. The edges of the transition from highlight to shadow are blurred. By the time you get next to the lamp, the shadow and the highlight almost merge. What's going on here? The light is really bright and the shadow edge is soft. Hmmm. Well, there are a couple of things happening.

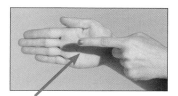

Shadow Edge   FIGURE 4.7

First, the light has become much larger in relation to the size of the subject so the transition from highlight to shadow is spread out (**Figure 4.8**). The result is an almost shadowless image similar to what you see on an overcast day in which the whole sky is the (really big) source of light. Second, as the light gets brighter the exposure on the camera has to be lowered to compensate. The background becomes darker.

The larger a light source is in relation to the subject, the softer the quality of the light. Large light sources make soft light. The transition from highlight to shadow is spread over a large distance. Small light sources create harsh light and sharp shadow edges.

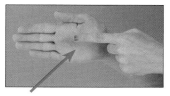

Shadow Edge   FIGURE 4.8

Instant soft light

Soft light is great for portraits of women and children. The long shadow edge transition minimizes texture in skin and enlarges the catchlights in the eye. It is very pretty. Best of all, it is easy to achieve. Either wait for an overcast day or slip a *diffusion panel* in front of the light source. Think of diffusion panels as on-demand clouds or port-a-clouds.

FIGURE 4.9

Sunny-day soft light

Outdoor sunlight streaming through tree leaves creates areas of very bright highlights and deep shadows, resulting in a high-contrast scene (**Figure 4.9**). The sun on Cara's face and legs is so bright that the detail in her skin disappears completely due to overexposure. Closing down the aperture on the camera to compensate would make her outfit go completely black. Look at her black robe draped over the chair. You can see folds in it. The exposure is correct for the shadows because these details show. So how can the contrast be lowered?

FIGURE 4.10

FIGURE 4.11

Remember that the only way to lower contrast is to add light to the shadows. The solution is to bring in a diffusion panel that is large enough to soften the light falling on Cara. In this case, it's a 42 x 72-inch Chimera frame with a full translucent panel on it (**Figure 4.10**).

Now the patches of bright sunlight and the shadows cast by the leaves blend into soft light (**Figure 4.11**). The panel's fabric reduces the amount of light reaching Cara by 1½ f/stops. If we open up the camera's aperture by that amount, the exposure adds light to the shadows, thereby lowering the contrast on Cara. At the same time, the increased exposure brightens the background not covered by the panel by 1½ stops, as well. The light hitting the stone wall behind her is much brighter now, complete with blown-out highlights. Brightening the background in a photograph by reducing the light hitting the subject and then increasing the exposure to compensate is called *subtractive contrast control*.

Harsh then soft studio light

Any light you find in nature can be duplicated in the studio—and it's not hard to do. In this section, you'll see how to place a single flash to replicate the effects of sunlight on both a clear and an overcast day.

Photographs do much more than tell the story of their subject. They also share exactly how it was lit. (Well, if someone has been playing around in Photoshop, it may not be *exactly* how the subject was lit.) Learning to read the lighting cues in a photograph goes a long way when you are creating the lighting yourself. Specular highlights reflect the source of light in the subject. Look for them on the hood of a car, on the glass of a window, in the water of a pond or lake, and in the eyes as they catch the light (**Figure 4.12**).

Specular highlights show you the size of the light shining on the person. A big catchlight reflects a large source and that means a gradual *shadow edge transition*, the indicator of soft light. A pinpoint of light in the eye would lead you to look for a quick, sharp shadow edge. Sometimes you can uncover retouching done on photographs by examining the catchlights. If the shadow edge transitions don't jibe with the specular highlights, you can be almost certain that Photoshop has touched the photograph. Now that you know how light works, your photographs with long, smooth shadow edges won't have teeny tiny catchlights in the eyes, will they? Of course not.

Shadow edge   Catchlights

Diffused value   Specular highlights

FIGURE 4.12

Harsh light, high contrast

This photograph of Marie is lit with harsh light (**Figure 4.13**). The tell-tale signs are the sharp transition from dark to light in the shadow cast on her cheek by her nose and on her shoulder by her chin. The tiny catchlight in her eye shows the size of the light source.

The high-contrast harsh-light image is made with a single flash set twenty feet from Marie and positioned forty-five degrees to her left and forty-five degrees above her (**Figure 4.14**). The flash is both the *origin of light* and the *source of light* because there isn't a modifier (such as a diffusion panel) between it and the subject. At twenty feet, the 5½-inch reflector is about the same relative size as the sun.

Here's an easy way to see if your light will deliver sun-like quality. Hold your thumb at arm's length from your eye. If your thumb blots out the light, it will be very close in quality to the sun. I guess this really is a "rule of thumb."

Harsh light / high contrast

FIGURE 4.13

FIGURE 4.14

Soft light / low contrast

FIGURE 4.15

FIGURE 4.17

Origin of light

Source of light

Bounce panel

Diffusion panel

FIGURE 4.16

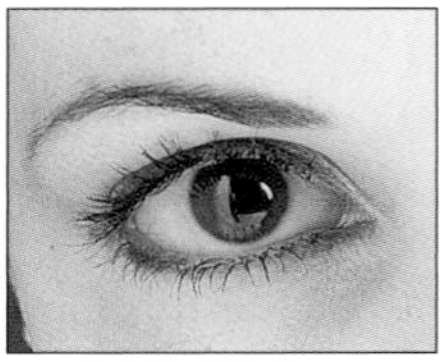

Soft light / high contrast

FIGURE 4.18

Soft light, low contrast

This photograph shows Marie in soft light with low contrast (**Figure 4.15**). The shadow edge transition is spread over a wide distance. The change from highlight to shadow is almost undetectable because of the low contrast. Again, the catchlights in Marie's eyes show the size of the source of light.

Three changes have been made—two on the set and one in the camera. Two *incident controls*—a *diffusion panel* and a *bounce panel*—have been added. Incident controls modify light before it reaches the subject. Some other changes have happened by adding the incident controls. The diffusion panel becomes the source of light. The source of light always illuminates the subject. In this setup, the flash is the origin of light. It lights the source. The bounce panel, in this case another Chimera panel covered with silver lame, catches light from the source of light and the origin of light to fill in the shadows, seriously lowering the contrast (**Figure 4.16**).

Take a closer look at Marie's eyes (**Figure 4.17**). The silver bounce panel shows on her right, and there is another reflection on the lower part of her iris. The white floor adds even more fill light.

Finally, as in the earlier example diffusing the light outdoors on Cara in Figure 4.11, the exposure on the camera has been increased to compensate for the brightness reduction caused by adding the diffusion panel.

Soft light, high contrast

Removing the bounce panel from the set takes light away from the shadow side of Marie's face and the contrast increases (**Figure 4.18**). Adding light to the shadows lowers contrast. Removing it from the shadows increases contrast. Contrast, and the quality of light, are all subjective decisions made by the photographer. Once you have set the diffused value (exposure on the camera), everything else is relative to it and under the rule of your every whim.

Creative Lighting

Learn to see your muse, as the camera will record it. One way to truly shortcut this process is to hook your camera up to your computer so you can see each image large on the screen. (See Chapter 3.)

Open a JPEG or RAW photograph in Photoshop. Zoom in to see the actual pixels at 100% and check your focus. Look at the catchlights in portraits. Be aware of the contrasts in the photograph. Is there a shadow that has lost detail? Are there any blown-out highlights (aside from the specular highlights)? Where would a little more light make a big difference? Those differences can be so subtle—you may only notice them by comparing them to other photographs.

Take a look at the photograph of Atlanta Falcons cheerleader Nikky Williams (**Figure 4.19**). Look at her left arm. It has a deep shadow. Her hair on that side falls into shadow and looks dull. The addition of a silver 42 x 72-inch bounce panel behind her adds a rim of light to her hair, along her arm, and along the edge of her gown (**Figure 4.20**).

FIGURE 4.19

FIGURE 4.20

Light different

Break down your lights after each shoot. Or a least move them off set and, in the case of electronic flash, disconnect them from the power packs. That removes the temptation to treat each subject the same as the one before. Each subject, especially when that subject is a person, is different. Remember Apple's "Think Different" ad campaign? Make your slogan "Light Different." Consider this photograph of Lauren. When we met, I was completely taken with her strong angular face, high eyebrows, and blue eyes. The editorial shoot called for three quarter-length poses (**Figure 4.21**). After we'd finished with the assignment, I moved in for close-ups. The lighting is two 2 x 3-foot Chimera Super PRO soft boxes. They are forty-five degrees from the lens to subject line and about two feet away. This is a soft, lower-contrast light that you won't find outdoors in "natural" light. And it is very compelling. A close look at Lauren's catchlights tells the setup's tale. Notice the highlight around her upper lip and the specular highlight showing off the shape of the lower one (**Figure 4.22**). Break rules. Light differently.

FIGURE 4.21

FIGURE 4.22

Play

I can't begin to describe how important play is in creative lighting. Try stuff. Shoot a photograph into your computer and study it. Change something. Shoot another and scrutinize that one. Keep going. Make notes or, even better, take photographs of the setup with a point-and-shoot camera. Never stop asking, "What would happen if...?"

I'll close with a happy result of light play. I had a *cucoloris* (also called a *cookie* in the motion picture industry) made of metal screening that had been burned with a blowtorch. I wanted to see what it looked like when photographed (**Figure 4.23**). I put up a blue background paper then placed the cookie in front of a bare-bulb flash head. That makes it a very small origin of light. The result is a sky full of clouds (**Figure 4.24**). I had no idea that would happen. Now I have another technique in my lighting kit.

Play. The rewards are indescribably useful and, well, lots of just plain fun.

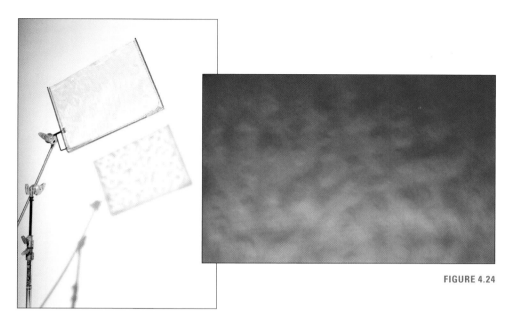

FIGURE 4.24

FIGURE 4.23

Thanks

The techniques in this chapter came from several years of being around the late Dean Collins. Many (if not most) of the photographers of my generation owe Dean for our knowledge of how light works and how to make it work for us and the camera. He gave us the definitions describing light.

FIGURE 4.25

Here's a photograph of Dean grabbing a couple of beers out of the darkroom sink during a party at my studio in March of 2002 (**Figure 4.25**). I hadn't used the darkroom since 1999 for processing and printing. It was great for parties, though. The darkroom has since been converted into a digital workroom, and I wrote this book sitting where the enlargers once stood. Things change. Photographs remind us of what is gone. For more on Dean, visit software-cinema.com.

CHAPTER 5

Musings on Clouds

PHOTOGRAPHY CAN BE HARD WORK, physically and mentally: lugging cameras, lights, grip equipment, and computers; collaborating with clients, models, and stylists; and working within the vagaries of weather on location.

Some photoshoots are more strenuous than others. I sometimes find creative purpose outdoors, alone, lying on my back looking at clouds and seeing shapes in them. Occasionally, I lift the camera from my chest, frame one of these atmospheric apparitions, and make its photograph. I then enjoy a well-deserved respite from those photographic exertions. I close my eyes and briefly nap. When I open them again, the clouds have created a whole new skyscape for my enjoyment. I study it, capture more images, and to avoid becoming overtired by these efforts, nap once again. The process is refreshing, creative, and restful as well.

Taking casual photographs of clouds—from below while lying on my back on a beautiful day, or from above when sitting in an airplane's window seat—shows me majesty and never-ending change. I wonder in the moment. Such moments are unique to me and irreplaceable in the world. These formations will never happen again. And I have photographs to remember them by!

Shoot the Sky

Go shoot some clouds of your own. Don't worry about how long it takes. I'll wait.

Back in the studio, bring your clouds back down to earth by downloading them to your computer. When creativity raises its mighty head, I look to Lightroom to choose the imagery. Reviewing my archives for clouds is easy because of the metadata that is added to each photograph during and immediately after import. More on metadata is in Chapter 6. Here's how Lightroom helps me choose the hero for the project.

Finding clouds

Click the Grid view in the Library module. Spin down the Library triangle, then choose All Photographs. Spin down the Find triangle and click the double down arrow to the left of Find's search field. For Text, choose Caption and for How, choose Contains. Type "clouds" in the search field. It's good to know that the metadata in Bridge calls the Caption field Description, so entering "clouds" in Bridge will result in it being in the Caption of Lightroom's metadata. As I said, more on all of this later (including how to do it). Lightroom reads the database for the word "clouds" contained in the Caption field of the IPTC data. The results appear in the Grid. The Library panel tells the story: 156 photographs (out of 34,185) contain the word "clouds" (**Figure 5.1**).

METADATA AFTER THE FACT

Say you have been making digital photographs since long before Photoshop supported metadata (version 7), and before that you scanned film. So there are tons of images in your library. I keep all of my digital negatives on a large RAID. They are backed up on non-writable optical discs as well. How do I add metadata after the discs have been burned and keep the integrity of the archived optical discs? The answer lies in Lightroom's database.

New metadata added to images using Lightroom can be exported to the original RAW, JPEG, or TIF files on the RAID or hard drive. Best of all, the files on the hard drive don't have to be re-burned to discs because the changes are kept in Lightroom's catalog. Keep the catalog backed up at your studio and in an offsite location. The metadata stays current and is always good to go.

FIGURE 5.1

I'll highlight all of the clouds shown in the Library's Grid view (Edit > Select All, or Command [PC: Ctrl] + A) and make them into a new collection called Clouds (Library > New Collection, or Command [PC: Ctrl] + N). Additional photos can be added to an existing collection by highlighting them in the Grid and dragging them to the collection. The green circle with a plus sign indicates photographs are being added (Mac). Lightroom even adds a preview of the topmost image (**Figure 5.2**). Nice!

FIGURE 5.2

> ## COLLECTIONS
>
> Collections are groups of photographs that reference the actual photo in the Library. They are very useful for getting similar photographs from many different shoots into the same place for ranking, adding additional metadata, and choosing "The One," as well as making web galleries, prints, proof sheets, and slideshows.
>
> The images in a collection retain the sort order in effect when the collection is made. The photographs can be reordered by dragging. To remove a photo from a collection, choose Photo > Remove from Collection, or press Delete while in the Grid view. This does not send the original to the Trash (Mac) or the Recycle Bin (Windows).

Editing the collection

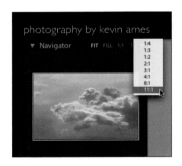

FIGURE 5.3

Spin down the arrow in the Collections panel and click on Clouds. That collection is now loaded in the Grid. I like to look at the work large. I'll press E to move into the Loupe view. The size of the displayed image is controlled in the Navigator panel. Choose Fit or Fill, or choose a ratio from the drop-down menu (**Figure 5.3**). Lightroom, like the amplifiers in the movie *Spinal Tap*, goes to eleven!

Hold down the Command (PC: Ctrl) key and press the left arrow to move through the collection. Look at each one for a few seconds. Trust your intuition here. If you like it, give it a single star rating by pressing 1. The rating appears just above the Filmstrip in the Toolbar. Go through the collection, rating your favorites. When you finish, click on the one-star rating in the Filmstrip view.

FIGURE 5.4

By default, you'll see the images rated with one or more stars. To see only one-star (or lower) images, click the drop-down menu arrow next to the words "and higher." Toggle the Filter off by clicking the switch to the right of the purple rating (**Figure 5.4**). Continue the process until you have found your group of heroes.

Enter the Loupe view from the Grid by tapping the E key. What do you see? Get a mirror. Hold it up to the edge of the Loupe panel. Rotate the image: Command (PC: Ctrl) +] for clockwise or [for counter-clockwise. What do you see now? Do you love it? Study your options in the monitor and mirror.

Rotate it again. How does it look upside down? Keep going. Move the mirror under the Loupe view. Hit Command (PC: Ctrl) + the right arrow to move to the next cloud photograph. Rotate it. Go through the hero. Choose one you love. You have found "The One."

The symmetries will never cease to astound. One type of symmetry is called a tessellation, a mosaic created when a shape is copied, flipped horizontally, then repeated. The whimsy of clouds, and their reflections forming tessellations, is the focus of this chapter. Let's explore.

A Bigger Sky

You can use any photographs of clouds—and I encourage you to go outside, lie down, and shoot the sky (don't forget to nap)—or you can download the folder labeled "Chapter 5" from amesphoto.com/learning. The book code you'll want is DPN8414.

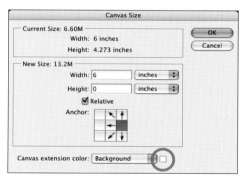

FIGURE 5.5

STEP ONE
Open 2255-0324.tif in Photoshop CS3 by double-clicking the image thumbnail in Bridge.

STEP TWO
Press the F key once to put Photoshop into Full Frame mode. Duplicate the Background layer by hitting Command (PC: Ctrl) + J. Highlight the Background layer and fill it with white by pressing the D key to set the default colors, then hold down the Command (PC: Ctrl) key and press Delete (PC: Backspace), or from the Edit menu choose Fill and select White from the Use menu. Set the Opacity to 100%, then click OK.

STEP THREE
Create more room for the tessellation by choosing Image > Canvas Size (Command [PC: Ctrl] + Option [PC: Alt] + C). Click the Relative checkbox. The Current Size of the clouds is six inches wide so enter 6 in the Width box. Click the right-hand box in the middle row in the Anchor box. That puts the white space to the left of the clouds. Make sure that the Canvas extension color is white, which is shown by the box to the right of the menu (**Figure 5.5**). Click OK.

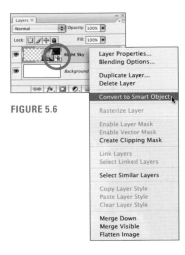

FIGURE 5.6

STEP FOUR

Double-click the name Layer 1 in the Layers palette. Rename the layer Right Sky.

STEP FIVE

Right-click (Mac: Control-click) to the right of the layer's name and choose Convert to Smart Object (**Figure 5.6**). The command is also available from the Layers palette flyout menu accessed by clicking in the upper right corner just under the X icon. The layer has the Smart Object icon in the corner of the thumbnail.

MULTI-BUTTON MOUSE

Okay, Mac users. It's time. Replace that one-button legacy from the last millennium. Drop the bucks and buy a Mighty Mouse from Apple.

Right-clicking has been an integral part of the Windows OS since about forever. Mac OS X has always had contextual menus—only you had to hold down the Control key and click to call on it. No more. From now on the *Notebook* will often just use the term "right-click" for getting contextual menus for both Mac and Windows. One-button traditionalists will just have to remember to add the Control key.

STEP SIX

Right-click to the right of the layer's name again and choose New Smart Object via Copy. Rename this layer Left Sky.

STEP SEVEN

Enter Free Transform by pressing Command (PC: Ctrl) + T (Edit > Free Transform). Right-click (Mac people: see why it's time?) and choose Flip Horizontal. Either click the Commit checkmark in Free Transform's Options bar (it's directly under Photoshop's menu bar) or press Return. Press V to choose the Move tool. Start dragging Left Sky to the left, then add the Shift key. That constrains the layer to moving horizontally (**Figure 5.7**).

FIGURE 5.7

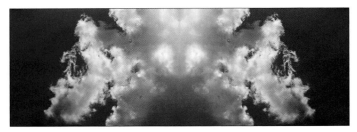

SMART OBJECTS

Introduced in Photoshop CS2, Smart Objects are copies of the content in the Layers palette placed elsewhere in the file. They can be vector art from Illustrator, layers from Photoshop, even RAW files placed in the layers stack. Smart Objects allow a new level of non-destructive editing. When a Smart Object is scaled down using Free Transform, it can be sized right back up with no loss in quality. See for yourself. Open Smart Object.psd in the folder for this chapter.

1. The Tiffany layer is active. Open Free Transform (Command [PC: Ctrl] + T). Click the link icon between the W and H boxes in the Options bar. Enter 5% in either box and click the checkmark or press Return.

2. Highlight Tiffany Smart Object by clicking in the layer's thumbnail. Again, go to Free Transform and check the link to constrain the proportions. Enter 5% in either the W or H field, then tap Return. There are now two tiny Tiffanys on the screen.

3. Highlight the Tiffany layer. Hold down the Shift and Option (PC: Alt) keys and drag the top right corner of the bounding box toward the top right corner of the document. Stop when the size is about where it was when the file was opened. Eeeewww. Looks pretty bad.... Okay, it's downright awful, not to mention completely unusable (**Figure 5.8**). Hit Return.

4. Highlight Tiffany Smart Object. Enter Free Transform. Click the link icon and enter 100% in either the W or H field. Press Return (**Figure 5.9**). Amazing creatures, those Smart Objects, aren't they?

Use Smart Objects anytime you want to test positioning—size or rotation—without affecting the quality of the layer.

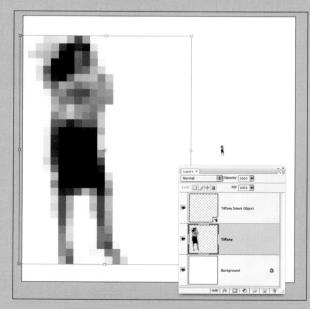

FIGURE 5.8

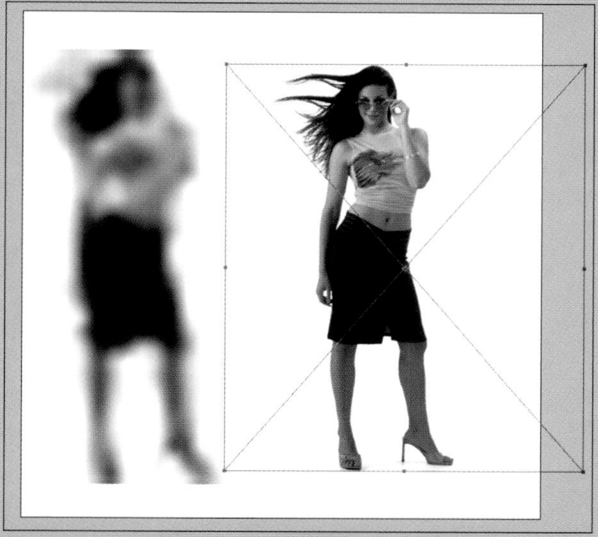

FIGURE 5.9

FIGURE 5.10

STEP EIGHT

The pattern is interesting. It's time to play. I see hair at the top, then shoulders and arms. The image seems too wide. The question is how to *see* how much to overlap them. Change the blending mode of Left Sky to Difference (Shift + Option [PC: Alt] + E). (Yes, I spend way too much time using Photoshop, as evidenced by knowing the keyboard shortcuts for the blending modes. Sheesh.) Drag Left Sky over Right Sky. Hold down the Shift key to keep the move horizontal. Don't worry about the funny colors. Look into the composition to see the patterns (**Figure 5.10**).

STEP NINE

Choose Rulers from the View menu (Command [PC: Ctrl] +R). Drag a vertical guide from the left ruler over the area where the two layers overlap. Get the Rectangular Marquee tool (M). Drag a selection from the top of part of the blue sky over to the guide and all the way to the bottom of the image (**Figure 5.11**).

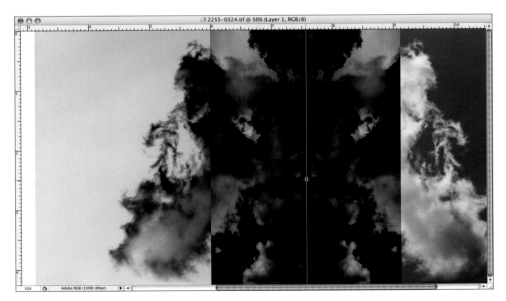

FIGURE 5.11

STEP TEN

Hold down the Option (PC: Alt) key and click the Add Layer Mask icon (third from the left at the bottom of the Layers palette) to hide the excess image area from Left Sky. Click the layer's thumbnail, press V for the Move tool, then press Shift + Option (PC: Alt) + N to return the layer's blending mode to Normal. Press Command (PC: Ctrl) + ; to hide the guide. So far, so good (**Figure 5.12**).

FIGURE 5.12

STEP ELEVEN

I'm seeing a cloud goddess here and liking the image except that her head is only half there. Not good. Back to work. Increase the top canvas size by two inches. (Want help? See Step Three. The only differences are the bottom center box in the Anchor area is checked, and 2 is entered in the Height field.)

STEP TWELVE

Now this is cool. Command-click (PC: Ctrl-click) Right Sky so it and Left Sky are highlighted. Right-click to the right of either layer's name and choose Convert to Smart Object. A new Smart Object appears, named Left Sky. Rename it Cloud Goddess. If you want to get to the original two Smart Objects, double-click this layer's thumbnail.

STEP THIRTEEN

Right-click to the right of the name Cloud Goddess, then choose New Smart Object via Copy. Enter Free Transform (Command [PC: Ctrl] + T). Right-click inside the bounding box and pick Flip Vertical. Hit Return to commit the transformation. Drag the upside-down Cloud Goddess Smart Object layer up, adding the Shift key to keep it moving vertically. Voilà! She's headstanding on her own head! Interesting, though not exactly what I had in mind (**Figure 5.13**).

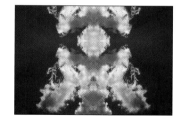

FIGURE 5.13

STEP FOURTEEN

This image wants more sky! Get the Rectangular Marquee tool (M) then drag a selection from the top right corner as close as possible to the clouds on her right shoulder. Press Command (PC: Ctrl) + J to copy the selection to its own layer. Label it Left Sky. (I know it's on the right side; it won't be in a moment.) Go to the View menu, choose Show, and check Smart Guides if they are not already selected.

STEP FIFTEEN

Convert Left Sky into a Smart Object. Get the Move tool (V). While holding the Shift key, drag Left Sky to the left until it just covers up the left edge of the Goddess's left shoulder. Enter Free Transform. Grab the center handle on the right edge of the bounding box and drag to the right until the vertical magenta Smart Guide appears, showing the right edge aligned with the edges below it (**Figure 5.14**). (This is so cool and very useful!) Press Return to commit the change.

FIGURE 5.14

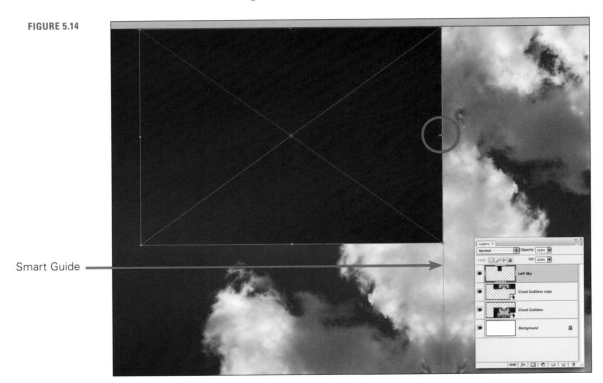

Smart Guide

STEP SIXTEEN

Right-click Left Sky in the layer stack and choose New Smart Object via Copy. Rename it Right Sky. Select Command (PC: Ctrl) + T to open Free Transform. Right-click inside the bounding box and choose Flip Horizontal. Hit Return. Drag Right Sky to the right until the Smart Guide appears on the left edge showing it is aligned with Left Sky. Command-click (PC: Ctrl-click) on Right Sky. Convert them into a new Smart Object. Rename it Sky.

STEP SEVENTEEN

The Goddess's head is covered by the newly tessellated sky. Click the Add Layer Mask icon at the bottom of the Layers palette. The mask appears at the right of Sky's thumbnail. It's active because it has an extra border around its white-filled thumbnail.

> ### LAYER MASKS: WHAT'S REVEALED AND WHAT'S CONCEALED
>
> Layer masks selectively show or hide what's on a layer. When the layer mask is white, everything on the layer shows. The layer mask added to Sky is filled with white. All of the sky on the layer is visible. Make the layer mask black by pressing Command (PC: Ctrl) + I, which is the keyboard shortcut for the Invert command under Image > Adjustments. The sky is hidden by its black layer mask. Press Command (PC: Ctrl) + I again and continue the project.

STEP EIGHTEEN

Get the Brush tool (B) and set it to 300 pixels with 0% Hardness. Controlling the brush from the keyboard is easy and efficient. The right bracket key makes it bigger; the left bracket key makes it smaller. Shift + [makes the brush softer by 25% each time the left bracket key is tapped. Shift +] makes it harder in 25% increments for each key tap. Press D to set the default colors (black is the foreground color; white is the background color). Center the brush in the visible part of the Goddess's head and paint over the sky around where the top of her head will be. As the brush paints black on the layer mask, the sky is hidden. The head on the Cloud Goddess layer copy is revealed. Paint until you are happy with the top part of her head. If you reveal too much, tap the X key to exchange black for white and paint over the excess on the layer mask. All that's left is to get rid of the extra white space on the left and clean up some of the edges where the layers meet.

STEP NINETEEN

This is the only time I ever use the tragic—I mean Magic—Wand tool. Press W or click it in the toolbox. Set the Tolerance to 1, with the Anti-alias and Contiguous boxes checked. Click in the white space to select it.

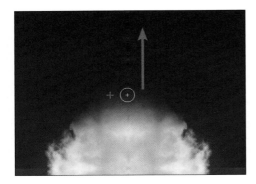

FIGURE 5.15

Press Command (PC: Ctrl) + Shift + I to inverse the selection (Select > Inverse). Choose Image > Crop. The white space is cropped out.

STEP TWENTY

The final edits have to be done on a rasterized copy of the Smart Objects. Make a copy of the visible layers by pressing Command (PC: Ctrl) + Option (PC: Alt) + Shift + E. Photoshop copies all of the visible layers to a new one. Name it Final. There are artifacts in the sky where the tessellated layers meet. Choose the Healing Brush (J). Start at the top left side of the head. Option-click (PC: Alt-click) to sample from the misty clouds, then center the Healing brush over the joint between the sky halves and heal up (**Figure 5.15**).

STEP TWENTY-ONE

Heal the lines from the edges to the clouds by her ears. Sample above an ear, center the Healing brush on the merge line, and heal out to where the incoming healing stopped. Repeat for the other side of the head. Clean up any other areas that bother you. Save the file as Cloud Goddess. psd (**Figure 5.16**). There's another project coming up where we work with her again.

Well, there you have it. The Cloud Goddess is an image that had its beginning shooting clouds and napping in the afternoon sun of a warm Atlanta spring. It came to be while musing in Lightroom with a mirror. Tell me, is photography a great career or what? I'll show you how to finish the Cloud Goddess in Chapter 17. Join me, won't you?

Excuse me, I see a particularly coy cloud formation overhead....

FIGURE 5.16

PART TWO

Management:
From Computer to Archive

Digital photographers create hundreds, then thousands, of files. Managing them can be an issue...

CHAPTER 6

All About Metadata

THE INTERNAL INFORMATION about an image—its creation time, exposure, name, title, description, photographer, and so on—that's been stored in the file itself is metadata. It all sounds a little, well, metaphysical, and the fact is the more data that's embedded in a digital photograph the easier it is to find that image, no matter how many years in the future you begin your search.

So much information can be added to a digital image that the mind boggles. Here's what information is included in metadata, how it's laid out, where it goes, and how to add it.

It Is Greek...

Meta is Greek, meaning after. *Data* means information. So metadata is information added to the photograph after it is captured. Metadata is pervasive in the digital world. Practically every music file, video, or still photograph has some kind of metadata appended within it.

EXIF

FIGURE 6.1

The camera records the image's pixels then adds the first metadata, writing it into the file. It's called EXIF (pronounced "x-if") information. EXIF metadata contains the creation date, camera brand, model, serial number, exposure settings, ISO, white balance, focal length, the photographer's name and copyright, and in some cases GPS (Global Positioning System) information regarding the location where the image was captured. EXIF metadata is written directly into the file, whether the capture is JPEG or RAW. Bridge CS3 displays EXIF information graphically as a camera might in the Metadata Placard accessible from the Metadata tab's flyout menu or from Bridge's Preferences in the Metadata pane. Additionally, it is available by spinning down the disclosure triangle in the Camera Data (EXIF) panel (**Figure 6.1**).

IPTC Metadata

Metadata in digital image files has been around for quite a while. The International Press Telecommunication Council (IPTC) set standards for adding information to digital files in a consistent format back in the days when news photographers carried Leafscan 35s with them on assignment to digitize their photographs in order to transmit them to their newspapers over telephone lines. Adobe has made Bridge, Photoshop CS3, and Lightroom compliant with the current IPTC standard for XMP (Adobe's Extensible Markup Platform) and the legacy Information Interchange Model (IIM) used back in the day. You'll see how all three work together later in the chapter.

Additional metadata can be added using Adobe Bridge CS3, which ships with Photoshop CS3, as well as in Lightroom. The important point to remember is that metadata added immediately after capture will accompany all of the subsequent photographs made from the file. The more metadata in a digital image, the richer the information to search on and the easier it is to find exactly the photograph you want—quickly.

Metadata, Adobe style

There are currently around 150 different flavors of RAW capture files supported by Adobe applications. To avoid any possibility of accidentally corrupting a digital negative, Adobe opted to keep metadata in separate "sidecar" files carrying the extension .xmp. These sidecar files are tiny text files that hold all of the metadata about a RAW file, including settings made in Camera Raw. You can see the XMP files by choosing View > Show Hidden Files from Bridge's menu (**Figure 6.2**). Command (PC: Ctrl) + F10 is the keyboard shortcut to show hidden files. Hide them again from the View menu by unchecking Show Hidden Files.

They are always on display in a computer's operating system, either in the Finder or My Computer. Remember to keep the sidecar files with the RAW files when moving, copying, or archiving them. The easy way to know you have the RAW files and their XMP sidecar files ready to go in the OS is to check to see if there is an even number of files selected (**Figure 6.3**).

RAW files that are moved or copied using Bridge automatically take their sidecar XMP files with them even when they are hidden.

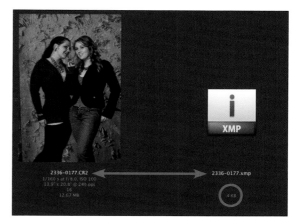

FIGURE 6.2

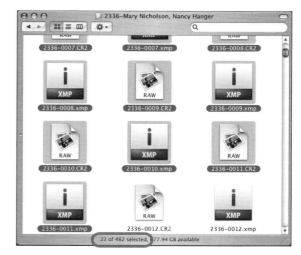

FIGURE 6.3

Metadata entry and display

Metadata can be added with Lightroom, Bridge, and even in Photoshop using File > File Info. There is an issue. The names for the metadata fields aren't completely consistent among these three applications. There are reasons, including backward compatibility with legacy files, that have metadata added in Photoshop with File Info, File Browser, Bridge (version 1) or older IPTC IIM. Since all of the fields don't correspond, it's good to know where the data is displayed from app to app to app.

The metadata map

It's important to know how to make a metadata map that shows where each field shows up in the three different programs. As they evolve, field mapping might change, so here's how to always know what fits where.

STEP ONE

Open Photoshop. Press Command (PC: Ctrl) + N to open the New dialog. Choose Web from the Preset menu. 640 x 480 is fine. Leave it as RGB, 8-bit, and a background of white. Name it Metadata Map.psd. Click OK.

Now hold down the entire left-hand side of the keyboard—alright, it's only Command (PC: Ctrl) + Option (PC: Alt) + Shift—and press I, or select File > File Info from Photoshop's menu bar. The metadata window for the document opens. (You can download a copy of Metadata Map.psd, complete with its metadata, from amesphoto.com/learning. Click on the cover of *The Digital Photographer's Notebook*. The book code is DPN8414.)

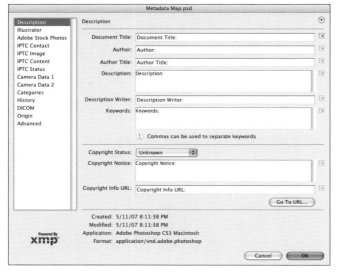

FIGURE 6.4

STEP TWO

By default, the Description field in the left-hand pane is highlighted. Fill in all of the fields on the right with their names. For instance, the Document Title window gets "Document Title:" in it. Do this for all of the fields in the Description pane. Leave Copyright Status at Unknown (**Figure 6.4**).

Click the IPTC Contact field to display the IPTC Contact pane. The first two fields, Creator and Creator's Job Title, are already populated with data from the Description pane. Enter a forward slash (/) and type in the field names. Creator would contain "Author: / Creator." Complete all of the fields in this pane (**Figure 6.5**).

Go to the IPTC Image pane. The first field won't accept any entry because it is a date field. Leave it blank. Fill in the rest of the fields. The ISO Country Code is a three-letter code, so enter ISO.

Click on IPTC Content. Fill in the Headline and IPTC Subject Code fields. Description, Keywords, and Description Writer are the same as in the Description pane, with the minor exception of the missing colon in this pane's field name.

Select IPTC Status. Add the slash and Title in the first field. Fill in the empty fields.

Finally, choose Origin. Leave the Date Created field blank. Add Credit and Transmission Reference to their respective, already populated fields. Leave Urgency at None (**Figure 6.6**). Click OK, then save the file to your working folder for this chapter. You'll need it for the next step. When the Photoshop Format Options dialog opens with Maximize compatiblity checked, click OK. This function creates a copy of the layers that can be read by other programs that can't read layered Photoshop files. Lightroom is one of the apps that needs this checked to read a PSD file. Make this dialog go away and always maximize compatibility by changing Ask to Always in Preferences > File Handling > Maximize PSD and PSB File Compatibility.

STEP THREE

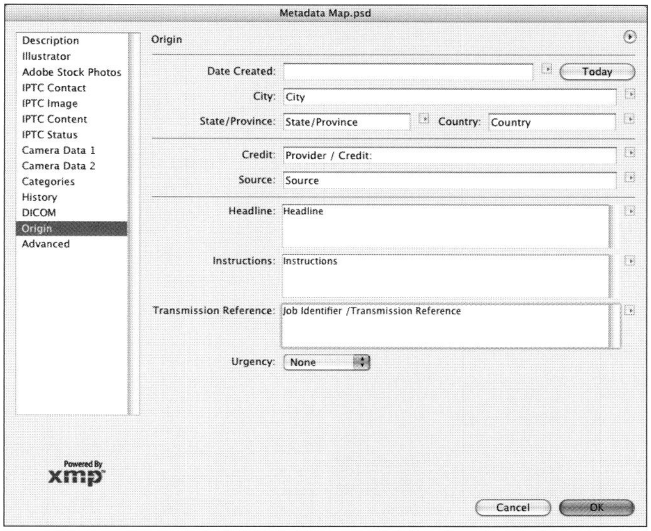

Open Bridge by either clicking the Go to Bridge icon located just left of the word Workspace in Photoshop's Options bar, choosing File > Browse from the menu bar, or pressing Command (PC: Ctrl) + Option (PC: Alt) + O. Choose the default workspace by pressing Command (PC: Ctrl) + F1

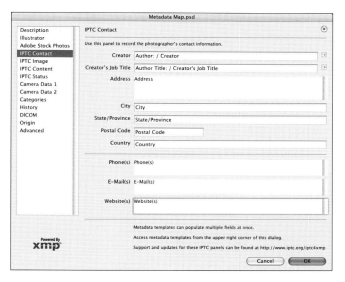

FIGURE 6.5

FIGURE 6.6

(or selecting Window > Workspace > Default). Go to the Window menu and uncheck Preview Panel. Now click the Metadata tab. Click the tab's flyout menu and choose Preferences, then highlight Metadata (**Figure 6.7**). Spin down the disclosure triangles for both IPTC (IIM, legacy) and IPTC Core. Be sure that all of the boxes for both are checked. Click OK.

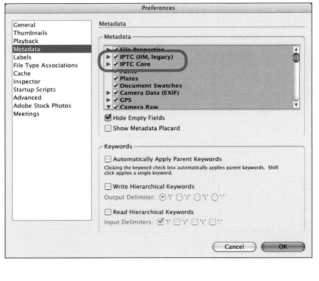

FIGURE 6.7

FIGURE 6.8

Mapped fields revealed

STEP FOUR
Spin down the IPTC (IIM, legacy) and IPTC Core panels (**Figure 6.8**). Close all of the others. Click the Folder tab, then double-click the folder where you saved Metadata Map.psd. Click the thumbnail to highlight it.

STEP FIVE
Hold down Command (PC: Ctrl) + Option (PC: Alt) + Shift + I to show the File Info dialog. Here's the payoff: The information entered in the panes of File Info are shown in the IPTC panels in the Metadata tab (**Figure 6.9**). Click on each of the File Info panes and see how what you entered is displayed. The Description pane carries legacy IPTC (IIM) data. Where appropriate, the Description pane entries are repopulated to the IPTC panes and vice versa. They correspond almost exactly to the IPTC Core display in the

Metadata tab in Bridge. Changes made in the IPTC panels will reflect in their respective panes in File Info and the Metadata tab in Bridge. Now you know where metadata displays in Bridge and how it gets there.

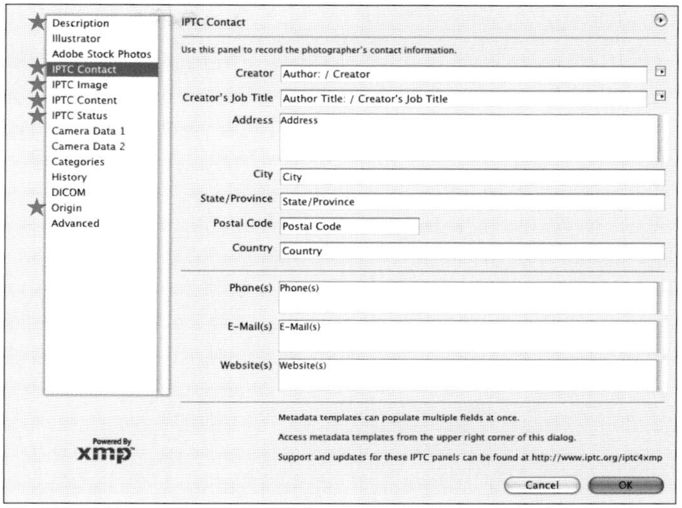

Lightroom metadata

Lightroom is more than the photographer's mini lab. It also can be the catalog of a life's work, thanks to its powerful database. The key to finding photographs created over the years is the metadata added both on import and shortly thereafter. So how does Lightroom handle metadata? Glad you asked. Read on.

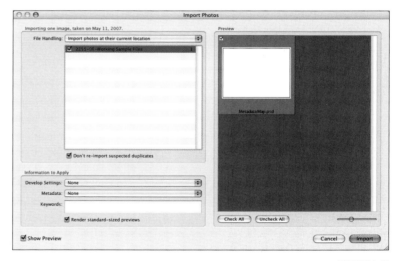

FIGURE 6.9

STEP ONE

Open Lightroom and enter the Library module by pressing Command (PC: Ctrl) + Option (PC: Alt) + 1. Press Command (PC: Ctrl) + Shift + I (or select File > Import Photos from Disk) to open the Import Photos from Disk dialog. Navigate to Metadata Map.psd's folder. Click Choose. Set up the Import dialog by choosing Import photos at their current location in the File Handling menu (**Figure 6.10**). Check Don't re-import suspected duplicates. Set both Develop Settings and Metadata to None. Leave Keywords blank. Render standard-sized previews may be checked or not. Click Import.

FIGURE 6.10

STEP TWO

Metadata Map.psd appears in the Library's Grid view. Click it to highlight it. Click the word Histogram in the right panel to close it. Command-click (PC: Ctrl-click) on Quick Develop to close the rest of the panels. Click Metadata

FIGURE 6.11

to see only that panel. Change the drop-down menu to the left of the word Metadata to All. Lightroom's field names appear in the left column of the panel. File Info / IPTC appear in the right columns under the headings Contact, IPTC, Image, Workflow, and Copyright. The one thing to make note of is that Lightroom's Caption field is the Description field in Photoshop and Bridge (**Figure 6.11**). Other than that, it's straightforward.

That's the metaphysics of metadata. The next section of the *Notebook* shows how to create and then apply your own template to an entire folder of digital negatives, as well as customize metadata for individual files quickly and simply.

Your Personal Template

The metadata map created in the previous section shows what information goes in each field of the Description and IPTC Core panes of the File Info dialog box, and where they appear in the Metadata tabs of Bridge and Lightroom. Now I'll show you how to make templates for all of the digital photographs you import using Bridge or Lightroom. It's a good idea to have templates for both apps. There are times when they come in handy. Finally, I'll show you how to put specific information in the metadata of individual photographs.

Metadata for all

There are two ways to create metadata templates with the basic information that wants to be included in every digital negative in Photoshop and Bridge. Lightroom uses the same information, though setting up a template is a different process.

STEP ONE

In Photoshop, create a new document by typing Command (PC: Ctrl) + N. The size you chose last time is already in the dialog box here. Hit Return. Press Command (PC: Ctrl) + Option (PC: Alt) + Shift + I to open the File Info dialog. The Description pane is displayed. Fill in the Author, Author Title, and Description Writer with your name, title, and name again, respectively.

Leave the Keywords section blank. Enter your information into the Copyright Notice and Copyright Info URL fields. The keystroke for the copyright symbol © is Option + G on the Mac. Windows users, make sure your Number Lock (Num Lock) key is down. Hold down the Alt key and type 0169 on the keypad. When the Alt key is released, the © symbol appears. Leave the Copyright Status at Unknown (**Figure 6.12**).

I have an action that applies some sharpening and color alias reduction, and changes the Copyright Status to Copyrighted. I run it on every file I build from a digital negative from Bridge or Lightroom. The © symbol that appears in the document header when the Copyright Status is Copyrighted tells me I have already run the action. The action is included in the downloads for this chapter. The set is called Sharpening. The action is named USM > Alias > ©. I run this action on every file I open from Camera RAW that hasn't been sharpened in the Detail tab (ACR) or module (Lightroom). The details on sharpening RAW files are in Chapter 11.

STEP TWO

Go to the IPTC Contact pane using the keyboard shortcut Command (PC: Ctrl) + 4, or click IPTC Contact in the column on the left of the dialog. Fill in all of these fields with your own information (**Figure 6.13**).

STEP THREE

The IPTC Image and Content panes (Command [PC: Ctrl] + 5 and Command [PC: Ctrl] + 6, respectively) are for specific data about individual photographs. Nothing gets entered in them for this template. Notice that the Description Writer field has been filled in with the data you entered in the Description pane.

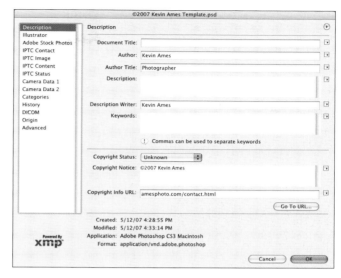

FIGURE 6.12

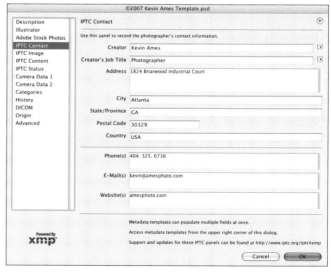

FIGURE 6.13

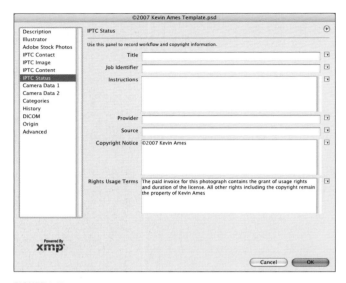

FIGURE 6.14

FIGURE 6.15

Press Command (PC: Ctrl) + 7 to move to the IPTC Status pane. Fill in Provider, Source, Copyright Notice, and Rights Usage Terms (**Figure 6.14**).

STEP FOUR

Select the Type tool (T) and set it to your favorite font at 60 points in size. Click in the document and type ©2007 Your Name. Of course, if it's a different year… remember we are using the WABAC Machine on occasion (heh, heh). Click the Commit checkmark or press the Enter key that is part of the numeric keypad. The other Enter adds a new line (carriage return).

STEP FIVE

Save this template by clicking the flyout triangle and naming it in the Save Template dialog. Click OK. Saved templates are visible in the flyout menu of File Info in both Photoshop and Bridge. My current-year template is named with my last name first, so that it's at the top of the list, which makes it easier to apply. The previous years are available in case I scan an older image and want to add that year's copyright. Starting the name of the current-year template with any letter will move it to the top of the stack. The © symbol comes after Z in the alphabetical pecking order (**Figure 6.15**).

STEP SIX

Save the Photoshop file as ©2007 Your Name Template.psd. It will come in handy if you want to add your template to Photoshop or Bridge running on another computer. Open the file, press Command (PC: Ctrl) + Option (PC: Alt) + Shift + I to open File Info in either Photoshop or Bridge, and follow the directions in these steps. To use it in Lightroom, read on….

Lightroom metadata preset

Lightroom calls 'em presets instead of templates. This one is easy, thanks to the team at Adobe, who understand the absolute necessity that Lightroom, Photoshop, and Bridge all play well with one another. If you ever meet any of these amazing people, be sure to thank them.

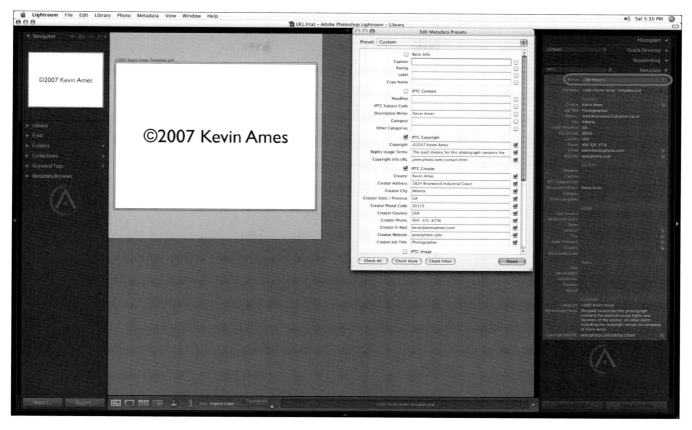

FIGURE 6.16

STEP ONE

Import the newly created ©2007 Your Name Template.psd into Lightroom using the same steps as shown earlier in this chapter.

STEP TWO

Highlight ©2007 Your Name Template.psd by clicking it in the Grid. The information you entered in File Info is displayed in Lightroom's Metadata tab. Go to the Preset menu at the top of the metadata display. Choose Edit Presets.... The Edit Metadata Presets dialog appears with all of the metadata from the file entered and checked (**Figure 6.16**).

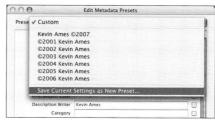

FIGURE 6.17

Choose Save Current Settings as New Preset... from the Preset menu at the top (**Figure 6.17**). Name the new preset Your Name ©2007. That puts it at the top of the menu in Lightroom. Click Create. That's it.

FIGURE 6.18

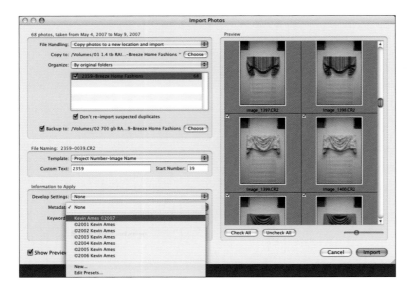

FIGURE 6.19

Adding metadata

There are different workflows for adding metadata to groups of photographs: You can add it during import, or you can append templates folder by folder in Bridge or Lightroom.

Adobe Photoshop Downloader in Bridge

By far the most efficient way to add basic metadata is to put it in the file as the images are imported from the camera or card. Chapter 2 covers importing digital negatives from Bridge using Adobe Photo Downloader. In that case, it reads the templates created for Bridge earlier in this chapter. Choose your template from the menu in the Apply Metadata section, then click Get Photos. The basic metadata is added on import (**Figure 6.18**).

Importing into Lightroom

Adding basic metadata to digital negatives being imported by Lightroom is as simple as it can be. Choose the template to apply in the Import Photos dialog box. Done (**Figure 6.19**).

Appending a template in Bridge

Open a folder of RAW files in Bridge. Press Command (PC: Ctrl) + A to select all of the files in Bridge. Click the Metadata tab, then click the flyout menu disclosure triangle and select Append Metadata. Choose the basic metadata template you just created and saved. Bridge writes the template to all of the selected files (**Figure 6.20**).

FIGURE 6.20

Shoot specific metadata

Image-specific metadata is added to the largest group of digital negatives first. Then to smaller groups, and finally to individual images. The first group to get metadata was all of the imported photographs. Every one of them got the basic metadata contained in the template.

Bridge

Select a group of photographs that will get the same information. Spin down the IPTC Core metadata pane in Bridge's Metadata tab. Fill in the Headline field with a one-sentence summary of the selected photographs. Add as much information as you can to the Description field. One of the things I include is whether or not I have a model release. Later I can search by "Model Release: Yes" to see photographs I can use commercially.

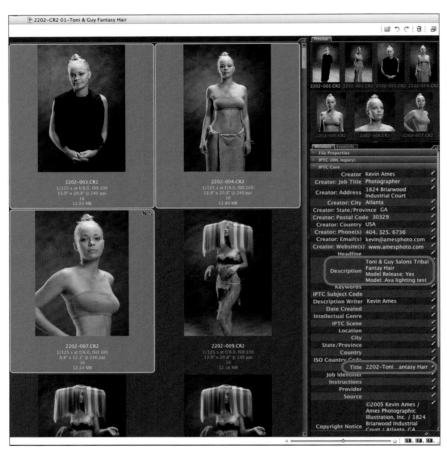

FIGURE 6.21

Even though there are two different models in this folder, I'll start by selecting them all and adding the overview of the project in the Description field. In this case it is Toni & Guy Salons, Tribal Fantasy Hair, Model Release: Yes because I have releases on both of them. I'll add the project number and folder name in the Title field: 2202-Toni & Guy Fantasy Hair.

Next, I select only the photographs of the first model, Ava, by clicking on the first image, holding down the Shift key, and clicking on the last image of her. The selected thumbnails are also displayed in the Preview pane. I'll enter her name and that these photographs are lighting tests (**Figure 6.21**).

The more information you add, the easier it will be to search for the file later. Detailed notes, including wardrobe description, catalog numbers, store, etc., can be made on a laptop and saved as a text file. The data can then be pasted into the Description.

METADATA IS PUBLIC INFORMATION

Information placed in digital negatives becomes public the minute a JPEG is emailed or a file is released for publication in any form. Don't add anything to the metadata of a file that you want to remain private. When I work with professional models, their name and talent agency go in the photograph's metadata. Their contact information—address, phone number, email, IM, etc.—go in my address book. Use caution not to reveal sensitive information.

Lightroom

Metadata in Lightroom works similarly to Bridge. It's important to keep in mind that Lightroom is a database, while Bridge is a powerful file browser. Lightroom's catalog contains all of the metadata about every photograph, whether it is available on a local hard drive or network server, or in an offline archived optical disc. Bridge has to access an image to read or modify its metadata.

The photographs of Ava and Heather that received metadata in Bridge are open in Lightroom. I have selected the thumbnails of Ava. There is nothing showing in the Metadata tab (**Figure 6.22**). What gives?

FIGURE 6.22

FIGURE 6.23

FIGURE 6.24

FIGURE 6.25

Lightroom adds and read the metadata into its database either on import or when metadata is added in Lightroom. The metadata in question was added in Bridge. Since the folder of images is online, the data is there; Lightroom just doesn't know it yet. I'll select all of the thumbnails (Command [PC: Ctrl] + A), then choose Metadata > Read Metadata from Files (**Figure 6.23**). Lightroom's taskbar shows the progress of the update (**Figure 6.24**).

Lightroom updates and displays the formerly missing metadata for the selected files (**Figure 6.25**).

I didn't add Heather's metadata in Bridge so that I could show how adding metadata differs in Lightroom. I'll select the first thumbnail of Heather in the Grid by clicking it. The Metadata tab populates. It has the information I added to the entire shoot in Bridge. I'll put her data in the Caption field by clicking on it. (The Description field in Bridge is the Caption field in Lightroom.) I'll add Model: Heather Graham, Click Models and Talent, Atlanta, GA. With Heather's first thumbnail still selected, I'll scroll to the last one, hold down the Shift key, and click. Finally, I'll click the Sync Metadata button at the bottom of the panel. The Synchronize Metadata dialog box opens. This is the last chance to make certain you want to overwrite the metadata.

If the word "mixed" appears next to a field, the metadata in at least one of the selected thumbnails is different from the others.

In this example, the Caption in the first selected thumbnail contains Heather's information while the others don't have it yet, so it reads "mixed" (**Figure 6.26**).

The dialog offers the opportunity to uncheck entries that might be showing the warning, as well as change the data before completing the sync. All is well, so I'll click Synchronize (**Figure 6.27**). Accumulating Metadata appears in the taskbar, then finishes. Done.

If a quick trip back to the same folder in Bridge reveals that the new metadata is missing, it can be easily updated. In Lightroom, choose Metadata > Save Metadata to File. Alternatively—and my choice, because I forget to do things like this—is to tell Lightroom to always export metadata to the original XMP sidecar files by going to Preferences > Catalog > Metadata, then checking Automatically write changes into XMP. Adobe says this slows Lightroom up a bit. As I see it, it's worth the small sacrifice in performance for the reliability of the metadata between platforms. This also updates Camera Raw settings for adjustments made in Lightroom's Develop module.

The key to remember is that these Adobe photographic applications—Bridge CS3, Photoshop CS3, and the photographer's mini lab, Lightroom—are designed to work and play well together with only a little help from us, their photographers.

FIGURE 6.26

FIGURE 6.27

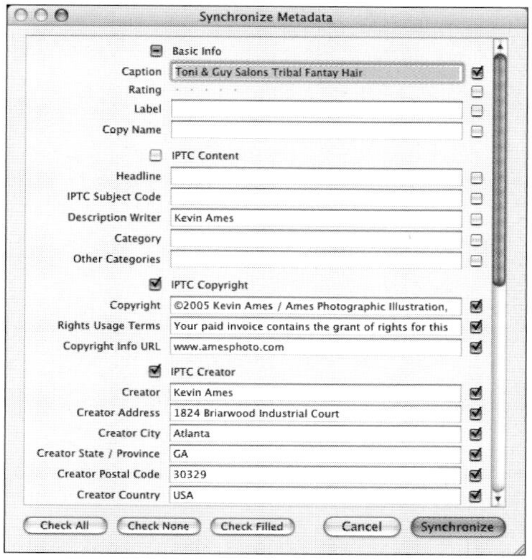

Keywords

Another important type of metadata is keywords. They are special and have their own tab in Bridge and pane in Lightroom. It is important to use exactly the same keyword every time. Think about it from a computer's point of view: If the assigned keyword is "children" and you search by "child" or "kids" (a word English-speaking Americans would understand as children, even though a "kid" is really a baby goat), nothing will be found. Computers don't make this kind of leap. On the other hand, when a standard set or catalog of keywords is used for adding keywords to a photograph—and used again for the search—confusion is eliminated.

There are sample keyword sets already in the Keywords tab or pane in both apps. I prefer to make my own. At the bottom of the Keyword pane are icons for New Keyword Set, New Keyword, and Trash to delete either a keyword or a set, depending on which is highlighted. Select the thumbnails to which you want to add keywords in Bridge or Lightroom, then click the checkbox next to the appropriate keywords in your set. That's all there is to it. Keywords can also be applied manually to multiple files by choosing File > File Info from Bridge's menu. Type them into the Keywords section of the Description pane, separating them by either commas or semicolons. Click OK. The Keywords field will be displayed in the Metadata pane, along with the keywords you chose in the Keywords tab or entered in File Info. Keywording is a very involved and specialized art/science that is beyond this edition of the *Notebook* to cover completely. More information is available at these websites—for news on keywording: www.iptc.org/NewsCodes/; for keyword catalogs: www.controlledvocabulary.com.

Catalogs made easy

The great thing about adding metadata to digital negatives before they are archived is that—with the exception of Photoshop's Save for Web, Web Photo Gallery (with Preserve All Metadata unchecked in the General section), and Lightroom's Web Galleries—all of this information is available every time you use the image. That means copyright, usage, details about the shoot, and even the edit history accompany the images everywhere they go digitally. The information is especially useful for finding that one special digital negative of Aunt Mary rafting the River of No Return in Salmon, Idaho, using Lightroom's search features. Your digital photographic life will be an outrageously organized thing of beauty when you make adding metadata an essential part of your workflow.

There is just one more thing…

Lightroom's catalog carries the most current metadata—information about the content and camera raw settings. Synchronizing this database with Bridge and then backing it up assures that metadata will always be current between both applications, even if files have to be restored from DVD archives. Chapter 8 covers this in depth.

CHAPTER 7

The Naming of Digital Negatives

NAMING DIGITAL PHOTOGRAPHS runs the gamut of conventions, from a date-based system to one using subject names. The real purpose of naming is to make certain the physical results of a shoot—DVD archive discs, model releases, receipts, and other paperwork—are never lost, and to ensure that the photographs can always be found.

Naming Conventions

The system used to name and keep track of anything is its naming convention. There are several. The Dewey Decimal System used in libraries is one. Making a file drawer with the year on it and twelve folders inside (one labeled for each month) is another. Alphabetical organization by a supplier's name is a way to organize a file drawer by vendor. In bank statements, sequential or serial numbering is used along with the year and the month to keep track of checks—especially the ones that have not cleared.

Dates

Using dates to name and file things is very human.

Photographers are, first of all, human. Human beings live sequentially in time. What we did is *past*. What we are doing is *now* and what's next is in the *future*. We remember things and put a time marker on them. Certain events are so powerful. A birthday, marriage, or birth of a child, for instance, is often remembered unfailingly through the years. Each of us relates to dates and sequences that are significant to us as individuals.

There are global events that all of us will always remember. The World War II generation's global event was the attack on Pearl Harbor on December 7, 1941. The Baby Boomers remember the assassination of President Kennedy on November 22, 1963, and Neil Armstrong's first step on the moon on July 20, 1969. Generation Xers know exactly where they were when the Challenger exploded on the morning of January 28, 1986.

Some photographers use dates as a naming convention on their photographs. 2006_09_12-0027.NEF is an example of using the date in an image file. The computer will sort the images first by year, then month and day, and finally, the image itself.

Events

Another way some photographers name their files is to precede the sequence number by an event or project name, such as: Saras_third_birthday-0113.ORF. Wedding photographers will often use the name of the bride and groom then the image or sequence number like this: black_chapman-0688.DCR.

NO APOSTROPHES PLEASE

There are punctuation marks and symbols, including the apostrophe, that work with some computer operating systems and not with others. It's most important that the naming convention follow these rules so the images can be used on any computer running any operating system:

1. Avoid spaces. Use underscores (_) or dashes (-) to separate words or numbers.

2. Don't use any other symbols, including and not limited to ~, !, @, #, $, %, ^, &, *, (,), \, /, :, ;, ", ', or ?.

Dates and events

It's normal for us to want to cram as much information into the name of a digital photograph as we possibly can to make it easier to find in the future. Consider, if you will, photographs of a trip to Nantucket Island, Massachusetts. The file name might be 2006_09_10_Nantucket_Island_Great_Point_Lighthouse-128.CR2. That name is really long. It's so long, in fact, that Bridge has to truncate it to fit it under even a fairly large thumbnail (**Figure 7.1**).

FIGURE 7.1

Logical sequences

All three of the naming conventions described above are valid and useful, especially from the human point of view. They all have one significant shortcoming: What is the next logical date after 2006_09_12? It is 2006_09_13. This works very well if a photographer shoots every day of the year without a day off—ever. If not, there is no way of knowing what the next date will be. This causes a break in the sequence.

Naming by event has the same problem. What is the next logical wedding couple after Black_Chapman? Jones_Arkwright? There simply isn't one. The date-and-event naming convention has the same issue.

Logical sequences are universal. Everyone knows what comes next in the series. For example, I write "A B C," then ask, "What's next?" You would reply, "D." That is an alphabetical logical sequence.

The numerical sequence 2, 4, 6, would get 8 as the next in line, and 10 after that.

Event, project, or job numbers

In the naming convention I use, anything I photograph is assigned the next number in sequence. It doesn't matter if it's a personal project, a self-assignment, a favor for a friend, or a job for a client. Each shoot gets a unique number. I don't have to remember the number either. That's the computer's job. Serializing photographic projects gives order to the file order on hard drives, the archive DVDs, and the jacket where additional physical media is stored. It's easy to re-file something in exactly the right order. An additional benefit is that anyone looking at a hard drive, disc wallet, disc box, or file drawer can see if anything is missing.

Here are some things to think about when setting up a serialized numbering system:

- Start with one. You already have lots of files on your hard drive, not to mention projects that were shot on film. The human part of you wants everything in chronological order. You desperately want the very first project you ever shot to be number 1. It is the first, after all. I have one word of advice: Resist. Insisting on getting every photograph you ever shot in order before you number them serially means that you'll *never* do it. It's too big a project, and there's really no reason to do it that way except that it's how we, as humans, think. Pick the most current project you have shot. Assign it project number 1. Then move on.

- Use at least three leading zeros. Computers don't know where a number fits in order without them. When you assign the first project number 1, it should look like this: 0001.

- Use a dash or an underscore immediately after the project number to differentiate the project from the digital negative. A file named 00200001.NEF seems good to us humans because we *know* that the first four digits are the project number and the last four are the image number. Computers are really stupid. What we *know*, they are clueless about. For instance, say you used this numbering system without a dash or underscore and had dutifully numbered twenty projects. Now you want the computer to show what's in the first one, so you tell it to find all photos in 0001. Well. The computer will do exactly that. It will show every photo in project number 1 alright, and it will show the first photo from the other nineteen as well because they all have 0001 in them. The dash or underscore differentiates the project number from the image number. Correctly done, the first photograph of the twentieth project is 0020-0001.NEF. To see the photos from the first project tell the computer to find 0001-.

- Clean up the backlogged projects using the next available project number. After completing your current project as 0001-, you see a folder from little Sara's birthday party when she was three. Assign it 0002-. Rename the images accordingly and move on to the next project. Computers are stupid and they are really good at sorting things. They truly don't care that Sara graduates from high school next June.

- Work on one backlogged project a day. It won't take much time and I don't care how many projects you have on your hard drive. Chances are it won't take an entire year to get them under control at the rate of one a day.

It's in the metadata

The last chapter went through metadata in what you might believe was excruciating detail. There is a big payoff to entering metadata for each photograph: It makes the image easy to find and you don't have to have a big honkin' long filename for the image. The metadata for the Nantucket lighthouse photographs has all the information that could possibly be wanted.

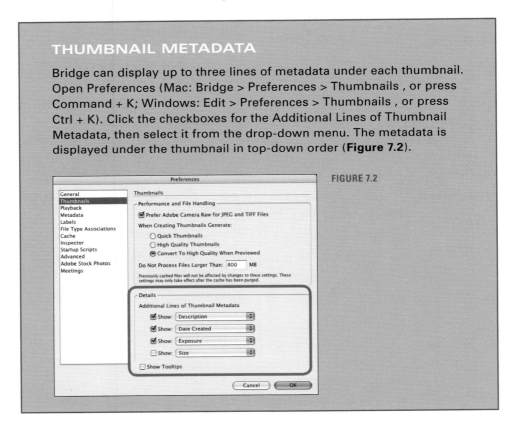

THUMBNAIL METADATA

Bridge can display up to three lines of metadata under each thumbnail. Open Preferences (Mac: Bridge > Preferences > Thumbnails , or press Command + K; Windows: Edit > Preferences > Thumbnails , or press Ctrl + K). Click the checkboxes for the Additional Lines of Thumbnail Metadata, then select it from the drop-down menu. The metadata is displayed under the thumbnail in top-down order (**Figure 7.2**).

FIGURE 7.2

Download the folder for this chapter from amesphoto.com/learning. The book code is DPN8414. (The download files for this chapter are JPEGs. The illustrations show the original RAW files. JPEGs were substituted to save download time.)

STEP ONE
Navigate to the folder in Bridge and click it. The thumbnails appear. Click the Metadata tab. The fields are blank. Click the image thumbnail for 2227-0128.jpg.

STEP TWO

Click on 2227-0128.jpg. The Metadata tab populates with EXIF and IPTC metadata. Look in the Description field of the IPTC section to see what the photograph is about. The Date Time and Exposure contain details about the capture (**Figure 7.3**).

FIGURE 7.3

Naming Made Simple

The KISS principle (Keep It Simple, Shooter) applies to naming files and folders. Simple names make for easy organization, retrieval, and ordering by a client, especially when they are coupled with detailed metadata.

Project names for images

Project names are serial numbers followed by a dash or an underscore, then the image number and, finally, the file extension. 2227- is the event name in the previous exercise. 128 is the sequential image number, and .CR2 is the file extension (or .JPG in the file you downloaded). The image name looks like this: 2227-128.CR2.

Project names for folders

The folder holding the digital photographs gets more information. It leads off with the project number, followed by the disc number (if the project spans more than one DVD) and a very brief project description. The description might be a model's name, an event, or a location. If the location is visited often, I include the year as a nod to my humanity. If there is no disc number, the entire project fits on a single DVD.

The folder name is entered into the Title field of the IPTC metadata. The disc number is excluded. When media that stores more data than a DVD becomes commonplace, the original folders will be combined and burned onto a single piece of new media. Leaving the disc number out of the Title field keeps the metadata current in an updated archive.

The Nantucket photography filled up two four-gigabyte cards. The digital negatives from the trip are stored on the hard drive in two folders named 2227-01-Nantucket 2005 and 2227-02-Nantucket 2005 because a DVD stores 4.7 gigabytes of data. All of the photographs I made during that trip are in these two folders. Individual photographs are differentiated from one another by the information in their respective IPTC Description fields. The disc number is included after the project number and before the description. The only difference between the folder name and the Title in the metadata is the disc number (**Figure 7.4**).

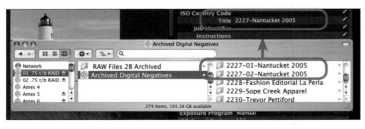

FIGURE 7.4

I love to shoot. I always have. Shooting film was expensive. Once, just before digital cameras came into their own, I figured that a single 35mm color slide cost a dollar, including film, processing, slide pages, and travel back and forth to the photographic lab. That meant that I was limited financially to the amount I could afford to shoot. Photographs made on medium- and large-format film cost upwards of five dollars apiece.

Now I shoot Canon cameras that deliver large files close to seventeen megabytes in size and are better than medium-format film. Currently I shoot onto four-gigabyte CompactFlash cards. A full four-gig card easily fits on a DVD that costs less than a dollar and a half, including label and envelope. I always make two

DVDs of each, so archiving 220 shots costs less than three bucks. That's not even a penny and a half per shot—a far cry, indeed, from when the sound the camera's shutter made was "Dollar!" every time it was pressed. Now I shoot more than ever...*lots more*. My bet is that you do, too.

Renaming Digital Photographs

Once a naming convention is chosen, renaming digital photographs using Bridge or Lightroom is easy. This section explains how to rename them step by step.

RAW or JPEG files from the camera

Let's be clear. The file the camera delivers, whether RAW or JPEG, is the photographer's digital negative. Digital negatives downloaded to a hard drive are named less than intuitively. Consider the name _V7Z4853.CR2. It has no meaning. Naming digital negatives is also important as part of the archiving process discussed in the next chapter. This section covers renaming digital negatives that were not imported using Adobe Photoshop Downloader (Chapter 2), shot tethered into Lightroom (Chapter 3), or imported directly into Lightroom from memory cards or disk (Chapter 8). These folders of photographs are already on your hard drive and have had project numbers added to them.

I shoot RAW exclusively. The steps and illustrations are written for that workflow. If you shoot JPEGs, that's fine. It works exactly the same way, except there are no XMP sidecar files for the JPEG format.

Bridge

STEP ONE
Open a folder of images in Adobe Bridge.

STEP TWO
Press Command (PC: Ctrl) + Shift + R to open the Batch Rename dialog box (or select Tools > Batch Rename). If no thumbnails are selected in Bridge's Content area, the chosen command acts as if they are all selected. This saves

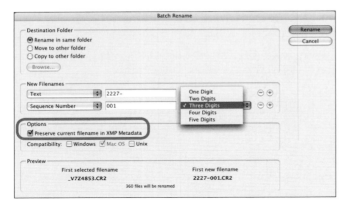

FIGURE 7.5

having to select all of the thumbnails for operations on all of them. It's a little thing that saves a lot of time and hassle in the long run. Choose Rename in same folder for the Destination Folder. Select Text from the drop-down menu in the New Filenames section. If there is not another menu below Text, click the + button and a new menu with Text selected appears. Choose Sequence Number from the menu. Choose Three Digits if you shot fewer than 1,000 images at the event. Finally, check Preserve current filename in XMP Metadata in the Options section (**Figure 7.5**). Preserve current file-name works with JPEGs, too. There is no XMP sidecar file in the JPEG spec, so the name is written directly into the file's header. The Preview section shows the first selected name, the new name, and the number of files to be renamed. Click Rename. Done.

FIGURE 7.6

Lightroom

Renaming in Lightroom is simplicity itself. Select all of the files in the Library module's Grid view by choosing Edit > Select All or using the keyboard shortcut Command (PC: Ctrl) + A. Choose Library > Rename Photos… (F2). The renaming preset made in Chapter 3 appears in the dialog box. Enter the project number in the Custom Text field and the number for the first image in the Start Number field. An example of the new name appears and the number of photos being renamed is displayed in the header of the dialog (**Figure 7.6**). Click OK. Done.

Event Number Journal

Event numbers can be recorded by hand, on a spreadsheet, or in a database. The simplest method is to get an ordinary blank check register booklet from your bank, then enter the event number, a description, and a date, if you like.

Another way is to build a simple database in Microsoft Access for Windows or FileMaker Pro for either Windows or Macintosh.

Another easy electronic method is to use an Excel spreadsheet. I have included a basic event journal spread in the downloads for this chapter. Keeping the journal on a spreadsheet makes adding the entries to a database in the future fairly easy (**Figure 7.7**).

By far the simplest journal of all is the folders pane in Lightroom. As each project is numbered in order and imported into Lightroom, it is cataloged. The folders appear in the folder pane in numerical order, and with their brief descriptions. If you don't remember what you shot on that trip to Nantucket, click the folder to see all of your amazing photographs (**Figure 7.8**).

Event Journal.xls

Event Number	Description	Notes
0001		
0002		
0003		
0004		
0005		
0006		
0007		
0008		
0009		
0010		
0011		
0012		
0013		
0014		
0015		
0016		
0017		
0018		
0019		
0020		
0021		
0022		
0023		
0024		
0025		
0026		
0027		
0028		
0029		
0030		
0031		
0032		
0033		
0034		
0035		

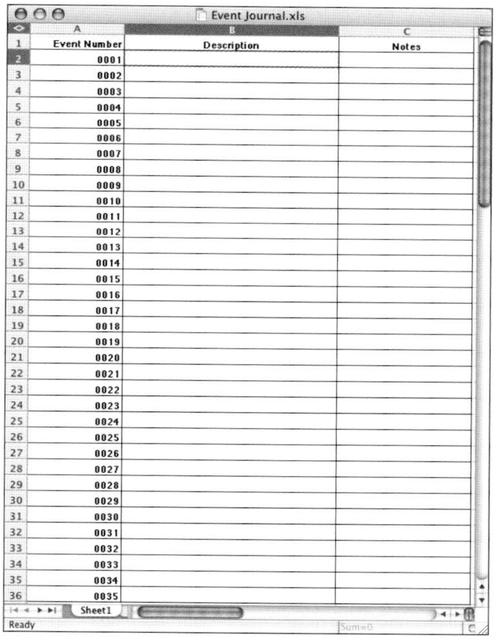

FIGURE 7.7

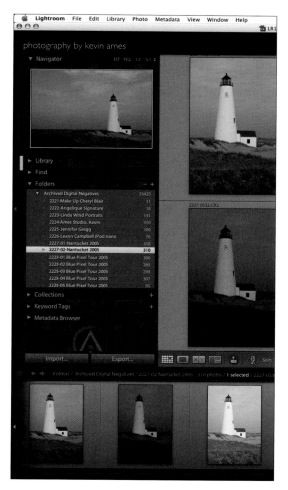

FIGURE 7.8

CHAPTER 8

The Bulletproof Archive Workflow

I AM CONCERNED. Very concerned about saving the visual history of this and future generations. A lot of photographers understand that with digital capture being the predominant medium, it is important to back up digital negatives. The truth is (and a potentially disastrous one at that) the backups rarely happen. Digital negatives (RAW or JPEG) are left on hard drives. One of the published features of a hard drive is its MTF: Mean Time until Failure. Do you really want to store your life's work on something that has a feature saying how long it will last until it fails?

Didn't think so.

Bulletproof isn't really bulletproof. The idea is that something bulletproof will stop a bullet or two, maybe three. It doesn't mean that if you keep shooting and hitting exactly the same place repeatedly that nothing will get through. Bulletproof archiving is like bulletproof glass or an armored vest. It gives the photographer methods for recovery after a disaster like a failed hard drive or a deleted folder of precious images.

We photographers are busy, well-meaning humans. The good intention of creating backups regularly is there. The process is not. This chapter of the *Notebook* explains the concepts of archiving, sets up the file structure, then shows step by step the procedures for making bulletproof archives.

Force of Habit

Regular backups are great. Practicing bulletproof workflow is much better. Making it a habit is best of all. Humans are habitual creatures. We photographers can use that trait to ensure that our digital negatives and their resulting projects are stored redundantly then cataloged for easy retrieval anytime in the future. If nothing else hits home for you, my reader, take this chapter to heart, then devote the time to making the principles a habit you do after every shoot.

About bulletproof archives

There are lots of systems for backing up digital photographs. The best ones share the same principles. They are triple redundant, verified, and scalable. These traits have been in place at my studio since the early nineties and have not changed, even though the software I use them with has evolved from the equivalent of traveling everywhere on foot to having a private jet. That's the scalable part. Will the system you adopt be able to evolve as software and storage media do?

Redundancy

The key principle to bulletproof archiving is having digital negatives in at least three discrete locations as soon after the shoot as is humanly possible. Initially those places will be external hard drives. Ultimately two of them will be non-volatile optical media—DVDs, for instance.

Immediately after the shoot, the memory card must be copied to two separate external hard drives. It is more efficient when both copies can be made at the same time. It is most efficient when the files are renamed (Chapter 7) and have basic metadata added to them (Chapter 6) during copying. Both Bridge (Chapter 2) and Lightroom (later in this chapter) offer this functionality.

Usually, though not necessarily before making optical backups, the digital negatives want to be enhanced for color and exposure and have more detailed metadata added to them. The key factor is that enhancements made prior to creating permanent archives on optical discs will be saved in the permanent archives. The pitfall is that as humans we want everything perfect before we commit it to permanent storage. As you will see, where once that was critical now it is not so important. As a matter of fact, using Lightroom as your main file management tool means that the archives can be burned, copied, and verified immediately after import.

Verification

So how do you really know the photographs you copied from the memory card are in fact actually there on your hard drives and optical media? You will not believe the number of photographers I have asked that question who have looked at me funny and said, "I copied them, so they have to be there. Right?" At this point in the conversation, there is a bit of doubt in their expressions.

The answer is: trust then verify. Trust that your operating system or import software works as promised. Then verify that no corruption is sneaking in. A side note here: CD- and DVD-burning software offer to "verify" the disc that has just burned. That assures the disc is a perfect copy of the data on the hard drive. If there is a corrupt photograph on the hard drive, this type of verification only proves that you have a perfect copy of that corruption.

Corruption usually happens during the copying process, either from camera to memory card, card to hard drives, or when shooting tethered. The first two corruption points are fairly rare. The third happens somewhat more often. The truth is that the corrupt file will never be the image of your out-of-focus shoes made by accidentally tripping the shutter while chimping a shot. Oh no! It will always be the most important photograph the galaxy has ever, er, not seen. A perfect example is this one of a Cape Air flight on final approach over the ocean for landing on Nantucket Island. (Cape Air is the real-life airline of the one in the TV comedy "Wings.") I was standing on Nobadeer Beach making photographs of the plane when (I swear it's true) a Godzilla-looking lizard reared up twenty stories out of the water taking a swing at the descending aircraft. I didn't verify the copies on the hard drives before I reformatted the card. Wouldn't you

FIGURE 8.1

FIGURE 8.2

FIGURE 8.3

just know it? The only file in the entire take that was corrupted was of the plane-swatting sea monster. Fortunately, it missed the plane because it got to its full height just after the plane passed.

True story. I have the picture to prove it. Sort of (**Figure 8.1**).

Creating bulletproof archives is the best habit a photographer can have. Better yet, make it your own personal addiction.

Structure

By definition, any system has to have a structure. Bulletproof archives for digital negatives have one, too. It is ever so slightly imposing at first. Once you get the habit, it's very straightforward.

Hard drives

The bulletproof archive uses two *external* hard drives or two *external* RAIDs or a RAID and a hard drive (**Figure 8.2**). Naming the drives can be as simple as HD1 and HD2 on the Mac or E and F on Windows. Mine are RAIDs named Hard Drive 01 and Hard Drive 02 since I use Macintosh computers (**Figure 8.3**). That naming puts them right under the boot drive, typically called Macintosh HD on the Mac. Logical drive letters can be assigned as close to the boot drive, C, on Windows.

Archived digital negatives want to be on external hard drives so they are available to many machines. This is a security/safety issue as well. If digital negatives are stored on internal drives, when the computer has to visit a repair facility, the photographs go along. Often technicians erase and reinstall software, particularly operating systems, as part of the servicing procedure. This is a potential DISASTER. (Sorry for shouting.) It is *never* a good idea to let the photographs leave the studio in a computer. Imagine if they are stored on a laptop and it gets stolen or dropped. Same bad result. Keep them on external drives.

The first hard drive or RAID wants to be the larger one if they are different sizes. It will house the digital negatives during the archiving—as well as after they are archived—and a copy of the Lightroom catalog. If you have already copied files to a drive, copy them to this one for the archiving process.

The second hard drive or RAID can be smaller. It is used to hold the temporary backups, a second copy of the Lightroom catalog, and the project archives.

Folder setup

STEP ONE

On the root of the first hard drive, create two new folders. Name the first Archived Digital Negatives and the second RAW Files 2B Archived (**Figure 8.4**).

FIGURE 8.4

STEP TWO

Open the RAW Files 2B Archived folder. This is the primary destination folder for images imported from memory cards. Make a new folder named 0001-Your Project's Name. Folders carry more information than individual digital negatives do. For more on this, see Chapter 7. The important point is that everything you shoot—personal, work related, portfolio, friend's engagement portraits, or a SOFE (that's a Significant Other Forced Event)—gets a job or project number. Keep them in sequence and let the computer sort them out.

The example here shows four projects—numbered 0001, 0002, 0003, and 0004—with more information about what's in the folder. I usually use the person's name I am photographing as my descriptor. Mac users: When naming folders, avoid apostrophes, ampersands, or any other character you can get by holding down the Shift key if it is even remotely possible that you will share with a machine running Windows. That's why I spell out "and" (**Figure 8.5**).

FIGURE 8.5

STEP THREE

Copy the empty folders you made in the folder RAW Files 2B Archived to the root of Hard Drive 02 (**Figure 8.6**). The destination folders for the first four projects are ready to receive the imported files.

FIGURE 8.6

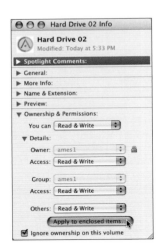

FIGURE 8.7

STEP FOUR (MAC USERS ONLY)

Highlight Hard Drive 01 on the desktop. Press Command + I for Get Info. At the bottom of the dialog is a section called Ownership & Permissions. Spin down its flippy triangle. It will read You can Read & Write. Spin down the Details flippy triangle. Make sure that the two Access menus and the Others menu all say Read & Write. Click Apply to enclosed items. Click OK when the warning dialog appears. Check Ignore ownership on this volume. Do this for Hard Drive 02 as well (**Figure 8.7**).

OS X is nothing if not rigorous when it comes to protecting data in its care. If a process—copying from a memory card, for instance—hangs, it is most likely a permissions issue. And remember to repair permissions on your Mac at least every month. (Applications > Utilities > Disk Utility. Select Macintosh HD, then click Repair Disk Permissions.)

Lightroom setup

Adobe Photoshop Lightroom differs from Bridge. Bridge is a file browser. It has to actually be able to open a folder of images to work with them. Lightroom is a database. It keeps previews available for sorting and rating in the Library module. Updates to metadata and exposure settings made in Camera Raw are included in the database as well.

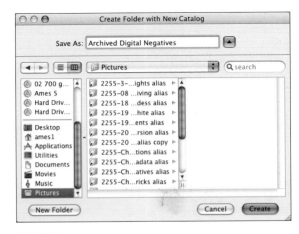

FIGURE 8.8

STEP ONE

Open Lightroom. Choose File > New Catalog... from the menu bar. The Create Folder with New Catalog dialog opens. Enter Archived Digital Negatives in the Save As window. Save it in the Pictures folder on the Mac or in the My Pictures folder on Windows. Click Create (**Figure 8.8**).

STEP TWO

Lightroom makes the new catalog and opens it. The name of the computer is displayed in the upper left-hand corner by default. Choose Lightroom > Identity Plate Setup... (PC: Edit > Identity Plate Setup). Click the Enable Identity Plate checkbox. Enter something along the lines of Photography by Your Name,

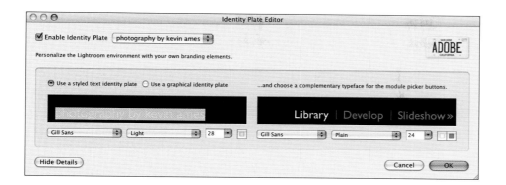

FIGURE 8.9

then highlight it and choose your favorite font. Keep the look of Lightroom consistent by selecting a typeface for the modules (**Figure 8.9**).

STEP THREE

Save the custom identity plate in the menu next to the Enable Identity Plate checkbox (**Figure 8.10**).

Identity plates can have graphics in them, such as a logo. I created one that I use in the Slideshow, Web, and Print modules. Since I have customized my end panels with my logo bug, having it in the header of the program (**Figure 8.11**) is way too much of a good thing, don't you think?

Okay. Enough about us. We are fabulous and now Lightroom shows it.

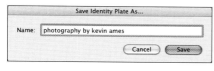

FIGURE 8.10

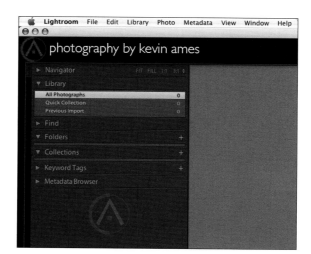

FIGURE 8.11

FLOURISHES, BOXES, YIN YANG, AND CUSTOM, TOO...

Lightroom 1.1 has thirteen panel end marks included. Access them by right-clicking (Control-clicking for Mac users who still haven't gotten a three-button mouse) one of them, then choosing a new one from the contextual menu. Or choose Go to Panel End Marks Folder and add your logo or graphic here. Then it is available in the contextual menu (**Figure 8.12**). My logo bug is 406 x 406 pixels.

The panel end marks can also be set in Preferences—Command (PC: Ctrl) + , (comma)—in the Panels section under the Interface tab.

FIGURE 8.12

STEP FOUR

Open Lightroom's Preferences by pressing Command (PC: Ctrl) + , then click Go to Catalog Settings at the bottom of the General tab. By default, the Automatically write changes into XMP is unchecked. Check this box (**Figure 8.13**). It tells Lightroom to export metadata additions, develop settings, keywords, ratings, and the like to an XMP "sidecar" file. This file is read by Adobe Bridge to apply your settings to files you ask it to display.

The box is unchecked by default because it does slow the importing process a bit. In my mind, having Lightroom and Bridge play nice with each other is well worth the small amount of extra time.

Importing digital negatives

Anytime processes can be done together, efficiency increases. The safari in Kenya (Chapter 1) resulted in close to four thousand digital RAW files. I got back to Atlanta in late August of 2001. The files took almost three weeks to rename, add minor metadata, burn to CDs (recording DVDs wasn't feasible then), duplicate, and verify. Recently I went through the workflow on them again just to see if improvements had in fact occurred. It took two hours.

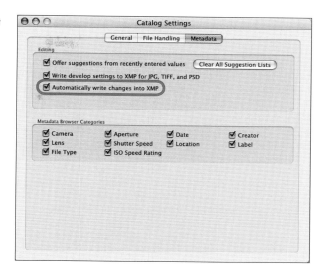

FIGURE 8.13

From memory cards

STEP ONE

With Lightroom open, insert a memory card into your reader. Lightroom recognizes the card when it mounts and automatically opens the Import dialog. Click the Show Preview box in the bottom left corner. A thumbnail of every image on the card is displayed. Each one has a checkmark indicating that it will be imported. The only time I uncheck a thumbnail is if it is completely black because the electronic flash failed to fire. I import and archive everything else, 'cause you never know when an out-of-focus image might just come in handy.

FIGURE 8.14

STEP TWO

Choose Copy photos to a new location and import from the File Handling menu. Under that, select the 0001-Your Project folder in the RAW Files 2B Archived folder on Hard Drive 01. Next, choose Into one folder from the Organize menu. Uncheck Put in subfolder. Check the next three boxes: Don't re-import suspected duplicates, Eject card after importing, and Backup to. Choose the 0001-Your Project folder on Hard Drive 02 (**Figure 8.14**).

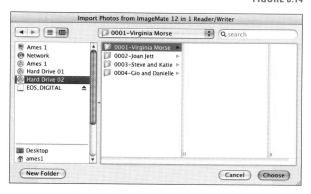

In the File Naming section, choose Project Number-Image Name from the drop-down menu. (The template was created in Chapter 3.) Enter 0001 for Custom Text, and enter 1 for the Start Number.

The Information to Apply section adds metadata by choosing the template you created in Chapter 6. In this example, it's Kevin Ames ©2007. I have yet to apply a Develop Setting during import, although if a client wanted to see black-and-white images as I was importing, that would be a good time to use Creative – BW High Contrast. Keywords can be added here, although it is better to use a controlled catalog of keywords rather than typing them in by whim.

The Render standard-sized previews checkbox puts reasonably high-resolution thumbnails into Lightroom's database. This will speed up the views in the Library module at the cost of slowing down the import and significantly enlarging the catalog. My thirty-six-thousand-plus Archived Digital Negative catalog's preview database is thirty-two gigabytes. That is a lot of overhead to carry if you are using a laptop.

Click Import (**Figure 8.15**).

FIGURE 8.15

Hard Drive 01

Hard Drive 02

STEP THREE

Occasionally, Lightroom displays a warning that files on the card don't appear to be photographs and shows a list. Click OK to continue the import or Cancel to close the dialog and stop the import. The dialog tells you what Lightroom is thinking; should there be files that are photos, though not in Lightroom-friendly form, you know in advance. This is unlikely since ACR 4 reads over 150 flavors of RAW files. The most probable time you'll see this dialog is when importing layered Photoshop files that have been saved with maximize compatibility turned off. This feature includes a flattened file in the Photoshop file (PSD) that allows Lightroom, as well as previous versions of Photoshop, to open the file even though all of the features of the current version aren't supported by prior ones.

The identity plate is temporarily replaced with a progress bar that also displays a thumbnail and new image name of the digital negative being imported (**Figure 8.16**). When the import finishes, the identity plate returns.

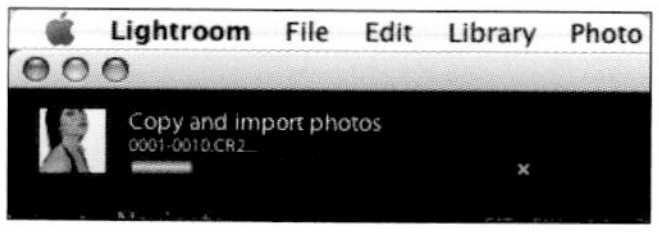

FIGURE 8.16

DOWNLOADING FROM A CAMERA

Lightroom will also recognize a camera that has been plugged into the computer. This is not the most efficient or safest way to transfer digital files. If the camera battery fails, corruption can occur. Cameras are pretty good at recording files. When it comes to playing them back into a hard drive, not so much.

STEP FOUR

Once the Grid fills up, scrolling to see the current photos coming in is a pain. In the center of the control bar is an icon that has a lowercase A on top of a Z with arrows circling it. This is the View Ascending Order icon. Click it to reverse their positions (so that Z is on top) and the current image being imported is displayed in the upper left corner of the Grid (**Figure 8.17**).

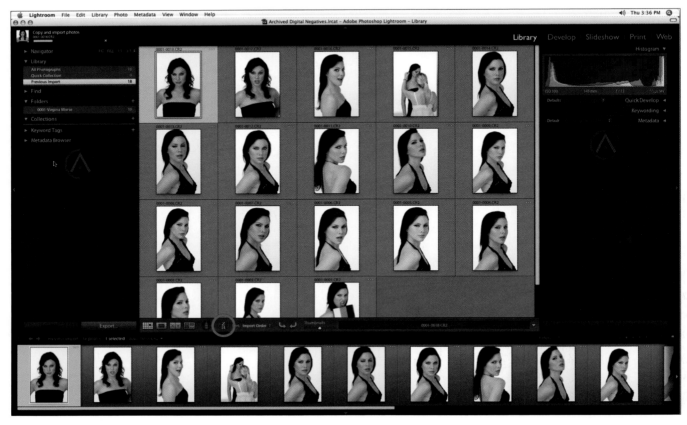

FIGURE 8.17

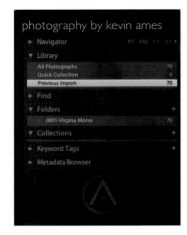

FIGURE 8.18

STEP FIVE

Add any additional metadata to the Caption, Keyword, and Title fields as discussed in Chapter 6.

The digital negatives are now in three places—on the memory card; in the 0001-Your Project folder within the RAW Files 2B Archived folder on Hard Drive 01; and on the root of Hard Drive 02 in the 0001-Your Project folder. Lightroom displays the previous import in the Grid. Under the Library pane, both the All Photographs and Previous Import panels display the same number of photographs. This is the only time it will be this way. From now on, the All Photographs panel tells exactly how many digital negatives are in the catalog, while the Previous Import tells just that. The Folders panel shows one entry—in this case, 0001-Virginia Morse (**Figure 8.18**).

Importing files already copied

Part of the archiving process is dealing with the files already copied from memory cards. Lightroom wants to add them to the Archived Digital Negatives catalog without having to copy them again. As mentioned earlier, if you are already storing images on an external hard drive, that's the one to use as Hard Drive 01.

STEP ONE

Move a folder of digital negatives from wherever it is on the hard drive into the RAW Files 2B Archived folder. Assign it the next number in sequence. For example, I will import RAW files I shot in 2005 of Joan Jett during the Music Midtown Festival as project 0002-Joan Jett. Remember, Lightroom does not care about the order of the sequence number. It sorts chronologically by the creation date stored in the EXIF metadata.

STEP TWO

Press Command (PC: Ctrl) + Shift + I to open Lightroom's Import dialog. Navigate to Hard Drive 01 > RAW Files 2B Archived > 0002-Your Project. Click Choose.

STEP THREE

Choose Import photos at their current location from the File Handling drop-down menu. The folder chosen will be listed in the pane underneath with a checked box that indicates it's set for import. Don't re-import suspected duplicates remains checked. Notice there isn't a File Naming option. Renaming happens after the import is completed. From the Metadata menu, choose a metadata template that has the correct copyright year. The date the photographs were made is shown just above the File Handling menu (**Figure 8.19**). Click Import.

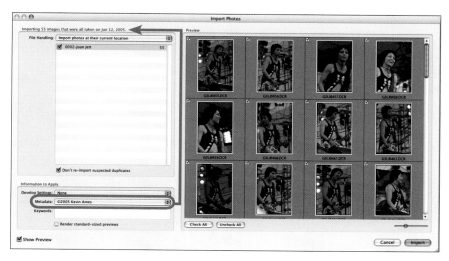

FIGURE 8.19

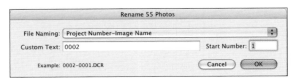

FIGURE 8.20

STEP FOUR

Press Command (PC: Ctrl) + A to select all of the thumbnails in the Grid. Rename the digital negatives by pressing F2, or choosing Library > Rename Photos…. (Lightroom follows Photoshop's convention of showing the keyboard shortcut to the right of a command selected from a menu. The keyboard shortcuts for each module can be accessed by pressing Command [PC: Ctrl] + ? or from the first choice in the Help menu.)

FIGURE 8.21

Lightroom remembers the naming template from the last import and displays it in the Rename dialog. It also tells how many files are being renamed. Type 0002 in the Custom Text field and 1 in the Start Number field. Click OK (**Figure 8.20**).

The Grid displays the new numbers in the thumbnails. The Library panel shows the previous import contains 55 photographs and the total number of images in the catalog is 125. The Folders panel lists both projects imported so far (**Figure 8.21**).

STEP FIVE

Add additional metadata to the Caption, Keywords, and Title fields.

Continue adding folders sequentially for each project you shoot. Add one project that's sitting on your hard drive per day; within a year or so you'll be completely caught up. Remember that this is a habit worth forming.

Archives

Since the foundation of bulletproof archive is redundancy, I am going to be redundant. The steps in the previous section deal with digital negatives on hard drives, and hard drives always fail. This section is the bulletproof part.

Optical Discs = DVD

Or a CD for those really small shoots. A DVD holds 4.7 gigabytes of data. A four-gig memory card fits nicely on a DVD. So I use DVDs.

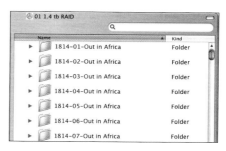

Oftentimes a shoot of a couple thousand RAW files will span several discs. After importing, which includes renaming, metadata addition, maybe keywords, and even enhancement in Bridge or Lightroom (see Chapter 13), I break them into DVD-sized folders, adding a disc number between the project number and the description. Here are the seven folders representing the seven DVDs containing the entire Out in Africa shoot as an example (**Figure 8.22**).

FIGURE 8.22

Blu-Ray, DVD-HD

These DVDs are still in the "format wars" stage of development. The burners are expensive, as is the blank media. Until one format declares "victory" and withdraws from the market and everyone you know has a computer that reads discs in the format of the real winner, stay away from these discs. This will sort itself out. Don't get excited about the promise of storing fifty gigs on a disc just yet. Wait, and let others live on this bleeding edge.

Burning software

I prefer to use third-party disc-burning software on my Macs, as opposed to the utility that is built into OS X. Same holds true on my Windows machines. In both cases, the tools come from Roxio (roxio.com): Toast on the Mac and Easy Media Creator on Windows. Since my workflow is predominately Mac-centric, I'll show how Toast fits in. Creator is similar in its function. Come on, we're only burning discs.

Burning the original disc

STEP ONE
Launch Toast or Creator.

STEP TWO
Drag the folder 0001-Your Project into the creation window.

STEP THREE

Make certain that the name of the disc in the burning software is *exactly* the same as the name on the folder (**Figure 8.23**, #1). This may be a problem in Windows, as some software shortens (truncates) disc names.

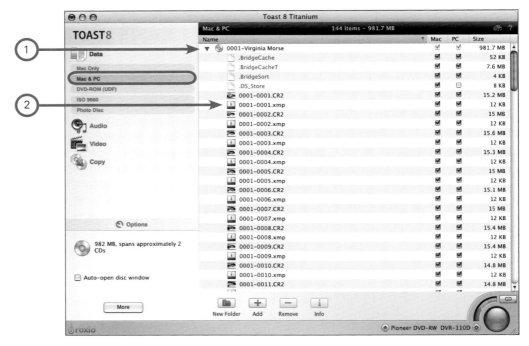

FIGURE 8.23

STEP FOUR

Check to see that the XMP sidecar files that accompany the RAW files are visible in the software's content area (#2).

Finally, fellow Mac users: Play nice with our Windows brethren. Click the Mac & PC compatibility button in Toast so we can all just get along. Windows users don't have to worry because Macs natively read discs they burn.

STEP FIVE

Burn the disc.

Copy the original disc

Here's where confusion creeps into this process. To copy the original disc means to make a copy from the original to another disc. It does not mean burn another disc. Here's why. The data flows from the CF card to Hard Drive 01. From there it is burned to the original DVD. That DVD is duplicated in a DVD duplicator and the *copy* is imported into a new Lightroom catalog named Verified DVDs (**Figure 8.24**).

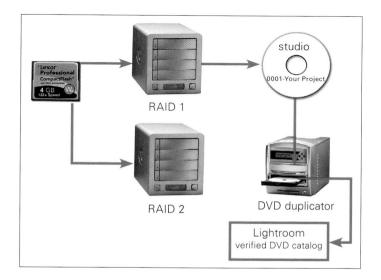

FIGURE 8.24

DVD duplicators are independent of any computer. Put the original disc in the top tray, close it, put a blank DVD in the bottom tray and close it, then press Copy Disc. Duplicators are available from discmakers.com and cost around $260 at the time I wrote this. This is the single accessory that really makes the Bulletproof Archive Workflow flow.

Verification

Both Toast and Creator offer the option of "verifying" the disc. This process confirms that the DVD is an exact copy of what's on the hard drive. If a file on the hard drive is corrupt, this verification process merely says that the DVD is a perfect copy of the corruption. Not so useful. So turn off that feature and follow along.

Lightroom setup

This part only gets done once.

STEP ONE

Choose File > New Catalog... in Lightroom. Name it Verified DVDs, then click Create. Lightroom quits, makes the new catalog, then launches itself with the Verified DVDs catalog open.

STEP TWO

Create a new identity plate named Verified DVDs.

Verify the copy

STEP ONE

Load the copy of the original DVD into the computer.

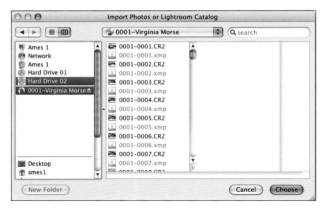

FIGURE 8.25

STEP TWO

Press Command (PC: Ctrl) + Shift + I to open Lightroom's Import Photos or Lightroom Catalog dialog. Choose the DVD 0001-Your Project. (The example shows mine, 0001-Virginia Morse.) Click Choose (**Figure 8.25**).

STEP THREE

Set up the Import Dialog by choosing Import photos at their current location from the File Handling menu. Check Don't re-import suspected duplicates. Select None from both the Develop Settings and Metadata menus. The Keywords section will remain blank as well. Be sure to check Render standard-sized previews. This is the key to verifying the DVD. Click Import. Lightroom opens each RAW file and renders a new preview from it off of the DVD, thereby proving the disc is good. The RAW digital negatives are now in five discrete places: 1) on the memory card, 2) in the 0001-Your Project folder within the RAW Files 2B Archived folder on Hard Drive 01, 3) in the 0001-Your Project folder at the root of Hard Drive 02, 4) on the original DVD, and 5) on the verified DVD copy of the original.

Clean up

It is now safe to reformat the memory card in your camera and delete the temporary backup folder from the root of Hard Drive 02, which leaves the RAW files in an almost bulletproof archive. One last housekeeping detail: Move the 0001-Your Project folder from the RAW Files 2B Archived folder into the Archived Digital Negatives folder—as of right now, they are archived.

DVD distribution

The archive becomes truly bulletproof when one of the two DVDs is stored in a secure off-site location. If your studio is in New Orleans, a good place for an off-site set of DVDs would be anywhere *above* sea level. Ideally, the off-site backups want to be where natural disasters are rare—someplace that doesn't have hurricanes, floods, wild fires, earthquakes, or anything where FEMA might be called in to help. I'm thinking Boise, Idaho. Face it, nothing ever happens to Boise.

How verification checks the process

Importing the second disc into a separate Lightroom catalog with Render standard-sized previews checked in the Import dialog generates a new preview from the file on the DVD, verifying it is good. If the copy made from the original DVD is good, so is the original. If the original DVD burned from the 0001-Your Project folder in the RAW Files 2B Archived folder is good, then the folder on Hard Drive 01 is good as well.

When verification fails

There are those admittedly rare times when a DVD won't verify. Here is what to do in order. Go to the next step only if the problem persists.

> **STEP ONE**
>
> If there is a problem, Lightroom will show a dialog at the end of the import indicating which files were not imported. Should this happen, write down the names of the files in the dialog. Click OK. Open the Import Photos or Lightroom Catalog window (Command [PC: Ctrl] + Shift + I), click on the DVD, then find the individual files. Command-click (PC: Ctrl-click) them to select them, then click Choose. The Import dialog opens. Click Import.

FIGURE 8.26

STEP TWO

If the warning shows again, check the original DVD as shown above. If the files import from it, the copy is bad. Make a new copy, delete the folder named 0001-Your Project in Lightroom by highlighting it in the Folders pane, then clicking the – (minus sign). A warning opens, asking if you want to delete the folder, and explains that it only removes it from the Lightroom catalog and not from the disc (**Figure 8.26**).

STEP THREE

If the original disc is bad, delete the 0001-Your Project folder in Lightroom's Folders pane. Import the folder 0001-Your Project from the RAW Files 2B Archived folder on Hard Drive 01. If it imports successfully, the original disc did not burn successfully. Repeat Steps One through Three in the "Burning the original disc" section above, then duplicate it and repeat Steps One through Three in the "Verify the copy" section.

STEP FOUR

If the folder on Hard Drive 01 shows problems on import, again note the files reported by Lightroom. Go to Hard Drive 02. Open the 0001-Your Project folder, then open the folder named Imported on June 29, 2007 (in this example. Your date will be different, of course) (**Figure 8.27**).

FIGURE 8.27

Find the files that have the same numbers as the ones you wrote down. Command-click (PC: Ctrl-click) them to select them, then right-click and choose Copy. Highlight the 0001-Your Project folder in the RAW Files 2B Archived folder on Hard Drive 01. Right-click and choose Paste. Click OK when the operating system asks if you want to replace the existing files. Delete the 0001-Your Project folder in Lightroom. (All of the troubleshooting is done using the Verified DVDs catalog.) Re-import the 0001-Your Project folder from the RAW Files 2B Archived folder on Hard Drive 01.

STEP FIVE

If the replaced RAW files are still not importing, check them in the Finder (Mac) or Explorer (Windows). If image thumbnails show up there, quit Lightroom and restart the computer. Launch Lightroom. The Verified DVDs catalog opens. Delete the folder 0001-Your Project. Re-import the 0001-Your Project folder from the RAW Files 2B Archived folder on Hard Drive 01.

STEP SIX

If the problem still exists, make a new folder in the RAW Files 2B Archived folder on Hard Drive 01. Name it 0001a-Your Project. Copy this folder to Hard Drive 02. In Lightroom, choose File > Open recent catalog... and choose Archived Digital Negatives. Import the memory card again, copying the RAW files to both drives following Steps One through Five in the "From memory cards" section. Burn a new DVD. Copy it and follow the verification steps. This is why memory cards are saved until verification is run.

STEP SEVEN

If the same files are still not importing, open Adobe Bridge and see if they can be read in ACR 4 directly from the memory card. They won't. And at least you'll be sure that the files on the card are corrupt. This is the digital badness that happens to photographers today. The photographs are ruined. During the days of film, scratches on the emulsion were the equivalent badness with the same result, a ruined photograph. Hopefully they are not your once-in-a-lifetime "Godzilla chasing a plane" photos.

Archive catalog

Wouldn't it be nice if you had a list of all of your archived digital negatives that was a definitive listing of all of the folders of images that have been through the archiving process? The answer, of course, is, "Sure would!" And you do. Look at the Folders panel in the Verified DVDs catalog. That's it. By importing the copy of the original DVD of each folder on Hard Drive 01, a catalog of the folders in the Archived Digital Negatives folder is maintained in the Verified DVDs catalog. You will always know if a folder is ready to move from RAW Files 2B Archived to the Archived Digital Negatives folder by checking the Verified DVDs catalog.

Form the Habit

I know what you're thinking: "Do I feel lucky?" Well, even if you do, your digital negatives are way too precious to trust to luck. I encourage you to work through this process for your next ten shoots and to add a project from your hard drive every day using this system. In ten days, you'll not only be proficient, you'll be hooked on the habit of bulletproof archiving. And believe me: When fate takes a shot at you and hits your hard drive, you'll be delighted with your armor.

CHAPTER 9

Lightroom Catalogs

PHOTOGRAPHERS ARE CREATIVE PEOPLE. We love creating about as much as we dislike—okay, hate—doing the repetitive work required to keep track of our creations. Sometimes we avoid the task of cataloging our work altogether, thinking, "I know where it is." (Or ought that be "rationalize our disdain for the mundane"?) Remember that the shortest pencil is better than the longest memory.

This section of the *Notebook* is about managing our digital negatives. Metadata and sequential naming, along with a robust system of archiving, are three quarters of the process. The last component is the catalog that takes the "I know where it is" out of mind and into a searchable database. The best part is that most of the work is done as the files are copying from the memory card and as metadata is added.

The Archived Digital Negatives Catalog

This catalog, created in Chapter 8, keeps track of each digital negative, whether RAW or JPEG. Most of the work done in Lightroom is in this catalog. It is the place where heroes are chosen, exposure experiments are conducted, color is explored, focus is checked, and information about the photograph is added. It's also where the images are sorted by date, location, and rating, then sent off to the web as a gallery, printed as a contact sheet or fine print, and presented as a slideshow.

The best thing about Lightroom is not only its ability to play nice with Photoshop CS3 and, particularly, Bridge; it's Lightroom's ability to back up changes made to XMP "sidecar" files.

Nothing really changes

The premise of a "digital negative" is that it is as immutable as a negative created on film. The output can be radically different while the underlying information remains unchanged.

This has always been true for film negatives. Prints could be toned, bleached, boiled, shaken, stirred (I have *no* idea what the last two might look like), or solarized. No matter what was done, the negative was unchanged.

This is also true for RAW files. Since the beginning of digital photography, RAW files have had to be converted (copied) into an editable file. The conversion is like shining light through a film negative to make a print. The data is copied to the new file while the RAW file, like the negative, remains unchanged. The difference is that the RAW file's preview *looks* changed because it reflects the settings made in Camera Raw or Lightroom.

The next project is for both Lightroom and Bridge. Download the folder of sample files for this chapter from amesphoto.com/learning. The book code is DPN8414.

STEP ONE
Make a new Lightroom catalog to use for exercises. Choose File > New Catalog…. Name it DPN Projects. When it opens, make a new identity plate using the same name (see Chapter 8).

STEP TWO

Press Command (PC: Ctrl) + Shift + I to open the Import Photos dialog. Choose Import photos at their current location from the File Handling menu. Leave the rest of the choices at their defaults. Click Import (**Figure 9.1**).

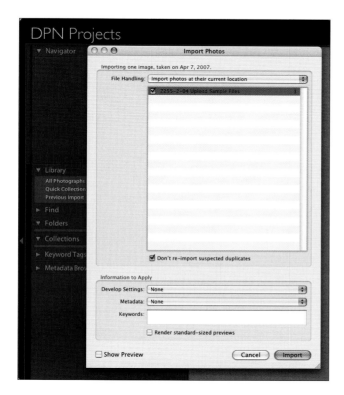

FIGURE 9.1

STEP THREE

Open Bridge. Navigate to the downloaded sample folder, then click it to display the same file that was imported into the DPN Projects catalog in Lightroom. Both Lightroom and Bridge are displaying the same image (**Figures 9.2** and **9.3**).

STEP FOUR

Open Lightroom's Preferences by pressing Command (PC: Ctrl) + , (comma). Click the Go to Catalog Settings button at the bottom of the dialog. Check Automatically write changes into XMP (**Figure 9.4**).

FIGURE 9.2

FIGURE 9.3

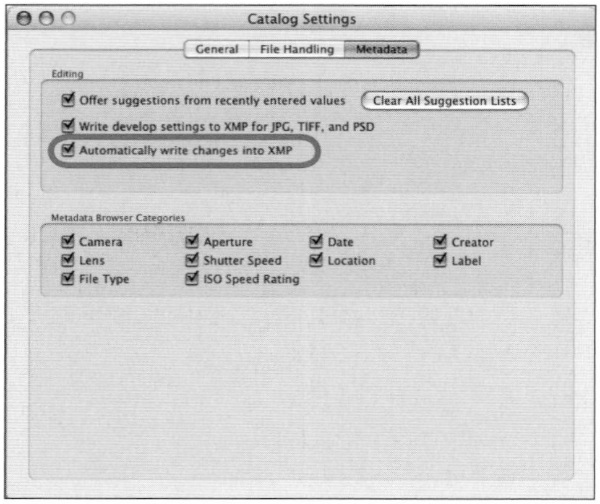

FIGURE 9.4

This setting may slow Lightroom down a little bit. It more that makes up for the price in speed by having automatic compatibility with Bridge. The truth is (especially if you have been using Bridge for a while) Bridge is where Photoshop projects start. Who can resist a quick tweak in ACR 4 before opening it? Photographers are natural-born change agents.

STEP FIVE

Modules in Lightroom can be chosen from the keyboard by holding down the Command (PC: Ctrl) + Option (PC: Alt) keys and typing 1 for Library, 2 for Develop, 3 for Slideshow, 4 for Print, and 5 for Web. Press the modifier keys and 2 to switch to the Develop module. The photograph was made about twenty minutes after sunset using a color temperature close to tungsten (3200°K). Show the right side panel and spin down the Basic panel. Click on the words As Shot. Choose Daylight. That's a good start. Move the Temp slider to 14080 (**Figure 9.5**).

FIGURE 9.5

LIGHTROOM PANELS: TO SEE OR NOT TO SEE

Lightroom is a single-monitor program. So it adapts to less screen real estate in amazing and useful ways. Here are the ways to see (or hide) these panels and to customize their behavior to your liking.

From the keyboard:

- Tab: Hides and reveals the side panels.

- Shift + Tab: Hides all panels.

- T: Shows toolbar.

- F: Cycles through Normal View, Hide Title Bar, Hide Title Bar and Menus.

- L: Lights Dim, Lights Out, Lights Normal (Dim and Out modes are for everything except the displayed image).

With the mouse:

- Click the Show/Hide Panel Group icon (flippy triangle).

- Right-click the outside edge of the panel group (beyond the scroll bar) and choose:

  - Auto Hide & Show: Displays the panel when the cursor is over it. Move the cursor away to hide the panel.

  - Auto Hide: Hides the panel when the cursor leaves it. A panel with this setting must be opened manually by clicking its triangle.

  - Manual: Just like the M setting on a camera. Click the triangle to hide or reveal the panel.

STEP SIX

Go to Bridge. Watch the preview. See it change to the settings made in Lightroom (**Figure 9.6**)?

FIGURE 9.6

STEP SEVEN

Highlight the thumbnail in Bridge's content area. Press Command (PC: Ctrl) + R to open the file in Camera Raw. The Temperature is set to 14080. Bridge and Camera Raw saw the changes Lightroom made to the RAW file's XMP metadata and updated themselves automatically (**Figure 9.7**).

FIGURE 9.7

Reciprocation

The Lightroom-to-Bridge-and-ACR 4 link is established. How about going the other way?

STEP ONE

The file is still open in Camera Raw. Click the HSL / Grayscale tab (fourth from left, including Basic). Click Convert to Grayscale. Click Done. The result shows immediately in Bridge (**Figure 9.8**).

STEP TWO

Return to Lightroom. What change do you see? Nothing changes, right? Go to the Library module. Choose Metadata > Read Metadata from File. The changes made in ACR 4 have been updated in Lightroom's database (**Figure 9.9**). One difference, then, between a file browser (Bridge) and a database (Lightroom) is that the file browser has to see the folder it is showing. The database stores the information. The file browser checks the folder when it becomes active and displays the current information. The database won't display changes made outside of Lightroom unless it's told to read them.

FIGURE 9.8

FIGURE 9.9

Metadata too!

Changes in Lightroom's metadata and keyword panels will show up in Bridge. Changes made in Bridge's metadata and keyword panel can be read in Lightroom. So will changes made in the File Info dialog in either Bridge or Photoshop. Needless to say, Photoshop picks up the changes in either program.

STEP ONE

Open the right panel if it isn't showing. Click the word Metadata to open that panel. Fill in the words Street scene in the Caption field. Enter 2352-Boston in the Title field (**Figure 9.10**).

STEP TWO

Return to Bridge. As soon as the window is active, the metadata panel updates with Lightroom's information. Notice that in Bridge the Description field holds the words that were entered in Lightroom's Caption field (**Figure 9.11**). Choose File > File Info.

FIGURE 9.10

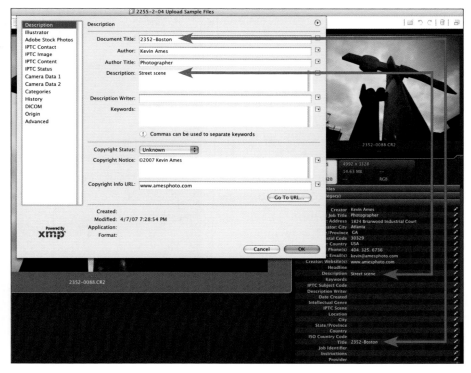

FIGURE 9.11

STEP THREE

Add the location information: Location: Harvard; City: Boston; State/Province: MA; Country: USA (**Figure 9.12**). When the Do you want to apply these metadata changes to "2352-0088.CR2"? box opens, first click Don't show again, then click Save.

STEP FOUR

Go back to Lightroom. Update the metadata by choosing Metadata > Read Metadata from File. Magically, the metadata entered in Bridge appears in Lightroom (**Figure 9.13**). (Hey, any technology that's so advanced you can't understand how it does what it does is magic in my book. Heh. And this is *my* book.)

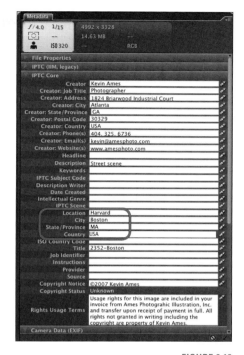

FIGURE 9.12

FIGURE 9.13

Resetting a RAW file

A RAW file can be returned to its original state directly as it came out of the camera by renaming, moving, or deleting its XMP sidecar file. The exception to this is that if the file has been renamed in Bridge with the Preserve original file-name box checked, the original name is gone forever.

STEP ONE

Go to Bridge. Choose View > Show Hidden Files. The file 2352-0088.xmp appears. Click its name, then rename it OLD-2352-0088.xmp. Press Return (PC: Enter). The preview immediately goes back to blue. Look at the metadata pane. It's blank except for fields filled in by the camera's EXIF metadata. The RAW file has been reset (**Figure 9.14**).

FIGURE 9.14

STEP TWO

Effectively there is no XMP sidecar file associated with the RAW file in this example. A new blank one has to be made. Highlight the thumbnail image. Open it in Camera Raw by pressing Command (PC: Ctrl) + R. Move the Temperature slider to the right ever so slightly until it reads 3200. Click Done. A new XMP sidecar file named 2352-0088.xmp appears in the content pane. The other one is still there.

STEP THREE

Go back to Lightroom. Choose Metadata > Save Metadata to File. Click Overwrite Settings in the dialog box (**Figure 9.15**).

FIGURE 9.15

STEP FOUR

Return to Bridge. The preview changes from its original blue to grayscale as Bridge reads the Develop settings from the newly updated XMP file for the RAW file 2352-0088.CR2 (**Figure 9.16**). Lightroom has also replaced the information missing from the Metadata tab.

New and updated XMP "sidecar" file

FIGURE 9.16

Closed loop

Our archived digital negatives are dynamic and evolving. As ideas generate from play, experience, or inspiration of the unconscious mind, we return to our images. Adjusting them, playing the "what if?" game, working with new crops, converting to black and white, even spending time simply watching them with creative intentions. Photographers live in the moment when shooting, and I believe we do the same when in front of the monitor. The tool often chosen is the one at hand. If an image is displayed in Bridge, the play likely happens with Camera Raw. The same is true when perusing in Lightroom's Library module. An idea strikes, an image is highlighted, Command (PC: Ctrl) + Alt + 2 is pressed, and editing begins in the Develop module.

So what does this closed loop mean to photographers?

Lightroom records changes applied to digital negatives in the Library and Develop modules. Bridge, Camera Raw, and Photoshop recognize changes in RAW settings and metadata. Changes made in Bridge, Camera Raw, and Photoshop have to be read by Lightroom so it can update its database.

The implications for cataloging are immense. For the first time, any change to metadata—settings or information—can be added, edited, or completely changed without concern for what might happen when a hard drive is lost.

The broken chain

Before Lightroom, there was no practical way to back up changes made to a RAW file. The files themselves were fine. They live on an external hard drive, have a backup DVD on site, and another stored remotely. The issue occurred when the photographer went into play mode, creating new images with ACR. Or she/he decided to add more information to the metadata to make searching easier. Oftentimes, that was done in cataloging software from a third party. The problem was that the catalog and the archives were separate. They could not share and update each other. Backing up the catalog software's database did not update the XMP sidecar files of the archived digital negatives. The chain of information flow was broken.

Lightroom has changed all that. For the first time, changes to the archived digital negatives are stored in a database that can read and restore XMP settings. This is a huge advantage in three ways.

- Initial archiving workflow becomes much faster. Lightroom renames and adds the base metadata to each digital negative on import. Adding the project number and a description to the Title field, filling in the Location, City, State/Province, and Country is quick and easy in either Lightroom or Bridge. The Description and Keywords can be added later. This reduces the time between importing and archiving to the two DVDs. Photographers are more likely to make bulletproof archives.

- Metadata can be much more robust. Before Lightroom, in order to archive your metadata, it had to be complete, as did enhancements of color and exposure before the bulletproof archives were made. With Lightroom, there is no practical limit to how much information can be added to a digital negative's metadata or how evolved its settings can be in ACR. This freedom becomes even more valuable as improvements are made to the Camera Raw engine that powers both Lightroom's Develop module and ACR. New settings can be applied to the oldest digital negatives and they can be archived for the first time dynamically.

- Archived digital negatives that are restored from DVDs can be updated to the current status of the Lightroom database. A catastrophe happens: The 750-gigabyte drive housing a couple of hundred DVDs' worth of digital negatives fails irretrievably. With a bulletproof archive, the catastrophe is downgraded to pain-in-the-neck status. Once the discs have been copied onto the new drive, the metadata and settings contained in the metadata are back to the state when the archive discs were burned, copied, and verified. Now, the metadata in XMP sidecar files can be restored from Lightroom.

The Verified DVDs Catalog

The second Lightroom catalog is the Verified DVDs catalog. This catalog is a list of the DVDs that have been verified. It's where you can check to see if a disc has been through the final and most important step of bulletproof archiving. If the disc is not in the folders list, it has not been verified. Discs are shown in red because Lightroom cannot access the DVD it imported (**Figure 9.17**).

It is also a database of the original state of the RAW files when they were archived. Compare a folder from the Verified DVDs catalog with the same folder in the Archived Digital Negatives catalog to see how the work has evolved from archiving to the present. As years go by, this will be a very interesting comparison. At this writing, comparing will require Lightroom running on two computers. Lightroom can have only one catalog open at a time.

The Projects Catalog

The third catalog is for projects. Projects are photographs that have been edited in Photoshop and/or delivered to clients. Work done from RAW files has to go through a similar process to creating bulletproof archives for digital negatives. The folder structure is similar, and the disc burning and copying are the same. A new Lightroom catalog is created named Projects with an identity plate of the same name.

Hard Drive 02 is for Projects. There are two main folders on it: Projects and Projects 2B Archived. (This works exactly like archiving digital negatives.)

FIGURE 9.17

When a client orders an image, its digital negative is either exported from Lightroom to Photoshop or opened in Photoshop from ACR 4. The work is completed and stored in a new folder with the same job number and description as the folder with the original digital negatives. The words Working Files are added after the descriptions.

This folder goes into a serial numbered folder inside the Projects 2B Archived folder. When the serial numbered folder has received enough working folders to bring its capacity to 4.5 gigabytes, it is burned to a DVD.

The DVD is burned and copied (**Figure 9.18**). (In this example, folder 0004 has two projects in it that will fill a DVD—2328-Nantucket Working Files and 2352-Boston Working Files. Note that the working files do not have to be in job number order. Drop them into the next available serial numbered folder, burn them to disc, then let the computer sort them out.)

The copy of the original DVD is imported into Lightroom's Projects catalog for verification. Once verified, the serial numbered folder representing the disc is moved from the Projects 2B Archived folder into the Projects folder. After verification of its DVD by importing the DVD into the Projects catalog in Lightroom, the folder 0004 is promoted into the Projects folder on Hard Drive 02.

A detailed step-by-step explanation of the Projects workflow is beyond the scope of this edition of the *Notebook*.

FIGURE 9.18

Backing Up Lightroom Catalogs

Lightroom catalogs are important. They take a lot of time to build. When they are used to place extra information in metadata—as well as rate, sort, and play with digital negatives—they become extremely valuable. Backing them up regularly is a serious Must Do.

Catalog settings

STEP ONE

The Catalog Settings dialog is available in Preferences or from the File menu (File > Catalog Settings...). The keyboard shortcut is Command (PC: Ctrl) + Option (PC: Alt) + , (comma). My Lightroom catalog currently has over thirty thousand images that took three-and-a-half days to import from the Archived Digital Negatives folder. I chose to render standard-sized previews, which accounts in large part for the length of time it took. Backups are important.

At the very least, back up the catalog weekly. The backup location is by default the same as the catalog itself. And by default the Lightroom catalog is housed on the computer's internal hard drive. That is as it has to be because Lightroom will not open a catalog stored on a network drive. Not a problem. These are backups and want to be on external drives anyway.

STEP TWO

From the Back up catalog menu, choose Once a week, upon starting Lightroom (**Figure 9.19**). When Lightroom asks if you want to back up the catalog, it offers a choice of skipping the process. Resist clicking this button. Click Backup (**Figure 9.20**).

STEP THREE

Quit Lightroom. Using the Finder (Mac) or Windows Explorer, copy the Archived Digital Negatives folder to the root of Hard Drive 01 for the first week. Next week, copy it from the hard drive on the computer to the root of Hard Drive 02.

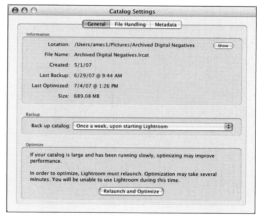

STEP FOUR

Burn the backup to a DVD and make a copy.

FIGURE 9.19

STEP FIVE

Verifying is a bit tricky. Lightroom cannot open a catalog that is on non-writable media like DVDs. Copy the catalog to the desktop and open it in Lightroom (File > Open Catalog…). If it opens, chances are the backup DVDs are good. Close the catalog in Lightroom and open the Archived Digital Negatives catalog from its normal location. Move the copy on the desktop to the Trash or Recycle Bin and empty it.

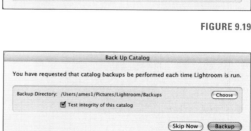

FIGURE 9.20

STEP SIX

Label the DVD with the data of the backup. Store one copy in the studio and one offsite.

FIGURE 9.21

Previews

Standard-sized previews are set in the Catalog Settings dialog under File Handling. If you choose to have Lightroom render standard-sized previews, this file can become large. Okay, it gets huge. I have 36,216 digital negatives archived. The previews take up over thirty-two gigs of space (**Figure 9.21**).

The Verified DVDs catalog is going to get big. Rendering standard-sized previews assures the DVD is good. Once the disc is verified, Lightroom can discard the previews.

STEP ONE
Open Catalog Settings and choose File Handling.

STEP TWO
Choose either After one week or After 30 days. Click OK. Lightroom keeps your preview cache a manageable size.

Finding Photographs

The whole point of a catalog is to find the exact photograph we want when we want it. Lightroom gets right to the point in the Library module.

FIGURE 9.22

The Find panel

Start using Find by clicking the checkbox to the left of the work Text.

Lightroom's Find panel searches by text anywhere or in eight categories—Filename, Copy Name, Title, Caption, Keywords, IPTC, EXIF, and Metadata. The sort rules are: Contains, Contains All, Doesn't Contain, Starts With, and Ends With.

My favorite is Text: Filename, Rule: Contains for sorting by job number (**Figure 9.22**).

When I don't have the job number or want to narrow it down to a subject, I use Text: Metadata, Rule: Contains, and then I enter what I remember. In this example, I'll enter Great Point (which is on Nantucket Island). The number of images in the Library is displayed in the All Photographs pane in the Library panel (**Figure 9.23**).

Additionally, the Find panel can search by dates and date ranges in order to narrow text searches.

After you have finished using Find, uncheck the Text and Date checkboxes so that other search methods have access to all of the photographs in the Library. You'll know a search is active in the Find panel by looking at All Photographs in the Library panel. When a smaller number (followed by a slash) precedes the number of photos in the Library, a search is active.

FIGURE 9.23

The Metadata Browser

The Metadata Browser is very cool and useful. It lists all of the cameras, lenses, file types, apertures, shutter speeds, ISO speed ratings, dates, locations, creators, and labels in the Lightroom database. Ever been asked, "What's your favorite focal length lens?" Spin down the Lens pane and see which one you use the most. "How much depth of field do you like? Do you shoot predominately wide open to blur the backgrounds, or do you like everything sharp by using a small aperture? Or does it fall somewhere in between?" I checked mine, and I appear to be an "f/8.0 and be there" photographer. F/2.8 came in second.

This tool is great, too, for finding missing metadata. Spin down the disclosure triangle by location, for instance. Anything listed under Unknown has not had metadata entered. The screenshot shows a lot missing, all of it shot before Photoshop could do a good job adding metadata (**Figure 9.24**). Now I spend a few minutes over morning coffee in the Metadata Browser filling in the missing information. Lightroom makes it easy to fill in the gaps.

Lightroom catalogs make photography even more fun. The best part is looking at photographs. I carry a copy of my Archived Digital Negatives catalog with me on the road so I can review my work; and as I am shooting and practicing the bulletproof archiving system, I can add to it. Care to join me?

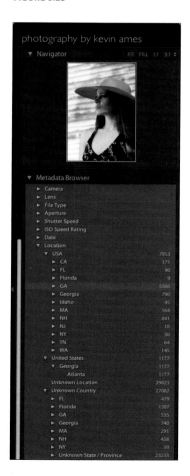

FIGURE 9.24

PART THREE
Showing Off:
From Archive to Review

The best part of digital photography is sharing your genius with the world…

CHAPTER 10

New Dogs, Old Tricks

I'VE BEEN USING PHOTOSHOP since version 2. There weren't as many of us and things were kind of bleak back then—no multiple undos, no layers, no Camera Raw, no 16-bit support, and no color management. It wasn't all bad, though; we had Levels and Curves. The techniques we used back then to color correct photographs, and adjust exposure and contrast still hold up to today's tastes in digital photography. The problem is that they've been put on the back burner—or taken off the stove entirely—to make way for prettier, more enticing fare. Everybody knew these basic recipes and wanted to cook with the new stuff in the latest version.

Well, it's eight versions into the future now. During that time, a whole lot of photographers have tasted one flavor or another of digital technique without ever having had anyone share good old vanilla with them.

Color correction in ACR 4 is either highlights, midtones, or shadows. For the two that ACR can't do, the tools "old dogs" use are second nature to us. We think everybody knows them when in fact they are brand spankin' new to photographers who have recently gone digital. Here are some old tricks for the new dogs in town.

It Starts with Color

Don't trick yourself into looking at the monitor and judging color. The human brain simply isn't going to let you. What color is snow on a bright sunny day? White? Nope. It has a blue cast that's a reflection of the sky. How about a white coat in open shade? It looks white to our eyes. In truth, it's blue because shade is blue. What color is a white tablecloth in a room lit by incandescent light bulbs? Look at the table and your eyes tell you it's white. Make it a photograph with a daylight color balance and it's yellow. Our brains do white-balancing color corrections on the fly. That is very convenient in life and, photographically speaking, it makes us lousy color correctors. The only accurate way is the numbers. Even today, with color management and calibrated monitors and printers, the fact is we can't really trust the color we think we see.

By the numbers

The best place to start, as in most everything photographic, is at the camera by setting the correct white balance, especially if the format of choice is JPEG. RAW allows the color balance to be set in post-production. Either way, the result is an approximation of the "correct" color. Color correction in its most basic form is making known neutrals—white, gray, and black neutral. Equal RGB numbers are free of colorcast. Here is a two-part technique that tweaks color for both original JPEG digital negatives and converted RAW files to make the neutrals neutral and the rest of the colors fall in line. I learned the first part from Eddie Tapp and the second from Ben Willmore.

Download the files for this chapter from amesphoto.com/learning. The book code is DPN8414. Open Colorcast.tif in Photoshop.

Highlight and shadow correction

STEP ONE

Click and hold the Eyedropper icon in the toolbox to open its menu. Getting tools from the toolbox is really the slow way to go. Each tool has a one-letter keyboard shortcut. The Eyedropper tool's keyboard shortcut is I. Choose the

Color Sampler tool. The keyboard shortcut is I + Shift + I. If you'd rather change tools by pressing the letter without using the Shift key, turn it off in the General pane of Photoshop's Preferences by unchecking Use Shift Key for Tool Switch. In the Options bar, change the tool's Sample Size to 5 by 5 Average (**Figure 10.1**). The Point Sample measures a single pixel. The average gives a more accurate measure of the color under the sampler.

FIGURE 10.1

STEP TWO

FIGURE 10.2

Click on the white patch to place Sampler #1. Click on the black patch to place Sampler #2 and, finally, click on the middle, gray patch to place Sampler #3. Press F8 to show the Info palette. The readings shown in the palette correspond to the Samplers on the patches. The Info palette shows that the overall color of the photograph is orange: the Red channel (R) in Sampler #1 reads 249, the Green channel (G) is 235, and the Blue channel (B) is 224 (**Figure 10.2**).

STEP THREE

Click on the fourth icon from the left at the bottom of the Layers palette, then choose Levels to add a new Levels adjustment layer above the Background layer. This layer handles the first part of the correction: neutralizing the highlights and the shadows. When correcting highlights, the channels with the lowest numbers are increased until they equal the brightest channel. Red is the brightest channel. Press Command (PC: Ctrl) + 2 to choose the Green channel. Click the highlight slider (the white one under the lower right edge of the histogram) and drag it to the left until the G under Sampler #1 reads 249. Press Command (PC: Ctrl) + 3 to set the Blue channel. Drag the highlight slider to the left until the B reads 249 in Sampler #1.

Notice that there are now two columns of numbers separated by a slash (/) under each Sampler. The left column holds the original color numbers. The right column shows the change made by the adjustment.

FIGURE 10.3

Shadow correction is similar except the higher values are lowered (darkened) until they match the lowest one. Look under Sampler #2. Red is 49, Green is 49, and Blue is 47. Blue started out at 42. When the Blue channel's highlights were matched to the Red channel, that correction changed the Blue shadow reading to 47. That B: 47 reading is now the lowest reading. Press Command (PC: Ctrl) + 1 to choose the Red channel. Click the shadow slider (the black one at the far left under the histogram) and move it to the right until the R under Sampler #2 reads 47. You can fine-tune the readings using the up and down arrow keys. Press Command (PC: Ctrl) + 2 for the Green channel. Move its shadow slider to the right until the G under Sampler #2 reads 47. Click OK. The highlights and shadows are neutral (**Figure 10.3**).

Midtone correction

The midtones show a nearly yellow colorcast with readings of R: 147, G: 142, and B: 134. As much as it would be lovely to fix this using the gamma slider in Levels, it simply won't work. Double-click the Levels adjustment layer's thumbnail to open it up. Move the gamma slider for the Blue channel to the left. As the Blue reading approaches 247, notice that the highlights—and especially the shadows—have moved way out of neutral. Click Cancel. This leads us to the second part of the correction that requires a bit of preliminary math: addition and division.

STEP FOUR

Average the values in the midtones by adding them together to get 423. Divide by the number of channels (RGB is three channels) to get the average, which is 141. Make a new Curves adjustment layer. If your Curves dialog box has a 4 x 4 grid instead of the 10 x 10 grid shown in the following screenshot, hold down the Option (PC: Alt) key and click in the grid, or click the Curve Display Options triangle and click the fine grid icon. Press Command (PC: Ctrl) + 1 to select the Red channel.

STEP FIVE

From the top right corner, count down one grid box and one to the left. Click at the intersection to place a point. Both the Output and Input fields will display 229. If they don't, you can change the number in the field by typing in the value or by using the up or down arrow keys to adjust the active field. Press Tab to toggle between them.

From the lower left corner, count up one grid box and one to the right. Click at the intersection to place a point there. Output and Input both want to read 26. These two points isolate the highlights at the top and the shadows at the bottom from the midtone corrections about to be made. Without them, the effect would be like moving the gamma slider in Levels. Place the isolation points in the same places for the Green channel (Command [PC: Ctrl] + 2) and the Blue channel (Command [PC: Ctrl] + 3). Click the Preset icon and save the isolated points as Midtone Correction. Next time you have to correct midtones, open Curves then choose the new setting from the Preset menu. This new feature in CS3 is a huge timesaver.

STEP SIX

Click somewhere in the center of the diagonal line running from the upper right through the lower left of the grid. Type 147, the Red channel's reading after the Levels adjustment neutralized the highlights and shadows, in the Input field. The color shifts. Hit the Tab key and fill the Output field with the average of the three, 141. This forces the off-color Red channel's midtone reading to the neutral average.

The Green channel in this example is 142. Press Command (PC: Ctrl) + 2 and repeat the procedure done for the Red channel. Finally, change the Blue channel's numbers (Command [PC: Ctrl] + 3) (**Figure 10.4**). When finished, the numbers in the right column under Sampler #3 will read R: 141, G: 141, and B: 141. This neutralizes the midtones without changing the highlights or shadows. Click the Eye icon on Curves 1 to see how large a difference this subtle correction makes. The photograph looks a lot better when the midtones are neutral. If you experience color shifts when printing, a midtone colorcast just might be to blame.

FIGURE 10.4

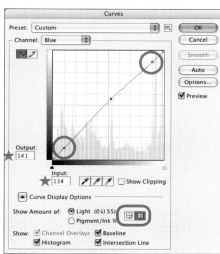

Workflow made easy

This would be a major pain to have to do for every photograph shot under the same lighting conditions. Fortunately, it's simple to fix using the adjustment layers in Colorcast.tif.

> ### STEP SEVEN
> Command-click (PC: Ctrl-click) both the Curves 1 and Levels 1 layers to select them. Open Joanna.tif from the download folder. Choose the Move tool by pressing V. Click and drag the selected layers from Colorcast.tif to Joanna.tif. Done (**Figure 10.5**). Hide and reveal Curves 1 and Levels 1 to see what a difference these old tricks really make (**Figure 10.6**).

The corrections for the highlights, shadows, and midtones are made. The photography is ready for delivery. Life is good!

FIGURE 10.5

FIGURE 10.6

No reference? No problem

In the previous section, I shared a couple of tried and true techniques from the days of yesteryear—or, at least, of yester-Photoshop (no, it's not a word; this is the practice of artistic license)—color and exposure correction techniques that relied on reference charts placed in the photographs. Including a chart in the first shot of every lighting situation is by far the best practice. Sometimes, though, it isn't possible, or you get caught up in the excitement of the shoot (like I do) and just plain forget. What's a photographer to do? Glad you asked. Here's another couple of old tricks for your digital toolkit.

The files for this section are in the folder for this chapter.

It's supposed to be white, not blue...

STEP ONE

In Bridge, navigate to the folder of samples for Chapter 10. Click it to open the thumbnails in the preview pane. Click the first thumbnail of Christina, press the Shift key, and click the last one to select all three (**Figure 10.7**). Double-click one of the image thumbnails to open them all in Photoshop CS3.

FIGURE 10.7

The wall behind Christina looks blue, although in reality it is white. I know: I bought the "high-hiding" Glidden latex paint at Home Depot, along with the rollers, extensions, and other implements of destruction, and painted it myself. Photography is all glamour all the time, don't you know? Heh, heh.

Since the wall started out white, it's supposed to be white in the photograph. I'll use it as the reference for color, though not exactly for exposure. My intention in making the series of photographs was to have the wall behind the model be close to RGB: 255, or pure white with no detail.

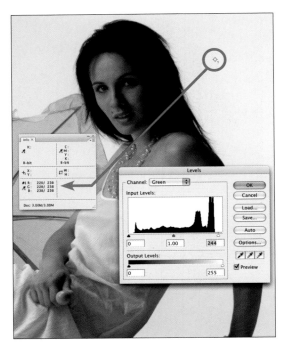

FIGURE 10.8

STEP TWO

2062-0003.JPG is active. Be sure the Color Sampler tool is set up as shown in Step One in the first section of this chapter. Click the Add New Adjustment Layer icon at the bottom of the Layers palette and choose Levels. A new Levels adjustment layer appears in the layer stack. If you're like I am, you forget to add the Color Sampler before you create the Levels layer. Apparently, there are lots of people like us. The old trick to adding a sampler while the Levels (or Curves) dialog box is open is to hold down the Shift key, then click to place a new Color Sampler. Shift-click on the wall behind Christina's head. The readings are R: 220, G: 228, B: 238. Reading 238, Blue is indeed the dominant color. Select the Red channel (Command [PC: Ctrl] + 1). Drag the highlight slider to the left until the readout for Red is 238. Do the same thing for the Green channel. When you have finished, the readings for Red, Green, and Blue will all be 238. The color of the background is neutral and it is underexposed (**Figure 10.8**).

STEP THREE

Highlights with detail (like the darker folds in her dress) want to fall somewhere around 248. The wall behind Christina is supposed to be white, or R: 255, G: 255, and B: 255. Since there isn't a reference card in the shot to set the exposure, another old trick comes to mind. Set the Channel menu in Levels to RGB. Hold down the Option (PC: Alt) key and begin dragging the highlight slider to the left. The preview goes black. Don't freak. It's supposed to. As the highlight slider moves to the left, the area under the sampler turns white. Keep dragging the slider to the left until white or yellow areas appear in the *red folds* of the dress. What do all these colors mean, anyway? Moving the highlight slider to the left brightens the image. The colors reveal information about each individual channel. When the preview is black, all three channels are below 255. As the image is brightened, colors start to appear, indicating the areas and channels that have become the brightest they can be: 255. When a channel reaches 255, it is said to be "clipped." That color is as bright as it can be. There is no detail in that color. Red in the preview means that the Red channel in those places is at 255. Remember where a red area is. Move the cursor over it to see in the Info palette that

Red is 255. Yellow indicates that both Red and Green are at 255. White means all three are at 255, as shown in the Info palette under Sampler #1. Click OK in Levels (**Figure 10.9**).

Apply the adjustment to other files

Clearly, it would be tedious to do this to every photograph from a session. Hey, we're photographers, not computer jockeys! There has to be an easy way to correct the rest of the photographs. Never fear. There is. (You knew that though, didn't you?) Here's the old trick.

STEP FOUR

Click the document header of 2062-0003.jpg and drag it to the right of the screen, slipping it under the palettes. Choose the Move tool (V). Click on the Levels adjustment layer. Drag it onto 2062-0002.JPG. The layer is *copied* and the corrections are applied to that image. It is active now. Click its header and drag it to the right over the first one. Click and drag the Levels adjustment layer in 2062-0002.JPG onto the last open image. Boom. Done (**Figure 10.10**).

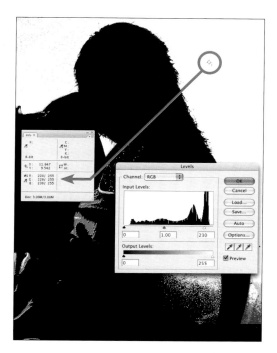

FIGURE 10.9

FIGURE 10.10

FIGURE 10.11

STEP FIVE

Save the JPEGs as PSD files in the same folder to keep the adjustment layers. That way, when the model changes her mind on how bright she wants to be in her photograph (and you know she will), you can make the changes quickly and get back behind the viewfinder (**Figure 10.11**).

Old is new

Photoshop has been around for quite a while now. I have assistants, for instance, that have never been in a black-and-white darkroom. They have never experienced the magic of an image appearing on a blank page of paper in a tray of clear liquid under yellow light. They don't know what burning or dodging means photographically.

Photographic knowledge is largely institutional. It gets passed from a photographer to an assistant who modifies it and then shares it with an understudy. Photoshop carries on in that tradition. Even better, the new dogs have tricks of their own in the digital arena. No matter where you are in the lifelong journey of learning and loving photography, take the time to sit down with those who know more than you do—and those who know less, as well. It's amazing how much everyone will grow.

CHAPTER 11

Adobe Camera Raw 4

DIGITAL CAMERAS SHOOT DIGITAL NEGATIVES. At first glance, that statement seems to be yet another example of my amazing grasp of the obvious. A traditional photographic film-based color or black-and-white negative could not be changed after being developed. Those negatives could, of course, be printed using a myriad of techniques to display their content.

RAW files have been traditionally thought of as the real digital negatives because they can't be changed either. Settings in RAW converters determined how the data was copied into a Photoshop-editable file—JPEG, PSD, or TIF.

Some RAW shooters look down their noses at JPEG shooters. I admit to having done some of that down-looking, too, because I simply could not understand why anyone would do the digital equivalent of taking a roll of film to the drugstore then shredding the negatives before even looking at the prints. JPEGs retain about $\frac{1}{8}$ of the information a digital single-lens reflex (DSLR) camera captures. So RAW files became digital negatives and JPEGs are called "camera originals" because they can be altered from their original state or even destroyed by over-manipulation in Photoshop.

JPEG and RAW Are Different

The beauty of shooting in RAW format is that it records all of the data the camera's sensor gathers; JPEG, not so much, as you'll see. First, there is some necessary backstory to tell, which explains what has gone before....

Bit depth

Bit depth is the amount of information each pixel captures. A bit depth of 1 has only two choices: black or white (**Figure 11.1**). A 2-bit file doubles the data to four steps: black, white, and two shades of gray (**Figure 11.2**). For each one-point increase in bit depth, the number of steps doubles. So a 3-bit image has six shades of gray, as well as black and white (**Figure 11.3**). On the printed page, a 4-bit image is almost continuous tone with white, black, and fourteen shades of gray (**Figure 11.4**). Compare it to an 8-bit file with 254 grays, plus black and white (**Figure 11.5**).

The chart shows the progression. Bit depths that are important to photographers are 8-, 12-, 14-, and 16-bit (**Figure 11.6**).

Output

Think of 8-bit as the *output* bit depth. There are 256 tones for each of the three channels—Red, Green, and Blue—which give us 16,777,212 color combinations,

FIGURE 11.1

FIGURE 11.2

FIGURE 11.3

FIGURE 11.4

FIGURE 11.5

including black and white. (Okay, here's the math: Multiplying 256 x 256 x 256 is really 16,777,216. Since there is only one true black and one true white, you'll have to subtract 4. Here's why: Since there are three channel—Red, Green, and Blue—there are a total of 3 blacks and 3 whites, one each per channel. Black is the absence of color. White is all colors at their brightest value: 255. Calculating the actual number of colors an 8-bit RGB file can potentially render means it can only have one black and one white, not three of each. This all comes from the More Than You Really Wanted To Know department.) The highest quality printers today can output thousands of colors from the 16-million-plus combinations available from an 8-bit file, so there are plenty of colors to choose from (**Figure 11.7**).

Bits	Tones
1	2
2	4
3	8
4	16
5	32
6	64
7	128
8	256
9	512
10	1,024
11	2,048
12	4,096
13	8,192
14	16,384
15	32,768
16	65,536

FIGURE 11.6

Capture

Think of 12-, 14-, and 16-bit as *capture* bit depth. Today, almost all DSLRs capture images in 12-bit. One (so far) records 14-bit, and the 16-bit capture space is currently the purview of medium-format camera backs. Canon's new 1D Mark III captures in 14-bit, meaning that each pixel records a whopping (the technical term for "a whole lot") 16,384 steps.

Medium-format backs that fit on cameras from Hasselblad and Mamiya, for example, might have fewer pixels. This is the case with a 16-megapixel back whose sensor measures 4080 x 4080 pixels and 36.7 mm square. The size of each pixel is larger so they can gather more light. More light means lower noise and higher bit depth. This is a classic trade-off of quality for quantity (resolution).

Compare the medium-format back described above to a full-frame DSLR (Canon 1Ds Mark II), whose sensor has pixel dimensions of 4992 x 3328 and a physical size of 36 x 24 mm. The Canon has 16.7 megapixels versus 16 megapixels in the Hasselblad back. That means the DSLR is better than the medium-format back, right? While it has more resolution by area, resolution alone is not the only factor when considering what is "better." The pixel density (resolution) is higher in the Canon, so the pixels are smaller. Smaller pixels equal lower capture bit depth (12-bit in this case) leading to more noise and fewer colors available than the medium-format back loaded with fewer, though significantly larger, pixels, which are capturing at 16-bit, or 65,536 steps each.

FIGURE 11.7

Editing

Sensors in modern DSLRs record at least 4,096 steps per pixel, which is seven times more information per pixel than a JPEG (8-bit) can store. A RAW capture records all of the data the sensor sees as unprocessed, grayscale data. Additionally, there is a record in the RAW file's metadata containing the location and color of each pixel on the sensor. The RAW converter uses that information to process the file into an editable 16-bit file. Consider 16-bit as your *editing* bit depth. Even though today's printers are limited to "only" thousands of colors of reproduction, it makes sense to believe they're going to get better. I want the best and most pixels available to output as progress marches on—as it inexorably does.

RAW versus JPEG

A JPEG is down-sampled from the RAW data by a converter within the camera. When you capture in the JPEG format, the conversion includes the white-balance information and an elevated contrast curve, so the resulting photograph looks like a color transparency (slide film). The camera then discards image information not included in the compressed JPEG.

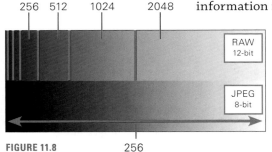

FIGURE 11.8

Images captured in RAW format aren't affected by the white-balance setting of the camera. Remember, RAW files are grayscale plus a metadata look-up table for the sensor. RAW files record light differently as well. Half of the information in a RAW capture is contained in the brightest f/stop of exposure. So a 12-bit (4,096 steps) image has 2,048 tones in that first f/stop. Thereafter, the amount of data is reduced by half for every f/stop reduction in brightness. The fourth brightest f/stop in a RAW file captured by a 12-bit sensor contains the equivalent number of steps as an entire JPEG (**Figure 11.8**).

The linear data in RAW files have several advantages over JPEGs. The greatest is that they can only be edited non-destructively. Think of true digital negatives as having unlimited undos—forever. Any value can be changed after the photograph has been taken. White balance, exposure, highlight recovery, fill light, blacks (shadows), brightness, contrast, and many other controls are available to adjust the way the RAW file data will look when opened as a 16-bit file for finishing in Photoshop.

The 16-bit difference, step by step

This exercise shows what happens to pixels when editing 16-bit files as opposed to the same edits made on 8-bit files. Full disclosure requires me to say that the results of major changes to an 8-bit file may never show in a print. If a print shows banding or posterization, the most likely cause is too much adjustment of an 8-bit file. Nothing exists without comparison, so let's do some side-by-side evaluations. First, what is the real difference between 16-bit and 8-bit? By the numbers, it's 65,536 minus 256, or 65,280 more tones in the higher bit-depth file. On the practical side, the difference can be significant, yet most likely won't be. It depends on how hard the pixels of an 8-bit file get hammered in Photoshop.

Download the files for this chapter from amesphoto.com/learning. Click on the cover of *The Digital Photographer's Notebook* and register if you haven't already. The book code is DPN8414.

STEP ONE

Open the Great Point Lighthouse.tif image. It's a 16-bit file made without adjustments from the original RAW digital negative. Make a duplicate of the file by choosing Image > Duplicate, and name the new file Great Point Lighthouse 8-bit.tif. Click OK. Choose Image > Mode > 8 Bits/Channel.

STEP TWO

Click on the 16-bit Great Point Lighthouse image to make it active. Add a Levels adjustment layer by clicking on the half-black/half-white circle at the bottom of the Layers palette and selecting Levels. Drag the highlight slider to the left until it touches the base of the right edge of the histogram. The Highlight Input Level should read 212. Move the center, Gamma slider left to brighten the image until the middle entry window reads 1.21. Click OK to accept the changes (**Figure 11.9**).

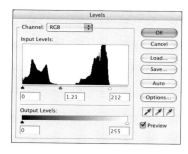

FIGURE 11.9

STEP THREE

Choose the Move tool (V) and drag the Levels adjustment layer onto the 8-bit version of the lighthouse photograph. The adjustment layer will automatically copy to the Layers palette of the 8-bit image and the new settings show in the image preview. Position the two documents side by side. You can tell which is which by the number displayed to the left of the closed parenthesis in the document header.

FIGURE 11.10

FIGURE 11.11

STEP FOUR

Select the 8-bit image and click the Histogram tab or choose Window > Histogram. Click the warning triangle in the upper right corner to refresh the view. See the gaps in the graph (**Figure 11.10**)? That's where pixels were destroyed by the Levels adjustment. Click the Eye icon next to the Levels adjustment layer to hide it, and refresh the histogram. The graph's solid now; the 8-bit file has been returned to its original state. Show the adjustment, refresh, and the gaps reappear. The gaps are called *combing*. Activate the 16-bit lighthouse image. Refresh the histogram. Notice there's no combing in the 16-bit file (**Figure 11.11**), even though the Levels adjustment is identical for both. The extra tones in the higher bit-depth file make the adjustment work without placing gaps in the histogram.

Adobe Camera Raw 4

There are things we just *know* can't get any better. That perfect day fishing, your favorite team wins the World Series, and good old Adobe Camera Raw 3. Well, hold on to your fly rod and championship sweatshirt. The best has gotten better—and by at least one order of magnitude, maybe even two.

The amount of functionality packed into the Camera Raw 4 plug-in is truly stunning. ACR 4 supports over 150 different flavors of RAW files, from DSLR camera manufacturers like Canon, Nikon, Olympus, Pentax, and Sony to medium-format cameras from Hasselblad, Leaf, Mamiya, and Phase One. It also supports many point-and-shoot cameras that offer RAW capture (as well as those that don't). Here's a quick overview of what's new, what's moved, and what you don't want to live without (**Figure 11.12**).

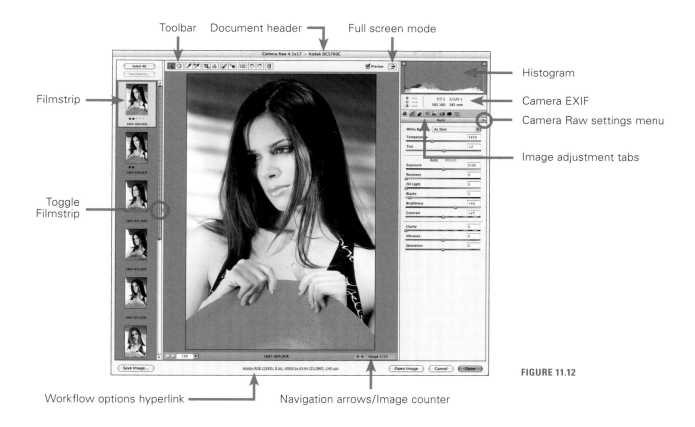

FIGURE 11.12

New to the toolbar

Camera Raw's toolset continues to mature, providing photographers with an easier and more efficient workflow. The first six icons on the toolbar (**Figure 11.13**) are old friends: Zoom tool (Z), Hand tool (H), White Balance tool (I), Color Sampler tool (S), Crop tool (C), and Straighten tool (A). Of the next three icons, two are tools that have been—up until now—a photographer's fondest wish: the Retouch tool (B) and the Red Eye Removal tool (E). The next icon opens Camera Raw's Preferences (Command [PC: Ctrl] +K). The following three are the familiar Rotate Left (L), Rotate Right (R), and the dangerous "Toggle mark for delete" icon. Completing the toolbar is the Preview checkbox and the new Toggle Full Screen Mode (F) button.

FIGURE 11.13

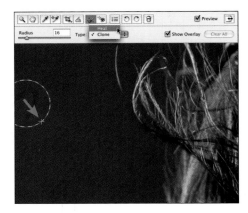

FIGURE 11.14

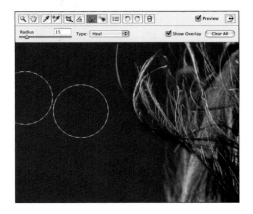

FIGURE 11.15

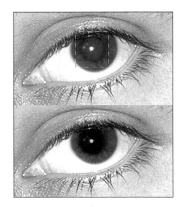

FIGURE 11.16

The Retouch tool

Sensor dust is an undeniable, unfortunate, and unavoidable reality of digital photographic life. In times gone by, every variation of a RAW file sent to Photoshop had to be individually retouched to remove dark spots caused by dust on the chip. The Retouch tool to the rescue! Yep. Healing and Cloning has finally come to Camera Raw! The humongous hair is easy to fix. (Okay, it looks humongous at 100% view, which is the view to use when dust-spotting RAW files.) Choose Heal from the Type menu, click in the center of the offending sensor detritus, drag until the red circle covers the offending mark, and then release the mouse (**Figure 11.14**). A green circle appears in an area of similar detail (**Figure 11.15**). This is the source of the healing or cloning. Click inside the green circle and drag it to choose a different source in case Camera Raw chose poorly (it rarely does). Click the edge of the red circle and drag to resize it. After dust-spotting for a while, your image will have multiple circles denoting the points of retouching. If this is annoying, uncheck Show Overlay. Clear All removes all of the work, allowing a fresh start. The Radius slider displays the size (in pixels) of the last circle that was dragged out. And, yes, the Retouch tool works on skin blemishes, too. Don't tell anyone.

Red Eye Removal tool

The flash on most point-and-shoot cameras is so close to the lens that its light goes into the eye and makes the retina, which is red, glow brightly back through the pupil. Hence the term *red eye*. The Red Eye Removal tool fixes this unfortunate and eerie phenomenon. This tool bows to the hobbyist who photographs for fun with point-and-shoot cameras and wants a quick non-destructive fix (**Figure 11.16**).

What has moved

Creating a new version of software offers the opportunity to clean up the interface to make the user experience more efficient. All of the ACR 3 functions are still available. Some are in a different place or under a new name, or have a new look (**Figure 11.17**).

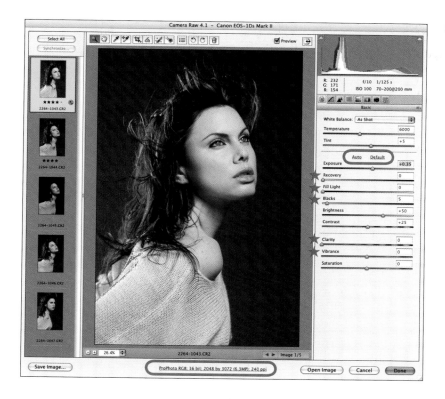

FIGURE 11.17

Shadow and highlight clipping

Formerly in the toolbar, the shadow and highlight clipping checkboxes have moved into the histogram. The RGB readings were displayed horizontally in ACR 3. This readout is now vertical (like the Info palette) and under the histogram on the left. EXIF data—information about exposure and focal length—shows just to the right of the RGB display.

Auto adjustments

The Auto checkboxes are now a hyperlink named Auto. Click it to see what Camera Raw thinks is a good balance of tonality (Exposure, Recovery, Fill Light, Blacks, Brightness, and Contrast). The Default setting returns them to the current Camera Raw settings. Thankfully, Auto is off by default in this iteration of ACR. Choose Apply auto tone adjustments in the Default Image Settings area of Camera Raw's Preferences (Command [PC: Ctrl] + K while in Camera Raw) to make Auto the new default.

Image adjustments

The image adjustment tabs from ACR 3 are now icons, and they're in the same location as the previous version's tabs except with a new arrangement. From left to right they are: Basic (formerly Adjust), Tone Curve (formerly Curve), Detail, HSL/Grayscale (new to ACR 4), Split Toning (new), Lens Corrections (formerly Lens), Camera Calibration (formerly Calibrate), and Presets (previously in the Settings flyout menu and called Save Settings...).

Save, Open, Workflow options

The Save Image button has moved to the bottom left corner. The Open Image, Cancel, and Done buttons line up along the bottom right.

FIGURE 11.18

The Workflow Options checkbox is gone. It has been replaced with a hyperlink between the Save and Open Image buttons that lists the color space, bit depth, pixel dimensions, and resolution. Clicking the link opens the Workflow Options dialog where the settings are made. There is a new checkbox, Open in Photoshop as Smart Objects (**Figure 11.18**). Check this box to change Open Image to Open Object.

Smart Objects

Checking the Open in Photoshop as Smart Objects box changes the default setting from Open Image to Open Object. Adding the Shift key changes it back to Open Image.

Save Image... works as it did in ACR 3. Click it, choose the destination, and name, if you wish, the file format to save in, along with compression and JPEG preview, then click Save.

Smart Objects were introduced in Photoshop CS2. They have taken on a much larger role throughout CS3. Camera Raw can now open up a RAW file (or a JPEG or TIF file—more on that later in this chapter) as a Smart Object in Photoshop without the help of Dr. Brown's Place-A-Matic. The Open button is much more versatile, thanks to a couple of modifier keys. With the Open in Photoshop as Smart Objects box unchecked in the Workflow Options, choosing the Open button opens the displayed RAW file, or RAW files selected in the Filmstrip, in Photoshop. Hold down the Option (PC: Alt) key to open the file without updating its metadata. Hold down the Shift key to place the RAW file in Photoshop as a Smart Object in the layers stack.

Image adjustment tabs

Basic

The Basic tab (**Figure 11.19**) (yes, they are still called tabs even though they look like panels) adjusts the white balance, tonality, and color saturation. Here are the new and renamed controls. Exposure remains the same, as do the Brightness and Contrast sliders. Shadows has been renamed Blacks. Four new sliders have been added: Recovery, Fill Light, Clarity, and Vibrance.

FIGURE 11.19

Exposure handled the overall brightness of the image in ACR 3. It still does, with two important changes: Recovery and Fill Light. Recovery tones down blown-out highlights. Fill Light brightens shadow areas.

I'll begin refining this RAW file of model Virginia Morse (NEXT Models and Talent Los Angeles) by moving the Exposure slider to the right while watching the histogram. When the pixels in the histogram reach the right edge, the highlight clipping indicator changes color, showing which channel or channels are at 255. If it is red, for instance, the Red channel is at maximum brightness (255). If it is yellow, then that means that both the Red and Green channels are maxed out. The Shadow clipping indicator is cyan, meaning that an area in the shadows has both the Green and Blue channels at 0 (black). Click either indicator to show the areas of clipping in the image. Red appears if any of the three channels (RGB) are at 255. Blue appears when all three channels are at 0. A white border around the indicator denotes it is displaying clipping in the image.

A better way to see this—and my preference—is to hold down the Option (PC: Alt) key while adjusting the Exposure or Recovery slider to see exactly which channels or combinations are clipping. When there is no clipping, the preview is black. Complementary colors—cyan (Green and Blue), magenta (Red and Blue), and yellow (Red and Green)—show multiple channels clipping. If white

FIGURE 11.20

FIGURE 11.21

shows when adjusting the Exposure and Recovery sliders, that indicates all three channels are clipped—R, G, and B equal 255, pure white. Moving the Recovery slider to the right brings down the clipped areas (**Figure 11.20**). This has the effect of brightening the whole photograph while maintaining highlight detail.

The preview is white when there is no shadow clipping. Colors show which channels or combinations of channels are clipping. Black appears on the preview when all three channels are clipped to 0 (**Figure 11.21**).

The Fill Light slider adds light to the shadows. It does not preview clipping with the Option (PC: Alt) key pressed, nor does it necessarily counter all of the effects of a higher setting in the Blacks adjustment. The before and after images of presidential candidate Barack Obama campaigning in New Hampshire demonstrate the power of this tool in high-contrast situations (**Figures 11.22** and **11.23**).

Basic's "Presence" sliders

The Presence sliders (Clarity, Vibrance, and Saturation) are options for making a photo "pop" (not Pop Art).

- **Clarity** is Camera Raw 4's new midtone contrast control, which adds depth by increasing local contrast.

FIGURE 11.22

FIGURE 11.23

- **Vibrance**, also new in ACR 4, affects the saturation so that clipping is minimized as a color is close to reaching full saturation. It also changes the saturation of less saturated colors so they won't impact on higher saturated ones. (I really just wanted to see how many times I could put a variation of "saturate" in a single sentence.) Vibrance is great for making skin tones more vivid without driving everything else into cartoon-like colors.

- **Saturation** moves all the colors equally from +100 (double normal saturation) to –100 (no color saturation at all, resulting in a monochrome black-and-white image).

Tone Curve

The first icon to the right of Basic is for Tone Curve (formerly Curve, and the second-to-last tab in ACR 3) (**Figure 11.24**). It is for fine-tuning adjustments made in the Basic tab. (Wanna bet that's the reason it's right next to the Basic icon?) What's new is the Parametric tab. This curve is used to tweak tones in defined tonal ranges in a photograph. There are four sliders in this tab—Highlights, Lights, Darks, and Shadows—controlling their respective sections in the curve (**Figure 11.25**). The left section of the curve is Shadows, next is Darks, then Lights, and finally Highlights on the far right. Lights and Darks change the middle values while Highlights and Shadows move the values at each end of the curve. The sliders at the base of the Parametric Curve change the size of the four regions. Point Curve is the original that debuted in ACR 3.

Detail

The Detail tab (**Figure 11.26**) adds two more sliders to the ones from ACR 3, Detail and Masking. Those two differences, along with some hidden preview screens, are significant. And, as the dialog says, "Zoom preview to 100% or larger to see the effects of the controls in this panel" (**Figure 11.27**). You won't see the effects at smaller views.

- **Amount** controls the intensity of the sharpening effect. The range is from 0 to 150. At 0, no sharpening is applied. The 150 setting is extreme and, by itself, pretty much unusable. Amounts higher than 100, used in combination with the other controls, improve the result. Compare an amount of 150 to the default setting of 25 (**Figure 11.28**).

FIGURE 11.24

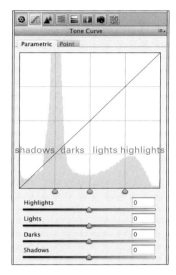

FIGURE 11.25

FIGURE 11.26

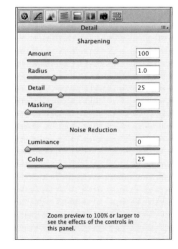

FIGURE 11.27

FIGURE 11.28

- **Radius** sets how many pixels beyond each side of an edge receive sharpening. Hold down the Option (PC: Alt) key while adjusting the slider to see how the affected area, and the effect itself, expand as the radius increases from .5 pixels (**Figure 11.29**) to 3.0 pixels (**Figure 11.30**) in these split views.

- **Detail** determines how the sharpening will work on the photograph. At 100, the result is very much like that of Photoshop's Unsharp Mask filter (**Figure 11.31**). Lowering the amount of the slider by moving it to the left reduces the haloing effect on edges in the image (**Figure 11.32**).

FIGURE 11.29

FIGURE 11.30

FIGURE 11.31

FIGURE 11.32

FIGURE 11.33

FIGURE 11.34

- **Masking** settings are from the default of 0 (no mask is generated) to 100. ACR 4 builds a mask to tone down the sharpening of smooth areas. This focuses the sharpening on edges within a photograph, making pre-sharpening quite useful. Compare a low Masking setting of 18 (**Figure 11.33**) to the full-on version (**Figure 11.34**).

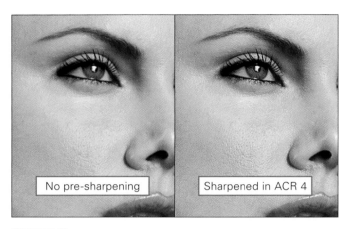

FIGURE 11.35

My suggestion is to work with the new sharpening tools and see how you want to adopt them. Otherwise, you might want to apply them to the preview image only by changing the setting in Camera Raw's Preferences. The Detail tab now offers terrific pre-sharpening for inherently soft digital captures before editing or sharing them with others (**Figure 11.35**). Sharpening for output is still best done in Photoshop.

The location of Camera Raw's Preferences has changed, too. They are now under the Bridge menu on the Mac and the Edit menu in Windows. If Camera Raw is open, the keyboard shortcut is Command (PC: Ctrl) + K. As before, the default is to apply sharpening to all images.

HSL/Grayscale

The HSL part of the HSL/Grayscale panel (**Figure 11.36**) is three separate tabs: Hue, Saturation, and Luminance. Each slider in the Hue tab controls the hue for its color (**Figure 11.37**). The color bar under the slider shows the range of color it can affect. Small moves in this tab make big changes to the photograph. Compare Virginia's lipstick color from 0 Red to –27 (**Figure 11.38**).

The sliders in the Saturation tab offer values from –100 to +100. A slider set at –100 makes its color grayscale (**Figure 11.39**). This is a great way to preview which slider controls exactly which color in the image. Simply move it to –100 and see where gray shows through (**Figure 11.40**).

The Luminance tab's sliders control the lightness and darkness for their respective colors. This is perfect for controlling tonality selectively in Camera Raw (**Figure 11.41**). I can give Virginia a tan by increasing the Red luminance while pulling back the Orange (**Figure 11.42**).

By the way, all of the sliders in ACR 4 can be returned to their default setting by double-clicking them.

FIGURE 11.36

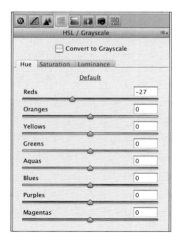

FIGURE 11.37

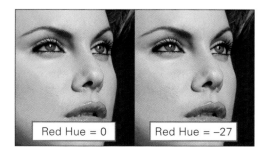

FIGURE 11.38

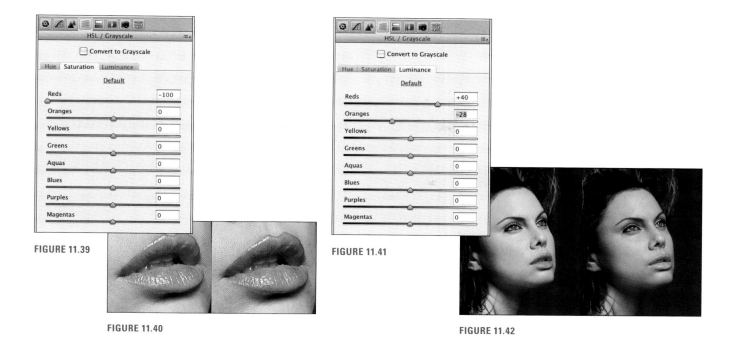

FIGURE 11.39

FIGURE 11.41

FIGURE 11.40

FIGURE 11.42

Black and white, Camera Raw style

Previous versions of Camera Raw let us do reasonable black-and-white conversions by first desaturating the image, then moving the sliders in the Calibration tab, and finally refining the deal in the Adjustment (now Basic) tab. ACR 4 moves beyond this workaround in the new HSL/Grayscale tab.

Check the Convert to Grayscale box to collapse the HSL tabs into another new feature of ACR 4: Grayscale Mix. The big story here is the color values. Camera Raw analyzes them and makes "optimum" settings. Click the Default link to return all the color values to zero. Click Auto to see again what Camera Raw thinks (**Figure 11.43**). Modifications are easy. Each slider tweaks only its color à la the Luminance tab. Uncheck the Convert to Grayscale box. Look at the colors. I want Virginia's lipstick to be a deeper tone. It's red, so I'll move the Reds slider to the left until it forms a nice contrast with her face. The changes I've made are now custom, and Camera Raw recognizes that by offering the choice of Auto, Default, or, of course, leaving everything at my new settings.

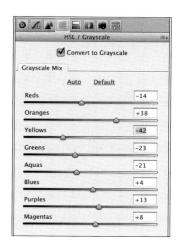

FIGURE 11.43

FIGURE 11.44

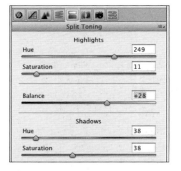

FIGURE 11.45

Split Toning

As long as the subject is black and white, there is another tab that fits right in: Split Toning (**Figure 11.44**). It's the icon to the right of HSL/Grayscale. This tab tones the highlights separately from the shadows, and controls the balance between the two. I've chosen a cool value for the highlights (think skin) and a warm one for the shadows (Virginia's hair and the background). The Balance slider is set to emphasize the lighter tones (**Figure 11.45**). Move it to the left to increase the influence of the shadow colors or to the right to favor the highlight colors. Behold the power of RAW by comparing color to grayscale to split tone (**Figure 11.46**).

Lens Corrections

Lens Corrections (**Figure 11.47**) handles issues that arise with lenses designed primarily for shooting film, an imaging medium that is not nearly as discerning as a digital imaging sensor.

FIGURE 11.46

Chromatic aberration causes one or more of the colors to fall in focus either in front of or behind the actual position of the sensor, resulting in a color halo or fringe. Use a high magnification—300% or so—and look at brighter edges against darker backgrounds. In this case, a pewter-colored handrail has a red fringe. Adjust Fix Red/Cyan Fringe and Fix Blue/Yellow Fringe until it disappears (**Figure 11.48**). Adding the Option (PC: Alt) key hides the effects of the other slider so the results of each slider's adjustment can be seen accurately. The Defringe menu focuses the effect on either Highlight Edges or, in this example, All Edges. The default setting is Off.

FIGURE 11.47

Lenses, especially wide angle lenses, tend to be darker around the edges. The Lens Vignetting adjustment fixes this. The Amount controls the brightening (positive numbers to the right) or darkening (negative numbers to the left). The

FIGURE 11.48

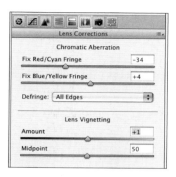

FIGURE 11.49

Midpoint slider aligns the effect with the areas wanting correction. Creatively, this is a great tool for doing that burned-down edges look from classic darkroom prints. Slide the Amount to the left and move the Midpoint to taste. Midpoint is grayed out until the Amount slider is moved to a setting other than zero (**Figure 11.49**).

FIGURE 11.50

Camera Calibration

Camera Raw uses profiles for each camera it supports to process the images. These profiles, along with the white balance set in the Basic tab, create the color in the photograph opened in Photoshop. The Camera Calibration tab (**Figure 11.50**) shows which version of Camera Raw first set the profile for a camera. If there are multiple profiles, it means the camera has been updated. Choose the profile that appears to give the most accurate color. If the choice is Embedded, it will use the profile in the TIF, JPEG, or DNG file. The controls in this tab will render non-neutral colors differently. Use the Hue slider first, then adjust the Saturation to alter the colors. The Shadows Tint control corrects for colorcast in the shadows. Move it to the left to add green or to the right to add magenta to the shadows (**Figure 11.51**).

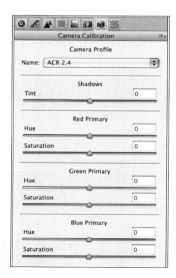

FIGURE 11.51

FIGURE 11.52

FIGURE 11.53

Presets

The Presets tab (**Figure 11.52**) is a huge workflow help. Once a group of settings has been determined (in the split toning for the photograph of Virginia, for example), it can be saved by clicking on the Presets tab's flyout menu and choosing Save Settings....

The preset can be applied to several images open in Camera Raw by selecting them in the Filmstrip and then clicking the saved setting listed in the tab (**Figure 11.53**).

JPEG: The New Digital Negative

The missing component that kept JPEGs from being elevated to full digital negative status was malleability. The thinking went like this: "Photoshop can completely and permanently change JPEGs. Because of that capability, they just aren't *real* digital negatives." There was no way to treat a JPEG as a digital negative without changing it permanently.

The advent of ACR 4 either silences the debate or reignites it, depending on your philosophical leanings. Acknowledging controversy is well and good. In the *Notebook*, I prefer to stick to what is the current state of the art. Not what it ought to be, or why did they do it that way? No value judgments, please. This is what works now—and how it works—so onward!

ACR 4 converts RAW files as it always has, only better. This version can also non-destructively adjust JPEGs, unlayered TIF files, and PSD files that have the Maximize Compatibility feature enabled. This setting is under Preferences > File Handling > Maximize PSD and PSB File Compatibility. My copy of Photoshop is set to always maximize compatibility. The setting slows down the act of saving a tiny bit, and it increases the file size by adding a flattened copy of the file. Lightroom does this automatically when exporting to a PSD file because it can't read layered files. Changes made to JPEG, flattened TIF, and compatibility-maximized PSD files in ACR 4 are applied to a copy of the photograph when Open Image is clicked.

Differences

Camera Raw treats JPEG and TIF files a bit differently than it treats RAW digital negatives. RAW files are always opened in Camera Raw. There simply isn't any other choice. JPEGs and TIFs are different. First, there is no XMP "sidecar" file. The ACR settings are written directly into the file's header. The Adjusted in Camera Raw icon appears in its thumbnail in Bridge. JPEGs and TIFs that have this icon will open in Camera Raw. Files without the icon will open in Photoshop CS3 if Prefer Adobe Camera Raw for JPEG and TIFF files is unchecked in Bridge's Preferences. Also, it is super important to note that versions of Photoshop prior to CS3 will treat these digital negatives as regular JPEG, TIF, or PSD files, where they can be opened and edited directly and destructively. Be very aware to see that JPEGs and TIFs edited in ACR are only opened in CS3 (or later versions).

Confusing? Yes, it is. The easiest way to preserve JPEG and TIF files as digital negatives is to first check the Prefer ACR box in Bridge's Preferences, then select all of their thumbnails in Bridge and press Command (PC: Ctrl) + R to open them in Camera Raw. Use Command (PC: Ctrl) + A to select all of the thumbnails in the Filmstrip, then make a tiny adjustment—say, nudge the brightness up one point—and then click done. The JPEG and TIF thumbnails now sport the ACR adjustment badge. From now on, Bridge CS3 and Photoshop CS3 will respect their "RAWness." If you use Photoshop CS3 as your preferred platform for ACR 4—usually by double-clicking thumbnails in Bridge—be sure to choose Preferences > File Handling and check Prefer Adobe Camera Raw for JPEG files.

I always shoot RAW so I have no use for editing JPEGs in RAW. For me, this feature is incredibly powerful when preparing 16-bit scans from my film archives for a client, in this case a manufacturer of pool and spa chemistry.

I set the scanner's software to capture all the data it can by setting the shadows to 0 and the highlights to 255 at 16-bit. They all look flat and dark (**Figure 11.54**). That's fine for the moment.

FIGURE 11.54

Optimizing scans

Open the scans folder that came with the files you downloaded for this chapter. If you skipped to this section, the instructions for the downloads are in the paragraph before Step One of "The 16-bit difference, step by step" tutorial earlier in this chapter.

STEP ONE

Open Preferences in Bridge CS3 by pressing Command (PC: Ctrl) + K. Choose Thumbnails and check Prefer Adobe Camera Raw for JPEG and TIFF files. If you double-click thumbnails in Bridge to open them in Camera Raw, don't. You have to open TIF files in Camera Raw by choosing File > Open in Camera Raw... from Bridge's menu, or right-clicking on a thumbnail and choosing Open in Camera Raw..., or using the keyboard shortcut Command (PC: Ctrl) + R. Double-clicking always opens TIF files in Photoshop.

STEP TWO

Highlight the two spa TIF files in Bridge and open them in Camera Raw by pressing Command (PC: Ctrl) + R. Move the Exposure slider to the right until the pixels on the right edge of the histogram barely touch the side. Keep an eye on the highlight clipping indicator (**Figure 11.55**).

Even if this is a large move, it's okay because the scans are 16-bit. They have the data to handle it without breaking down. Check where clipping actually happens by holding down the Option (PC: Alt) key and clicking the Recovery slider. This works with the Exposure slider, too. I use Recovery because if I see clipping I can move the slider to the right to remove it (or, in this case, minimize it using a setting of 3) (**Figure 11.56**). The clipping shows that the red channel along his right arm is 255. There are a

FIGURE 11.55

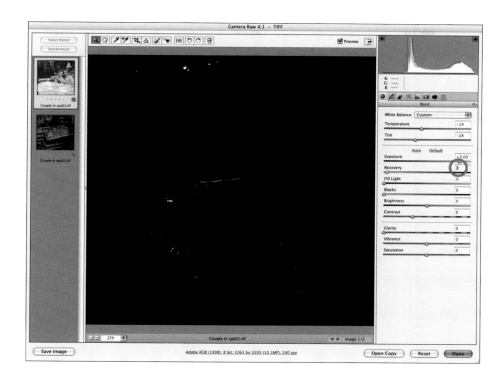

FIGURE 11.56

few cyan warnings (G+B at 255), some green warnings (R+G at 255), and an area of white (R+G+B at 255) sky through the trees. All in all, the brightness is fine.

A photograph of a couple in a spa in sunlight would have some areas of almost—if not completely—white specular highlights (see Chapter 4).

FIGURE 11.57

STEP THREE

There is one place in a color transparency (slide) that we know is neutral—the base of the film that has never been exposed to light. When scanning, I always include the edge of the film itself to aid in balancing the color. After setting the exposure, the film base isn't close to black. It has information in all three channels. Choose the White Balance tool (I) and click on the left film edge above my copyright notice. The edge is neutral and the couple gets warmer (**Figure 11.57**).

STEP FOUR

Place a Color Sampler (S) where you clicked to achieve the white balance. Mine reads RGB: 73. Hold down the Option (PC: Alt) key, then slowly drag the Blacks slider to the right. The screen is white. Stop when the film edge reads 25. You'll see a tiny bit of detail in the white. These are areas where individual channels are at 0. Where you see black, all three channels are at 0. Release the Option (PC: Alt) key while still holding down the mouse button. The image looks great! See what happens when you make the film base sampler read RGB: 0. The photograph has way too much contrast. The shadows and midtone details block up for a truly ghastly result (**Figure 11.58**).

FIGURE 11.58

STEP FIVE

Click Select All at the top of the Filmstrip. (In this case, the Filmstrip is appropriately named, since the images are actually from film. Really, though, for everything else it ought to be called the "Thumbstrip," don't you think?) Now click Synchronize and, finally, click OK. Uh oh...too bright. Reduce the exposure until the highlight clipping warning in the histogram goes black, then nudge the exposure up until it turns red.

STEP SIX

Place a Color Sampler on the film base. Notice it's close to neutral? The previous setting was a good start. Use the White Balance tool to tweak the color by clicking it on the film base by the Color Sampler. Move the Fill Light slider to the right until the Sampler reads around 25. Click Done. The settings are written into the headers of both files. Look at their thumbnails in Bridge. Notice the "I've been edited in ACR" badges in the upper right corners? That tells you the files are now digital negatives and ACR 4-friendly (**Figure 11.59**).

FIGURE 11.59

STEP SEVEN

To create the 8-bit TIF files for the client, reopen the files in Camera Raw. Click Select All at the top of the Filmstrip. Click on the Workflow Options hyperlink at the bottom of the Camera Raw dialog. Choose 8-bit and uncheck Open in Photoshop as Smart Objects. Click the Save Images... button, select the destination folder, set the format to TIFF, then click Save. You're done. If you want to see how well this works, open either of the newly saved scans in Photoshop by double-clicking them in Bridge (**Figure 11.60**). Check the histogram (**Figure 11.61**). No combing! Sweet.

FIGURE 11.60

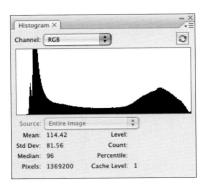

FIGURE 11.61

TANSTAAFL*

8-bit files are not RAW. Even though they can be adjusted in Camera Raw, that does not mean they have the depth of data required for all of the things that can be done in this wonderful tool. Large changes in white balance—changing a JPEG shot in daylight with a Tungsten balance on the camera, for example, back to daylight—or big moves in Exposure and Fill Light will most likely damage the file that opens in Photoshop to the point of posterization and/or banding. The good news is that the original is never harmed, although the resulting copy may look truly awful...or not.

*There Ain't No Such Thing As A Free Lunch. Coined by the late master of science fiction Robert Heinlein in his novel *The Moon Is a Harsh Mistress*.

CHAPTER 12

Lightroom Develops

IN FEBRUARY, 2008, Photoshop will celebrate the eighteenth anniversary of its arrival on the planet as a fresh version 1.0 app. Almost a human generation has passed since then. Photoshop has evolved quite nicely—thank you very much, Adobe!

Every generation looks at its progenitors and says it is time for a change. Usually, it's change only to be different. On rare occasions, it is truly change for the better. Enter the new version 1.0 application—Adobe Photoshop Lightroom, born appropriately enough on February 19, 2007, and already updated to version 1.1 a week before this chapter was written.

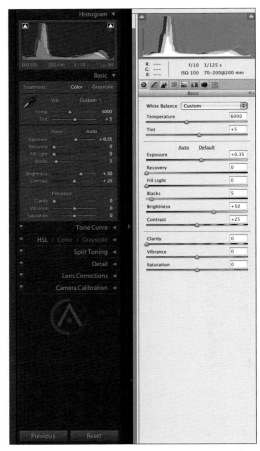

FIGURE 12.1

Similarities

Lightroom and ACR 4 have functional differences using the same toolset. All of the tabs in Camera Raw are panels in Lightroom. While ACR 4 no longer has a Convert to Grayscale offering in the Basic tab, Lightroom's Basic panel's first choice is Treatment: Color Grayscale. The Basic tab and Basic panel have the same tools in practically the same order (**Figure 12.1**).

New, Different, and Extras

Presets

Lightroom ships with a set of Creative, General, Sharpen, and Tone Curve presets in place. Move the cursor over each one to see its effect in the navigator preview. Click to apply one (**Figure 12.2**).

Create your own by making changes in the Develop tabs, then highlighting the User Presets folder and clicking the + (plus sign) to open the New Develop Preset dialog. The one shown here is based on the Creative – Antique Light preset (**Figure 12.3**). Remove a preset by highlighting it, then clicking the – (minus sign).

Snapshots

Anytime a group of settings is specific to a photograph and does not warrant a preset of its own, a Snapshot of the state of the developing steps can be made. Click in the Snapshots panel, then click +. Name the Snapshot.

Remove an unwanted Snapshot by highlighting it then clicking the – sign.

History

Everything done to an image in Lightroom is recorded and, unlike Photoshop's History palette, saved for future editing. This History is not limited to the last twenty steps, as is the default in Photoshop. This is unlimited undos

FIGURE 12.2

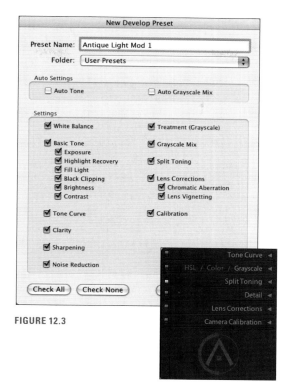

FIGURE 12.3

FIGURE 12.4

forever! Command (PC: Ctrl) + Z moves the History back one step for each keystroke. Command (PC: Ctrl) + Shift + Z goes forward one step for each keystroke.

Use History to review changes. When one is found that really works, it can be saved as a Snapshot or as a Preset. The Clear button empties the History panel.

Panel toggles

The Tone Curve, HSL / Color / Grayscale, Split Toning, Detail, Lens Corrections, and Camera Calibration panels have On/Off toggles located at the left of the header. Click to turn the effect of the panel on or off to see how it is affecting the photograph. Up is on. Down is off. Here, the Split Toning toggle is in the off position (**Figure 12.4**).

Lightroom has a very powerful set of developing controls including Curves, Hue, Saturation, Luminance, Color, Grayscale, and Histogram (yes, the histogram is a control, too, as you'll see in a minute). All of the tools are photographer-friendly. In other words, they work the way we intuitively think they should, rather than backwards in inverse-photo think: "Let's see, the little number, f/2, is the big aperture, and the big number, f/22, is the little aperture...." Lightroom is straightforward. It also has really great can't-mess-this-up-too-much limits built right in.

Download the folder for this chapter from amesphoto.com/learning. The book code is DPN8414.

New tools

Lightroom takes a fresh look at all of the underpinnings of Photoshop. It questions everything about how working with digital images—particularly digital negatives, be they RAW or be they JPEG—can be streamlined and, ultimately, made more intuitive to photographers, a growing number of whom have never shot film. Thomas Knoll wrote the first version of Photoshop. He is a photographer, so Photoshop has film as its model. Lightroom embodies the best of a generation of advances in digital photographic tools—and improves them.

Lightroom's Develop module is Adobe Camera Raw 4. Think of Camera Raw and Lightroom's Develop module as the same girl wearing a different outfit. ACR 4 is the business suit. All work and to the point. Lightroom's Develop module is the wonderful little black dress—flirty and fun, yet very serious when it comes to processing RAW files.

Histogram control

STEP ONE

Import the sample file into your DPN Projects catalog in Lightroom (see Chapter 9 for creating that catalog). The left panel that contains the Navigator, History, Snapshots, and Presets panes is hidden. Hide yours by clicking the solid disclosure triangle (I call this the flippy triangle) in the middle of the left-hand side of Lightroom's workspace to give the preview area more

FIGURE 12.5

room. Do the same thing for the Filmstrip at the bottom of the screen. Next, click the side-by-side comparison button in the control bar to set up the Before view on the left and the After view on the right (**Figure 12.5**).

STEP TWO

Right-click the histogram and choose Show Clipping (press J on the keyboard). White borders appear around the Shadow and Highlight clipping indicators, showing the feature is active. This histogram shows this is a full tonal range image with some blown-out highlights shown by the highlighted triangle in the top right border. The exposure information and focal length of the lens displays along the bottom (**Figure 12.6**).

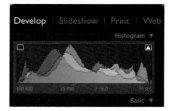

FIGURE 12.6

FIGURE 12.7

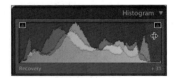

FIGURE 12.8

A red highlight clipping warning shows in the sky midway up on the left-hand edge of the abandoned car wash (**Figure 12.7**). There are no blocked-up shadows.

STEP THREE

Hover the cursor over the right side of the histogram. The area highlights with a lighter gray. Click then drag to the left. The whole histogram compresses in that direction. The word Recovery replaces the exposure info under the graph. As the histogram compresses, the Recovery slider in the Basic tab moves as well. Drag until Recovery reads +31 (**Figure 12.8**).

The red warning disappears. The highlight has been recovered without reducing the overall exposure (**Figure 12.9**).

STEP FOUR

Next, click on the pixels in the shadows at the left of the histogram. This area is now light gray. Drag to the left (or right) until Blacks reads +15. The shadows darken and the white warning triangle appears (**Figure 12.10**).

FIGURE 12.9

The blue shadow clipping warning appears (**Figure 12.11**). Drag in the other direction until the value reads +11. The warning is still there, though only for the deepest shadows.

STEP FIVE

Move the cursor to the right from the Blacks to Fill Light in the histogram. Click inside, then drag to the right to +10, revealing detail in the areas brighter than the shadows (**Figures 12.12** and **12.13**).

The next section to the right is the Exposure area. No change is warranted.

STEP SIX

Toggle the Basic panel closed with the keyboard shortcut Command (PC: Ctrl) + 1. The histogram stays open because it's pretty. And because it updates with changes made in other panels, in addition to being a handy little tool. Nice!

The Histogram control is great. As a matter of fact, exposure, highlight control, shadows, and fill light can all be adjusted right in the histogram without ever opening the Basic panel. Click, drag, done!

FIGURE 12.10

FIGURE 12.11

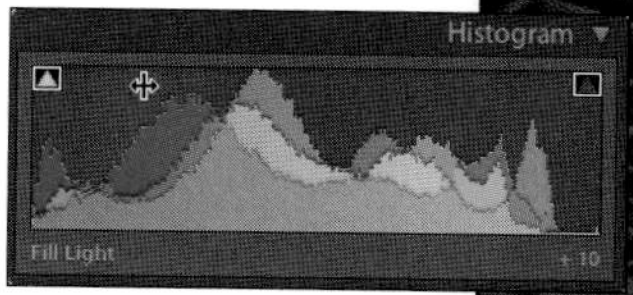

FIGURE 12.12

FIGURE 12.13

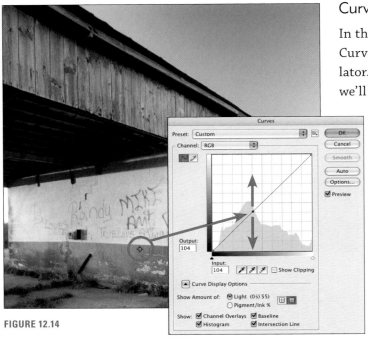

FIGURE 12.14

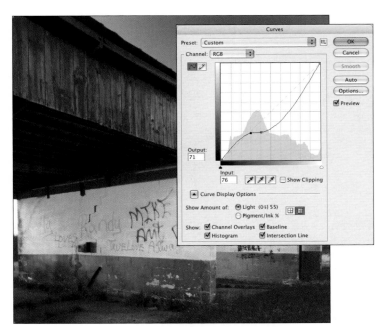

FIGURE 12.15

Curves

In the beginning there was Curves. And it was good. Curves is Photoshop's powerful tone and color manipulator. Work through this exercise in Photoshop, then we'll do it with Curves in Lightroom.

STEP ONE

Open the file 2260-003.psd in Photoshop. Press Command (PC: Ctrl) + M to open Curves. Click and drag over the photograph. The tone of the pixels under the cursor is shown as a hollow circle on the straight line in Curves. Command-click (PC: Ctrl-click) and the circle becomes a point (**Figure 12.14**). Press the up arrow key to make that part of the image brighter and the down arrow key to make it darker. The grayscale bar on the left side of Curves' graph shows highlights at the top and shadows at the bottom to remind which direction lightens (up) and which darkens (down).

STEP TWO

Working with Curves also requires knowing what not to do. Hold down the Option (PC: Alt) key and click Reset. Move the cursor over the photograph and Command-click (PC: Ctrl-click) in the same area as in Step One. Hold down the Shift key and press the down arrow three times. Click on the intersection one box below the point and one box to the left. Again, hold down the Shift key. Press the up arrow twice. The curve has a flat spot, resulting in desaturated tones (**Figure 12.15**).

STEP THREE

When the curve turns in on itself, major color weirdness occurs (**Figure 12.16**). Hold down the Shift key then tap the up arrow six times (**Figure 12.17**).

FIGURE 12.16

These effects are interesting, and even useful in editing images for creative effect in Photoshop. They really aren't so hot for enhancing digital negatives.

Tone Curves

Lightroom's implementation of Curves differs from Photoshop's because it changes only tonality—the underlying black, white, and gray values of the image. Lightroom's version retains the tone curve's versatility for contrast and brightness control while making it close to foolproof.

FIGURE 12.17

STEP ONE

Click on the Tone Curve panel to open it. Drag inside the image in the After preview. The first difference is that when the cursor moves over an image in the content area, nothing happens. There is no dancing circle à la Photoshop. Get it back, put it on tool-enhancing drugs, and take control by clicking the Targeted Adjustment tool bullseye in the upper left-hand corner of the Tone Curve panel (**Figure 12.18**).

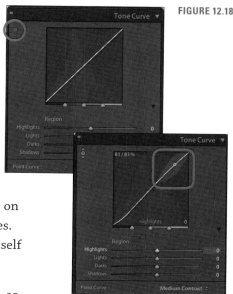

FIGURE 12.18

STEP TWO

Drag the mouse over the photograph. The dancing circle gracefully glides along the curve! There is something new. Notice that as the cursor moves over an area, a shaded area appears around it on the curve. This shows the limits that the curve can shift for these tones. There is no way for a curve in Lightroom to flatten out or turn in on itself (**Figure 12.19**).

Be aware that if the preview looks bad after you have moved the curve, so will the print. Little curve tweaks are usually all it takes.

FIGURE 12.19

FIGURE 12.20

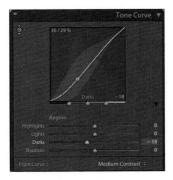

FIGURE 12.21

STEP THREE

The photograph would be stronger with the reddish cinder blocks at the bottom darker and the sky deeper as well. Now for the good part: Hover the cursor over one of the red blocks, click, then drag down. They get darker (**Figure 12.20**).

And the curve reflects the change (**Figure 12.21**).

STEP FOUR

Darken the sky by clicking in it and dragging down with the Targeted Adjustment tool. It stays on until you click on it again in the Tone Curve panel. Check the effect by clicking the preview toggle off, then on. It is located in the upper left corner of the panel. Finally, brighten the highlights just a bit. Click on the highlights in the Histogram and drag them to the edge of the Recovery zone. Press Command (PC: Ctrl) + 2 to close the Tone Curve panel.

Once again…done.

Hue, Saturation, Luminance, and Color (Oh My!)

The next panel down holds Lightroom's HSL, Color, and Grayscale tools. The choices across the top of the panel highlight which tool is active. All opens every one of them for a plethora of tweaking choices.

STEP ONE

Press Command (PC: Ctrl) + 3 to open the HSL / Color / Grayscale panel. Continue the work on the abandoned car wash. The cinder blocks want to be redder rather than merely reddish. Select Hue, then click on the bullseye in the upper left corner of the panel to get its Targeted Adjustment tool. A click on the second block followed by a downward drag does the trick (**Figure 12.22**).

The Red and Orange hue sliders change to –13 each. If your numbers are slightly different than mine and the bricks look red to you, it's good (**Figure 12.23**). If there is too much orange in the white brick: click, drag down, and it's done.

STEP TWO

The sky could use some deepening, too. Click Saturation in the panel header. It's just to the right of Hue. Drag upward in the sky to darken to taste. Notice that as the cursor moves over an area the corresponding slider highlights in the panel.

STEP THREE

The grass looks anemic. Choose the Color panel, click on the green swatch, and drag down. Woo-hoo! Instant turf builder.

If you're not sure which color swatch to pick, click All, then move the mouse pointer over the color you want to change. As it passes over different colors, those colors highlight in the Color panel. Click when you see the one to change.

The After preview is a dramatic improvement over the Before (**Figure 12.24**). Best of all, not a single slider was touched in the process!

FIGURE 12.22

FIGURE 12.23

FIGURE 12.24

There is one more thing...

Black and white

Some consider great black and white to be the holy grail of photography. Lightroom's handling of this quest is nothing short of incredible. I'd like to keep all of the work on the color version of my washed-up car wash. I want a copy of the color photo to convert to black and white. The old way would be to duplicate the image in Photoshop, save it with a different name, and wind up with two or more full-sized copies.

Not so in Lightroom.

There is quite a list of changes to make: black-and-white conversion, then a deeper sky, darker grass, brighter walls, and more legible graffiti. And it's all done without touching a single slider (heh, heh).

STEP ONE

Press the G key to go to Grid view in the Library module. Highlight the thumbnail of the car wash. Press Command (PC: Ctrl) + N to make a new collection. Name it Car wash. The photograph is now in a grid by itself.

Now it's menu time. Choose Photo > Create Virtual Copy. A new thumbnail appears highlighted in the Grid and the Filmstrip. The page curl in the bottom left corner says it's a virtual copy. Click to highlight it (**Figure 12.25**).

FIGURE 12.25

Virtual copies aren't pixels at all. They are tiny metadata text files in the Lightroom database that hold all of the adjustment settings. They are applied to a copy of the original when exported.

STEP TWO

Press D to return to the Develop module. Click the Reset button at the bottom right of the right-side panel.

STEP THREE

Click Grayscale in the HSL / Color / Grayscale panel to turn the colorful car wash into a drab vision of its abandoned self.

STEP FOUR

Start with exposure. Click in the center of the Histogram and drag to the right. The red highlight clipping warning appears so at least there will be pure white in the final print (**Figure 12.26**). Pundits say that's a good thing.

FIGURE 12.26

STEP FIVE

Next, make deeper midtones in this black and white. Press Command (PC: Ctrl) + 2 to open the Tone Curve panel. Click the Targeted Adjustment tool. Click in the more distant dark set of rafters and drag down. Then click on the lighter rafters in the front and drag down for bolder midtones (**Figure 12.27**).

Always check that the adjuster is clicked for the panel you want to use. Active adjusters add up and down triangles above and below the bullseye (**Figure 12.28**).

STEP SIX

The Grayscale panel is next. Choose its Targeted Adjustment tool. Click in the sky and drag down. Alright! It's really dark, producing nearly the same effect as a #25 red filter on the lens when shooting black-and-white film.

FIGURE 12.27

FIGURE 12.28

STEP SEVEN

Now click, then drag downward in the grass to lower the yellow and green values. The grass becomes lush and full of contrast. The green graffiti pops out, too. The blue shadow clipping warnings are fine. They mean some of the areas in the print will be as black as a printer can make them. That adds depth and richness. A quick press of the J key turns off the warning. The work here is done without ever touching a slider or Photoshop (**Figure 12.29**).

Does this sound too easy? Unbelievable? Or even a bit magical? I have to admit, this is almost as much fun as seeing that first black-and-white print appear in a tray of developer.

The Targeted Adjustment tool just makes sense. Using it on an image you're getting paid for means it makes cents, too, if not dollars—and lots of 'em. Tone Curve, Hue, Saturation, Luminance, and Color adjustments are as easy as click, drag, done. Best of all, this is totally non-destructive. Not a single pixel has been harmed in producing this chapter. And it can be saved as a preset to be applied to another lonely car wash in the future.

Could anything be simpler or more intuitive? How about being able to say, "Computer, make the photograph on the screen...pretty"?

Maybe in Lightroom version 2.0.

Done.

FIGURE 12.29

CHAPTER 13

Color Correction and Exposure Tweaks

I CONTINUE TO MARVEL at how much easier, better, and more fun all things digital have made photography.

I have often thought of the vagaries of shooting film. Before ever going on a shoot, I would buy a case or two of film and test it to see how it recorded color by photographing a Gretag-Macbeth (now X-Rite) ColorChecker chart. The lab would read the processed film with a spectrophotometer and tell me what gelatin filters I had to put on the front of the lens to ensure neutral color. On set, each light had to be measured with a color temperature meter, then covered with an appropriate gel to make it neutral.

Once a setup was complete and carefully metered for exposure, a Polaroid would be made as a pre-put-it-on-film check. The instant print (that "instant" lasted between ninety seconds and two or even three minutes, depending on the temperature) would be waved vigorously to dry it before close examination.

I distinctly remember explaining to clients and art directors viewing the Polaroid, "Don't worry, the real film won't look like that."

After a shoot it was common for photographers to have their labs clip a small portion of exposed film from each roll of film, then run them through the processor. A couple of hours later, based on meticulous scrutiny of these "clip" tests, the rest of the roll was chemically pushed to get more exposure or pulled for less exposure by the lab. This was often for another 50% of the price of processing, not to mention another couple of hours of time.

Shooting film took extra money and time, and it was positively nerve-wracking waiting to see if the film "came out." Fortunately, those days are behind us. Now it's a simple matter to tweak exposures and correct color in Adobe Camera Raw 4 or Lightroom.

About Color Neutrality

FIGURE 13.1

What is neutral? Loosely defined, it's when whites are white, grays are gray, and shadows are deep dark gray. The problem with the definition is the question, "What color is white?" Look around. Let's say for a moment that you are sitting in a restaurant lit by incandescent light and candles on the table. It's a white-tablecloth restaurant so the tablecloth is, in fact, white. Look at the table. What color is the tablecloth? Don't think about it. Answer with what you see. White. Right? The reality and the problem is that the human brain knows that the tablecloth is white. It "corrects" for the warm yellow-orange-ish light and says, "Yup. It's white." All of the rest of the colors in the room fall into place in spite of the color of the light. The human eye is a lousy judge of color neutrality.

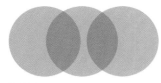

FIGURE 13.2

Digital color

Download the files for this chapter from amesphoto.com/learning. The book code is DPN8414.

Here's a question: Which of the dots in **Figure 13.1** is neutral gray?

Which one of the dots in **Figure 13.2** is neutral gray?

Which one of the dots in **Figure 13.3** is neutral gray?

FIGURE 13.3

Your answers (whatever they may be) are right for the way you see under the lighting conditions you're in as you read this right now.

The "correct" answer for the first one is neither one. The answer for the second is the one in the middle. The same is true for number three. Take my word for it or, better yet, measure it for yourself.

STEP ONE

Open Lightroom, then open the DPN Projects Catalog. Import the folder of samples containing question1.psd, question2.psd, and question3.psd.

STEP TWO

Click on question3.psd in the Grid. Press D to enter the Develop module. Hold the cursor over the far left circle. Note the RGB percentages. Move the cursor over the middle circle. Note the percentages. Finally, put the cursor over the right circle and note those readouts.

STEP THREE

Open question3.psd in Photoshop. Show the Info palette. Hover the cursor over the left circle and write down the RGB numbers. Do the same for the middle and right circles. The results are a higher percentage (Lightroom) or higher numbers (Photoshop) of Red and Green for the image on the left; the exact same percentages or numbers for the middle image; and a higher percentage or number of Blue for the right image (**Figure 13.4**).

The other two questions are copies of the same file, only with lower opacities.

FIGURE 13.4

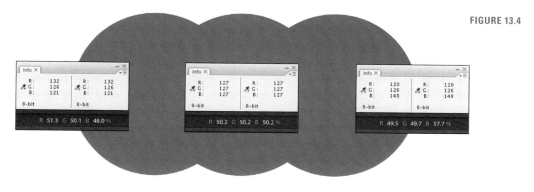

Going further

STEP FOUR

Go ahead and measure the other two files. The color difference is the same even with the added white from the lower opacity of the circle layers. What are the readings where the neutral overlaps the warm and cold circles in question2.psd?

Color neutrality in Photoshop, Camera Raw, or Lightroom is easy. When the RGB numbers or percentages equal each other, the tone is neutral.

Photoshop, ACR 4, and Lightroom

Photoshop and Camera Raw display color in 256 steps, from 0 (black) to 255 (white). Lightroom uses percentages; 0% is black and 100% is white. The reason for the difference in measurement is that photographers new to digital would more intuitively understand a scale of 0 to 100 instead of one from 0 to 255. I made a chart so I could easily get the equivalents between my familiar 256-step scale versus Lightroom's percentage readings (**Figure 13.5**). Until Photoshop offers an RGB 0-100 choice in the Info palette, the need to understand both systems continues.

FIGURE 13.5

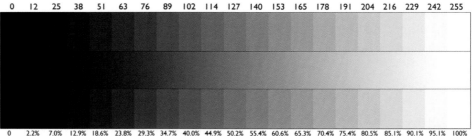

Photoshop & Bridge

| 0 | 12 | 25 | 38 | 51 | 63 | 76 | 89 | 102 | 114 | 127 | 140 | 153 | 165 | 178 | 191 | 204 | 216 | 229 | 242 | 255 |

| 0 | 2.2% | 7.0% | 12.9% | 18.6% | 23.8% | 29.3% | 34.7% | 40.0% | 44.9% | 50.2% | 55.4% | 60.6% | 65.3% | 70.4% | 75.4% | 80.5% | 85.1% | 90.1% | 95.1% | 100% |

Lightroom

I use both Lightroom and Camera Raw for color correction and exposure adjustments. I strongly believe it is critical for a working pro to be able to use both systems proficiently.

Color and Exposure Refinements

ACR 4 and Lightroom do the same thing, only a bit differently. There are sample folders for each program in the downloads for this chapter. They each contain photographs of the same girl in different outfits.

Adobe Camera Raw 4

Camera Raw is a workflow tool, no doubt about it. It's fast, powerful, and fairly easy to use. The Camera Raw team, headed by Thomas Knoll, has packed an unreal amount of functionality into this premier RAW converter.

Color correction

STEP ONE

Click on the ACR 4 folder in Bridge to populate the Content pane with thumbnails of the photographs.

STEP TWO

Click the first one, hold down the Shift key, and click the last one to select them all. Or use the keyboard shortcut Command (PC: Ctrl) + A.

STEP THREE

Press Command (PC: Ctrl) + R, or right-click and choose Open with Camera Raw....

STEP FOUR

Again, press Command (PC: Ctrl) + A to select all of the thumbnails open in ACR 4's Filmstrip. (The last three steps are high-speed workflow using the keyboard, easy as 1-2-3: Command + A, Command + R, Command + A. Ready to work.)

STEP FIVE

An X-Rite (formerly GretagMacbeth) ColorChecker Gray Scale balance card is held in front of model Joanna Lamb from Elite/Atlanta. The white swatch is closest to the source of light. That's a quick cue for me of the direction of the light.

I carry at least one of the full-size versions of the reference card and a mini version, as well, in my camera case. I do my best to photograph one of them each time the light changes. Sometimes when shooting outdoors I simply hold the mini at arm's length and make an exposure. A neutral reference is always useful.

Pick the Color Sampler tool (S). Click first on the white swatch, then again on the black. Sampler #1 reads the white and Sampler #2 reads the black (**Figure 13.6**). The white swatch is R: 241, G: 237, and B: 238. This is very close to neutral. As a matter of fact, it's only off by a small amount over 1%. Chapter 10 explains how color correction is done in Photoshop using Levels. It's a bit simpler in Camera Raw.

FIGURE 13.6

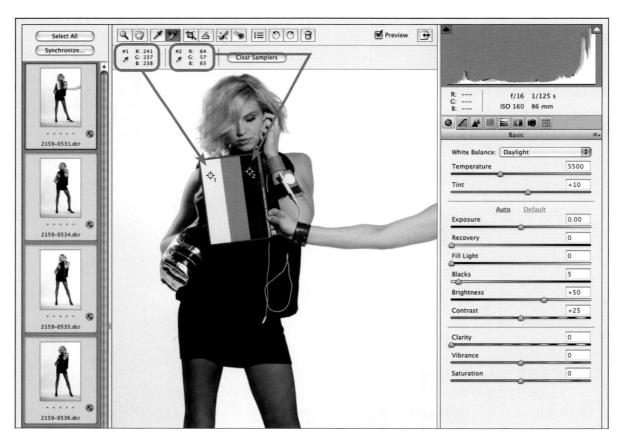

STEP SIX

Choose the White Balance tool (I). Move it over the white swatch and click. Camera Raw neutralizes the white to RGB: 237. The changes are applied to all of the files selected in the Filmstrip. If you forgot or forget (don't worry; you will) to select all of the thumbnails in the Filmstrip before making corrections, click the Select All button, then Synchronize.... Finally, click OK.

The blacks are within 2% of each other. It's important to note that Camera Raw and Lightroom can only neutralize one tone. If color balance is critical in the midtones and shadows, they can be made neutral using the techniques in Chapter 10.

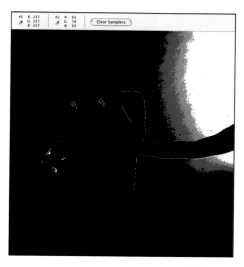

FIGURE 13.7

Exposure

RGB: 237 for a highlight—in this case, the white patch—is a bit dark. It is underexposed. This section deals with that, shadows, and more.

STEP ONE

Hold down the Option (PC: Alt) key. Click the Exposure slider. The Preview turns mostly black, showing an area of white surrounded by magenta circled by blue (**Figure 13.7**). These warnings are areas of potential overexposure. The situation here is that the background is supposed to be white. Move the Exposure slider to the right. Watch the numbers for Sampler #1. As the exposure is increased to brighten Joanna, the background moves closer to being completely white. When the highlights on the card reach around 253, the wall is all white except for her shadow (**Figure 13.8**).

Release the Option (PC: Alt) key. The Exposure is +.65.

STEP TWO

The increase in exposure has brightened the shadows (black) to R: 81, G: 76, B: 83. Once again, hold down the Option (PC: Alt) key. This time, move the Blacks slider to the right to lower these numbers to the high fifties or low sixties. The example shows R: 61, G: 55, B: 65 (**Figure 13.9**). Release the mouse and the Option

FIGURE 13.8

FIGURE 13.9

(PC: Alt) key. The temptation is to run the Blacks up to push the contrast. Resist. Lowering the shadow numbers much more will result in losing all the detail in Joanna's little black dress. Press P to see the before view. Her skin looks better in the after image. The dress has more detail in the before image (**Figure 13.10**).

STEP THREE

Bring back shadow detail. Drag the Fill Light slider to 12 to add just a bit of light to the shadows. This lowers contrast (see Chapter 4).

FIGURE 13.10

BRIGHTEST COLORS AND LOST DETAIL

When a color reaches 255, there is no detail in that channel. The following colors indicate which channels are at maximum brightness, reading 255. The Primaries (R, G, and B) are obvious. Here are the Complementaries.

Complementaries: Cyan = GB: 255, Magenta = RB: 255, Yellow = RG: 255

White = RGB: 255

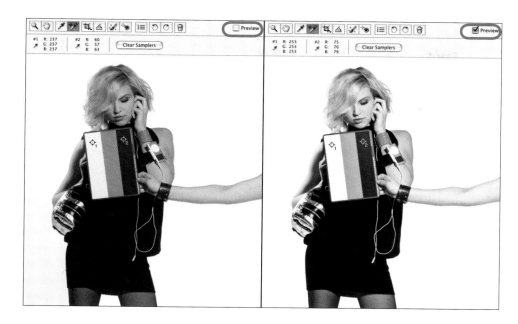

FIGURE 13.11

STEP FOUR
Move the Clarity slider to the right to 43. Press P to see the before and after images (**Figure 13.11**). Nice.

Lightroom

The power of Camera Raw is in Lightroom's Develop module....

Color correction

STEP ONE
Open the DPN Projects catalog in Lightroom.

STEP TWO
Import the DPN Projects folder from the downloads folder for this chapter.

STEP THREE
Select the preview of Joanna holding the ColorChecker chart in the Library's Grid view. Press D to enter the Develop module. Lightroom does not have Color Samplers.

FIGURE 13.12

FIGURE 13.13

STEP FOUR

Click the White Balance Selector (W), lovingly known as the "Turkey Baster" tool. Move it over the white swatch in the ColorChecker. The Loupe appears. The center square has a crosshair showing exactly the place being balanced. If a reference card isn't available, find a white in the photograph you want to correct. The values are R: 91.6%, G: 91.9%, and B: 95.1% (**Figure 13.12**).

Use the Scale Slider to increase the resolution of the tool. The farther right, the more refined the view. Were a reference card not available, this would allow you to select part of the white wire of Joanna's earbuds as a balance point (**Figure 13.13**).

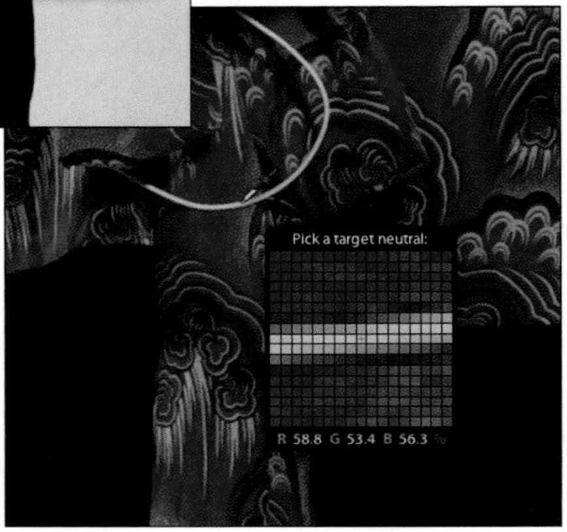

Click on the white swatch to neutralize the highlights. The values now read RGB: 93.1%. The blacks are as close as they were in ACR 4, with readings of R: 16.3%, G: 15.5%, and B: 16.5%.

Exposure

93.1 is underexposed. This set of photographs was made with the same expectations as the previous group. The wall is white, although not as brightly lit as before (**Figure 13.14**).

STEP ONE

Click the Before and After view button in the control bar. Hold down the Option (PC: Alt) key. Click the Exposure slider and move it to the right until the white swatch goes completely white. Release the mouse. The Exposure is –.95.

STEP TWO

Hold down the Option (PC: Alt) key again. Click the Recovery slider. The white areas around Joanna's shoulders are at RGB: 100% (**Figure 13.15**). Move the slider to the right until the halo breaks up. Release the mouse at a value of 3.

FIGURE 13.14

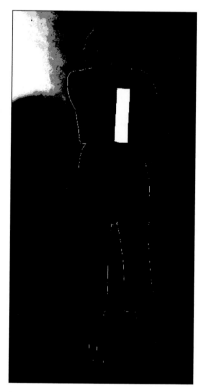

FIGURE 13.15

STEP THREE

Move the cursor over her pants at about mid-thigh. The RGB values are around 16%, which is a little dark for reproducing them with detail. And there isn't much detail in them anyway. Add some Fill Light by moving the slider to the right. If you like watching the numbers, highlight the entry field in Fill Light, put the cursor back in place on the pants, then tap the up arrow key. At 13 the crease in the pants shows and there is a difference in tone between the cuffs and her socks. The Tab key will cycle to the end of the entry fields (Saturation), then it hides and shows the side panels.

STEP FOUR

Move the Clarity slider to 50 and Vibrance to 41.

Synchronization

Color corrections and exposure refinements have been made to the photograph of Joanna and the ColorChecker. Next, these changes want to be applied to the rest of the take.

STEP ONE

Hold down the Shift key, then click the last thumbnail in the Filmstrip.

STEP TWO

Click Sync. The Synchronize Settings dialog opens. Click Synchronize or tap Return (PC: Enter). The previews in the Filmstrip update with the new settings. The Filmstrip displays the Settings Edited icon in the lower right corner of each updated thumbnail (**Figure 13.16**).

FIGURE 13.16

Corrections and tweaks are complete. Color correction has come a long way from Levels and Curves in Photoshop. On a final note, those techniques are valuable for fine-tuning neutrals in the midtones and shadows after using ACR 4 or Lightroom on the highlights.

CHAPTER 14

Takin' 'Em to the Net

THE INTERNET IS A GREAT PLACE to show photographs. A website rich with imagery is a joy to look at and return to as new work is added. Building websites, on the other hand, isn't quite so much fun. It can be tedious, detailed, and time-consuming work that could better be spent taking photographs. There has to be an easier way. Wouldn't you know it? There actually are a few….

Web Photo Galleries

Both Photoshop and Lightroom generate photographic websites from selected photographs and display them in the order the photographer chooses. There is a setup you have to do in both programs.

Download the files for this chapter from amesphoto.com/learning. The book code is DPN8414.

Lightroom

Lightroom's Web module creates either HTML or Flash galleries with photographs chosen in the Grid and saved as a collection.

HTML galleries can be read by any Internet browser—Safari, Firefox, or Internet Explorer, to name the most popular. Photographs in HTML galleries can be copied by right-clicking and choosing Download from the browser's contextual menu. They are not the most secure.

Flash galleries can only be read by browsers that have a Flash plug-in loaded. Some IT departments are still reticent to allow corporate users access to Flash. It is very secure when it comes to protecting photographs.

Setup

This project is part of an editorial shoot I did for an Atlanta magazine on formal wear for weddings. The shoot is over and the editor is anxious to get a look at the results. The files were converted to JPEGs from the original RAW files to save you from having to download several gigabytes of data.

STEP ONE
Open the DPN Projects catalog in Lightroom. Import the folder 2114-Wedding Fashions from the sample folders for this chapter.

STEP TWO
Select all of the thumbnails in the Grid by pressing Command (PC: Ctrl) + A. Make a new collection by pressing Command (PC: Ctrl) + N (**Figure 14.1**).

FIGURE 14.1

FIGURE 14.2

The new collection appears highlighted in the Collections panel along with a count of the photographs (**Figure 14.2**).

STEP THREE

The opening page is of the bride and groom together. Choose those thumbnails in the collection by clicking on the first one, holding down the Shift key, and clicking the last one in the series. Drag them in front of the groom in his tux. The next pages will feature the bride's dress. Highlight the photographs of the bride on the pink background. Drag them in front of the groom. I will often arrange the photographs so my favorite is the last one. Editors seem to remember the last one for some reason. Feel free to pick your favorites and place them last or first, depending on how you think the shot will be memorable.

Sharpening

STEP ONE

Digital captures are just plain soft on capture. These files want some sharpening. Select the first image of the couple. Press D to go into the Develop module. Tap Y to enter the compare mode. Open the Detail panel by pressing Command (PC: Ctrl) + 5. Click inside either the before or after preview. The image enlarges. Choose at least 1:1 in the Navigator pane in the left side panel when adjusting the controls in the Detail pane. Command (PC: Ctrl) + + enlarges the view. Command (PC: Ctrl) + – zooms out. Move the Amount slider to the right until it reads 94. Leave the Radius at 1.0. Detail controls how the sharpening affects the photograph. I want the photograph

FIGURE 14.3

FIGURE 14.4

to be sharp alright, though not at the expense of the softness of the bride's skin. Detail goes to 30, then the Masking gets cranked up to 45 to soften the effect of the sharpening on her skin (**Figure 14.3**). (See Chapter 11.)

Yes, those are orange-handled A-clamps tucking up extra fabric on the bride's dress in some of the photographs of the couple. The clamps will be removed in Photoshop if a photograph showing them is chosen.

STEP TWO

Apply the sharpening to all of the photographs. Click the right arrow in the Filmstrip at the bottom of the workspace. When the scrolling stops, the Filmstrip has reached the last thumbnail. Shift-click it. The word Previous at the bottom of the right side panel changes to Sync.... Click it (**Figure 14.4**).

STEP THREE

Click Check None at the bottom of the Synchronize Settings dialog. Now check Sharpening. Click Synchronize (**Figure 14.5**).

All of the images are sharpened. Each thumbnail in the Filmstrip displays the "I've been adjusted" icon in its lower right corner.

Web module

The editor's pick will be forwarded to the layout team. They will want to grab images to use as FPOs (For Position Only) to see how the photograph will look on the page. This is a perfect situation for using an HTML template.

Lightroom's Flash templates get set up the same way as HTML versions.

Gallery and Site Info

STEP ONE

Click the word Web to enter the Web module.

STEP TWO

Hover over the choices in the Template Browser in the left side panel. The layout for each one appears in the Preview pane. Click Earl Grey. It's a Flash template (**Figure 14.6**). Lightroom begins building a full-size preview.

STEP THREE

Command-click (PC: Ctrl-click) any of the open panes in the right side panel. They all close. (Command-clicking [PC: Ctrl-clicking] again will open all of the panes. This works in all of the panels in all of the modules.) I like to work my way through each one when setting up a Web or Slide show template so it doesn't look so busy.

STEP FOUR

Click the Gallery pane to open it. Select Lightroom HTML Gallery. Lightroom redraws the preview in HTML.

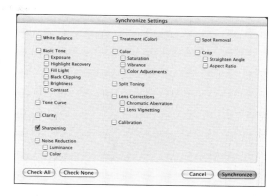

FIGURE 14.5

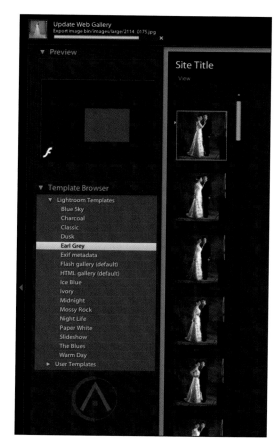

FIGURE 14.6

STEP FIVE

Click the Site Info pane to open it. Click in the Site Title entry window. Name it February Issue. Tap the Tab key to go the Collection Title field. Enter 2114-Wedding Feature. Tap Tab again. Collection Description becomes highlighted. Fill in the field with Bridal Editorial proofs – For Position Only – Not for Publication. Press Tab again and type ©2007 Kevin Ames. (The copyright symbol is Option + G on the Mac. In Windows, turn Num Lock on, hold down the Alt key, then type 0169 on the keypad. The numbers below the function keys will not work for this. Release the Alt key and tah-dah! ©!) Tab again and type kevin@amesphoto.com.

WEBSITE LOGOS

Adding a logo to a Lightroom website is easy.

1. Open your logo in Photoshop. (I'll use mine for this example.)

2. Choose Image > Image Size (Command [PC: Ctrl] + Option [PC: Alt] + I). Set the Height to 60 pixels. Leave the resolution at 300. Choose Bicubic Sharper (best for reduction) from the menu at the bottom (**Figure 14.7**).

3. Choose File > Save for Web and Devices… (Command [PC: Ctrl] + Option [PC: Alt] + Shift + S). Click the 2-Up tab, then choose PNG-24 from the Preset menu. Click Save. Name the file appropriately. Its extension will be .png.

4. Navigate to the saved logo in Bridge.

5. Go to Lightroom. Choose Identity Plate Setup…. Click Use a graphical identity plate.

6. Click into Bridge. Click the logo thumbnail. Drag it over to Lightroom's Identity Plate Editor. Drop it in the left window highlighted by a blue border (**Figure 14.8**).

7. Click OK.

The logo will be available in the Identity Plate section of Lightroom's Web, Slideshow, and Print modules. Since it is so small, it most likely won't print well.

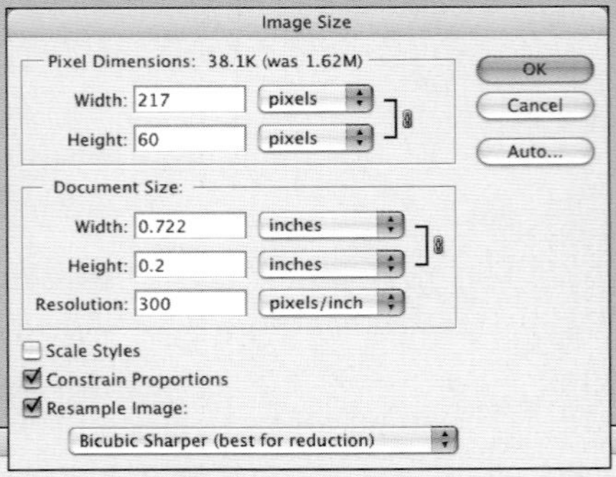

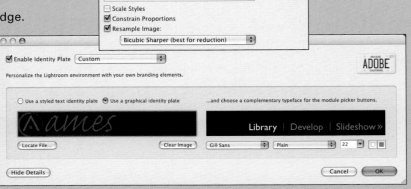

FIGURE 14.7

FIGURE 14.8

STEP SIX

Follow steps four through seven in the "Website Logos" sidebar to add my logo into an identity plate. The logo is copyrighted and I'm providing it for you to use in these exercises only. Click the Identity Plate checkbox. The logo can act as a link. A convention on amesphoto.com is that clicking the logo returns the browser to the home page. Enter amesphoto.com/index.html. That takes care of the Site Info pane (**Figure 14.9**).

Color palette

The logo really stands out in the preview (**Figure 14.10**). Not!

Some things have to change. Here's where it happens.

STEP ONE

Double-click on the Background color swatch. This opens the color picker. White is going to be the ticket. Drag the slider to the top (**Figure 14.11**).

That's better; the logo is legible (**Figure 14.12**).

FIGURE 14.9

FIGURE 14.10

FIGURE 14.11

FIGURE 14.12

FIGURE 14.13

STEP TWO

There are two basic colors on my website: a gray and a burgundy. Double-click on the swatch for Text. Click on the magnifying glass. Move it over the gray legs of the A in the logo. Click to sample the color (**Figure 14.13**). The color appears in the bar to the right of the magnifying glass. Click in the bar, then drag the color to the swatch panel in the bottom of the picker. Repeat for the burgundy color. All of the text turns burgundy. Click on the gray swatch.

STEP THREE

Double-click the Grid line swatch. Change its color to the gray of the logo. Close the picker, then click the Color Palette pane to close it as well.

FIGURE 14.14

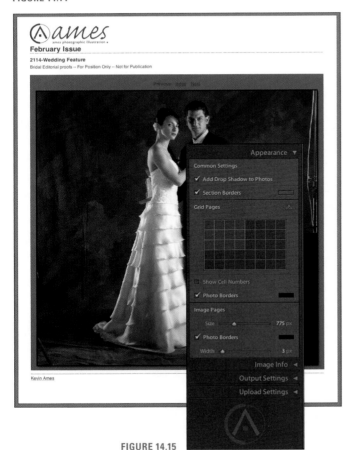

Appearance

STEP ONE

Open the Appearance pane. Change the color of the Section Borders to the logo gray.

STEP TWO

Drag in the Grid Pages layout so that four columns and three rows are highlighted. The preview updates to show the additional thumbnails. Uncheck Show Cell Numbers.

STEP THREE

Click one of the thumbnails. Hide the Filmstrip by clicking its flippy triangle. Set the Size under Image Pages to 775 pixels. That will be big enough for the designer to use the image for an FPO (**Figure 14.14**).

Set 3 for the Photo Borders Width (**Figure 14.15**).

Close the Appearance pane.

FIGURE 14.15

Image Info and Output Settings

STEP ONE

Open both of the Image Info and Output Settings panes.

STEP TWO

Choose Filename from the Title menu. Select Sequence from the Caption menu.

STEP THREE

Set the Quality slider to 80. Click the Add Copyright Watermark checkbox. Choose Copyright Only from the Metadata menu (**Figure 14.16**).

FIGURE 14.16

Upload settings

Lightroom includes an FTP client. How convenient! It gets set up like any other. If you upload to your own website you already know how to use this feature. 'Nuff said!

Export

Save the files to a location on a hard drive by clicking Export. Follow the prompts. The exported folder contains a complete website. Burn the folder to a CD. Anyone you give it to can open the folder on it and double-click the index. html file. The site will open for viewing in their computer's default browser. This is a very slick way to pass along a portfolio, especially one that uses Lightroom's Flash slideshow template.

Photoshop

Bridge is the gateway to Photoshop's Web Photo Galleries. Photographs are sorted, arranged, then finally sent off to have Photoshop complete the work. Setting up the Photoshop Web Photo Gallery is similar to setting up Lightroom's, though not nearly as refined.

Setup

STEP ONE

Open the folder 2114-Girls BFF in Bridge. Yep...shoes. When I'm photographing women, I ask them to say, "Shoe shopping," instead of the totally cheesy standard smile phrase, "Say cheese...." Eew. If shoes aren't a girl's best friend forever, I don't know what might be.

These are product photographs for the magazine's fashion pages. The editors will use the website for FPOs, while the full-resolution files are being outlined with the Pen tool.

STEP TWO

Press Command (PC: Ctrl) + A to select all of the shoe thumbnails. Click the second dot from the left (above the filename) to give all of them a two-star rating (**Figure 14.17**).

STEP THREE

Deselect all of the thumbnails by pressing Command (PC: Ctrl) + Shift + A.

FIGURE 14.17

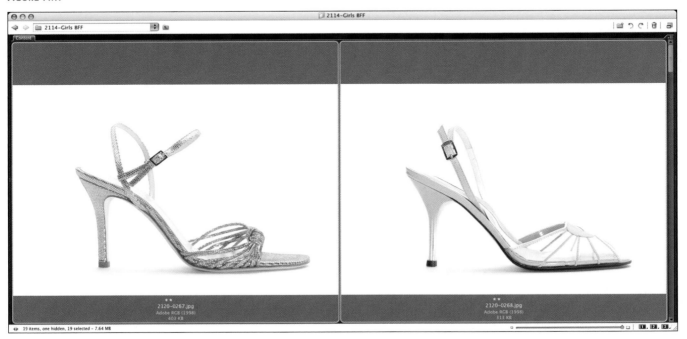

STEP FOUR

Some of the shoes in this set just don't belong. Click the two stars in the Filter pane (**Figure 14.18**).

Scroll down through the shoes until you get to 282 and 283. These just don't look like women's shoes by any stretch of the imagination. Click the one-star rating on each one. Poof, gone.

STEP FIVE

As a courtesy to the editors, group the shoes by high heels, flats, sneakers, then boots. Click the first of the three high heels between the red and lime green sneakers. Hold down the Shift key and click the third one. Drag them up between the pink heel and the first flat. Perfect. Deselect (**Figure 14.19**).

STEP SIX

Choose Tools > Photoshop > Web Photo Gallery....

FIGURE 14.18

FIGURE 14.19

General

Photoshop offers several templates in both Flash and HTML. They are listed in the Styles menu of the Web Photo Gallery dialog. Unlike Lightroom's templates, these are editable in Adobe Dreamweaver CS3. They are located in the Photoshop folder in Applications (Mac) or Programs (Windows). The path is Adobe Photoshop CS3 > Presets > Web Photo Gallery.

STEP ONE

Choose Simple from the Styles menu. Type my address in the Email field: kevin@amesphoto.com.

STEP TWO

Click Destination.... Make a new folder on the desktop called 2114_girl_bff. This is the folder that will be uploaded to the website, so it follows web naming conventions: all lowercase, and underscores for spaces.

STEP THREE

Click the Preserve all metadata checkbox. This helps protect photographs that have been registered with the United States Copyright Office.

Choose Banner in the Options drop-down menu.

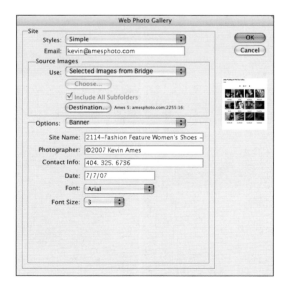

Banner

STEP ONE

For the Site Name, type 2114-Fashion Feature Women's Shoes – Proofs for FPO – Not for Publication.

STEP TWO

Fill in ©2007 Kevin Ames in the Photographer field.

STEP THREE

The phone number (404. 325. 6736) goes in Contact Info.

STEP FOUR

The date fills in automatically. Choose Arial for the Font and 3 as the Font Size (**Figure 14.20**).

Choose Large Images from the Options menu.

Large Images

STEP ONE

If the site you are building has only a few images (like this one does), leave Add Numeric Links checked. The finished site will have links to every large image running across the top of the large image page (**Figure 14.21**).

If you are posting an entire shoot of several hundred photographs, don't check this box! You'll get at least a couple of pages of links before the large photograph appears. And that's for every one of the hundreds of images on the site.

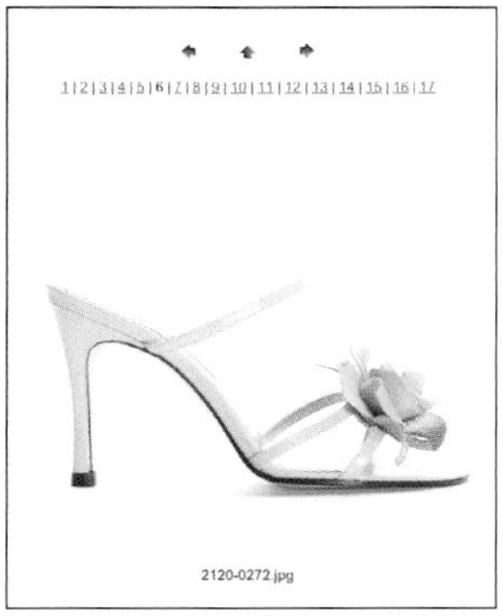

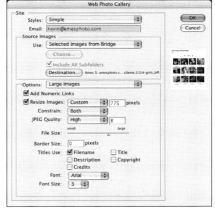

FIGURE 14.21

STEP TWO

Check Resize Images. Set Custom as the Size and enter 775, the same setting used before. Constrain wants to be set to Both. Set 8 as the JPEG Quality.

STEP THREE

Enter a number higher than 0 if you want to put a border around each large image.

STEP FOUR

In the Titles Use section, select the Filename. Once again, set Arial as the Font and 3 for the Size (**Figure 14.22**).

Select Thumbnails in the Options menu.

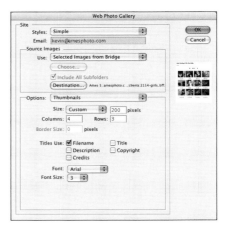

FIGURE 14.22

Thumbnails

STEP ONE

I like big thumbnails. Enter 200 pixels. The Size will change to Custom.

STEP TWO

Some templates don't support all of the functions in the dialog. That's the reason that Border Size is grayed out. Set 4 Columns and 3 Rows.

STEP THREE

Again, check Filename for the Titles Use section, and choose Arial for the Font with a Size of 3 (**Figure 14.23**).

Select Custom Colors from the Options menu.

FIGURE 14.23

Custom Colors

Can you say neutrals? Good. I like the way you say that. This is a website showcasing photographs. Bright colors are alright in the photographs themselves. As text, links, banners, or backgrounds, vibrant color is simply distracting to the view. Other words come to mind...can you say "odious"?

STEP ONE

Double-click on the Background swatch. Photoshop's color picker opens. Check Only Web Colors. Click the third gray patch from the bottom. Click OK (**Figure 14.24**).

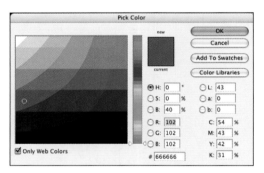

FIGURE 14.24

STEP TWO

Double-click the swatch next to Banner. Choose the same color.

STEP THREE

Choose black for text.

STEP FOUR

Choose the third one down from the top for the Link. (The gray reads RGB: 153.)

STEP FIVE

Set the one below white for the Active Link (RGB: 204).

STEP SIX

Choose black for the Visited Link (**Figure 14.25**).

Select Security from the Options menu.

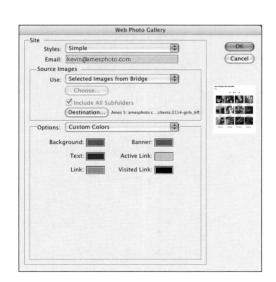

FIGURE 14.25

Security

STEP ONE

Select Custom Text from the Content menu. Type ©2007 Kevin Ames in the Custom Text field.

STEP TWO

Use Arial as the Font.

STEP THREE

It's possible to totally obliterate the image using the next four choices. That will protect the photograph, alright—at the expense of the viewer being able to see what you are showing. Be subtle. Set Font Size to 18 points.

STEP FOUR

Black is good for the Color. Set the Opacity to 12%.

STEP FIVE

Copyright law states that removing a copyright notice from a photograph is willful infringement. Cropping a photo to cut out the notice counts. Position the notice at the Top Left. Rotate it 90 Degrees Clockwise (**Figure 14.26**).

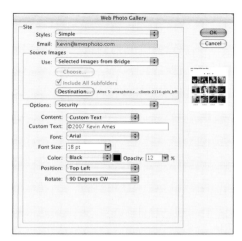

FIGURE 14.26

Create the website by clicking OK.

The thumbnails are easy to see. They pop off the page. Everything else is subordinate to them (**Figure 14.27**).

The large images dominate the page. The copyright notice is understated and not distracting. The colors support the photograph. This works well (**Figure 14.28**). The editors will love it!

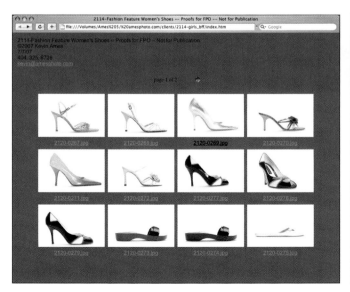

FIGURE 14.27

FIGURE 14.28

Customize Simple

Photoshop's Web Photo Gallery templates don't have a way to drop in a logo the way Lightroom does. It would be truly great if Photoshop could add a logo, a navigation bar, and a custom background, as well as reposition the fields so they weren't stacked up in the banner of the site. Gee, I wish it could look something like...**Figure 14.29**.

And for the enlargements, could the pages be simple with the filename along the top of the photograph, and could the navigation arrows be stylized logos? How about the banner being really understated, size-wise, while branding the image with the look of the rest of amesphoto.com? Maybe it might be like...**Figure 14.30**.

Of course, it would have to work the same way the Simple style does from the Web Photo Gallery dialog and be no harder than a regular Web Photo Gallery....

Rub the digital—er, magic—lamp and the genie will grant your wish if you know a smattering of HTML and are willing to open up the PDF that came with the downloads in this chapter. That PDF, by the way, is practically an entire chapter—all laid out like the *Notebook*—walking you step by step through finding the template in Photoshop and making the modifications in Adobe Dreamweaver. It even shares how to get a free 30-day trial of Dreamweaver. Want it? Double-click Kevin and Ted's Excellent PDF. (Ted, my editor, really made the PDF happen. He deserves credit, right?)

FIGURE 14.29

FIGURE 14.30

CHAPTER 15

Email Presentations

I DON'T KNOW ABOUT YOU. I get truly tired of scrolling through email to look at attached JPEGs. They go on and on and there isn't a convenient way to see them in any order other than the way they were attached. There's gotta be a better way!

Photoshop has an improved PDF presentation builder available in File > Automate > PDF Presentation…. In Bridge CS3, it's in Tools > Photoshop > PDF Presentation…. This tool is easy to use and simple to set up. For emailing presentations, it's unbeatable.

A Picture Is Worth...

Bridge picks

While the PDF Presentation tool is available directly in Photoshop, Bridge makes it a lot more versatile. Download the files for this chapter from amesphoto.com/learning. The book code is DPN8414.

Bridge setup

STEP ONE

Open Bridge CS3. Press Command (PC: Ctrl) + K to open Bridge's Preferences. Click Labels and uncheck Require the Command (PC: Ctrl) Key to Apply Labels and Ratings. Click OK.

STEP TWO

Open the folder 2328-Nantucket in Bridge. There are 39 photographs from a Thanksgiving trip to the island on display in Bridge's Content pane. They all have a one-star rating. The goal is to choose ten images to share, arrange them, then create a self-running, emailable PDF presentation. To save download time, the photographs are JPEGs converted from the original RAW files. RAW files will make PDF presentations in exactly the same way shown in these steps.

FIGURE 15.1

STEP THREE

Select Window > Workspace > Reset to Default Workspace. Uncheck all of the panes except for the Filters and Preview panes. Click and drag the Filters pane to the bottom of the Content pane. When the Filter pane is over the Content pane, the Content pane is bordered in blue. Continue dragging the Filter pane to the very bottom, and a single horizontal blue line appears. Release the mouse. The Filter pane is docked under the Preview pane (**Figure 15.1**).

STEP FOUR

Resize the Preview pane until it fills two-thirds of the window by clicking and dragging the two parallel lines in the middle of the bar at the left of the Preview pane. The content area is on the left. Enlarge the thumbnails as big as you can while still being able to see them all. Resize the Filter pane until it's barely showing under the Content pane. Click the first thumbnail of the

FIGURE 15.2

ferry boat. Shift-click the third image. All three are displayed in the Preview pane (**Figure 15.2**).

Awarding stars

STEP ONE

Decide which ferry photo tells the Nantucket story. My opinion is that it's between the first and the second one, just before the ship passes the Brant Point lighthouse. I'll grant that the third one is the better photograph of the ferry. And that's not the story I want to tell. Command-click (PC: Ctrl-click) the third thumbnail in the Content pane to deselect it. The two shots with the lighthouse are left in the Preview pane. 2328-003.jpg works best for me. Command-click (PC: Ctrl-click) the first thumbnail in the content pane. Press 2 to give the pick a two-star rating. As soon as there is more than one rating, the Filters pane shows the distribution.

FIGURE 15.3

STEP TWO

Select the five thumbnails of the Brant Point light-house. (Skip the clamshells for now.) Hover the cursor over an image in the Preview pane. The cursor turns into the Zoom tool with a big difference. Click it to show the Loupe tool. Click inside the Loupe. The cursor becomes the Hand tool. Drag the Loupe over the image to check sharpness. The arrow-shaped corner of the Loupe points to the center of the area it is magnifying. Drag the Loupe to a corner and it spins around to provide the best view. The normal view is 100%. Press Command (PC: Ctrl) + + to zoom in. The increments are 100%, 200%, 400%, and 800%. Press Command (PC: Ctrl) + – to zoom out by the same steps. Each photograph in the Preview pane can have a Loupe open. Click inside the Loupe to dismiss it (**Figure 15.3**).

STEP THREE

After Command-clicking (PC: Ctrl-clicking) the first four images in the Content pane, my choice is 2328-0068.jpg. Press 2. It's fine by me if you like a different one.

STEP FOUR

Click on 2328-0118.jpg. Shift-click on 2328-0131.jpg to select the rest of the images of the Great Point lighthouse next to one another. Command-click (PC: Ctrl-click) on 2328-0205.jpg to add it to the selection. My buddy Geoff loves his truck; if this were going to him, it would definitely get that second star. For everyone else, it looks like a Chevy ad. Presentations are tailored to the audience. So not this time. The interesting thing about the lighthouse is that it is solar-powered. Is that part of the story? Hmm. I think for now 2328-0118.jpg and 2328-0205.jpg get another star. They are both selected. Press 2.

STEP FIVE

Give another star to five more photographs. I'll do mine while you pick yours. Save the house for last. I have a story.

FIGURE 15.4

STEP SIX

Welcome back. All that's left is the house near Madaket beach. It's named the "Crooked House." It was the summer home of Fred Rogers of the classic children's television show "Mr. Rogers' Neighborhood." 2328-0861.jpg gets my star (**Figure 15.4**).

The arrangement

STEP ONE

Click on the two stars in the Ratings pane of the Filters panel. Only the photos rated with two stars show. Tap the Tab key to hide the Preview pane.

STEP TWO

Drag the Thumbnail size slider to the right until all ten images are displayed as large as possible. Finally, click and drag the photographs into the order you want them to show in the PDF presentation. When the light blue vertical bar appears, the thumbnail will move to its left (**Figure 15.5**).

FIGURE 15.5

CS3's PDF Builder

Once the photographs are chosen and arranged, making the PDF presentation is straightforward if not a bit anticlimactic.

Bridge's Photoshop toolbox

Any function called from Bridge's Tools menu uses the thumbnails displayed in the Content pane. If some images are selected, only those images will be used with the tool. That makes perfect sense. If all of the images are to be worked on, all of them are selected. That's logical, too.

Here's where Adobe's engineers are a photographer's secret weapon. To save us as much time as possible, any item in the Tools menu that calls up Photoshop will work with all of the images *even if none of them are selected*. Let's get Photoshop to work.

PDF Presentation setup

STEP ONE

Deselect all of the thumbnails in the Content pane by pressing Command (PC: Ctrl) + Shift + A.

STEP TWO

Choose Tools > Photoshop > PDF Presentation....

FIGURE 15.6

STEP THREE

The PDF Presentation dialog lists the filenames of the photographs from Bridge in the Source Files section. The Output Options want to be set to Presentation. Choose a Background color of white, gray, or black from the menu. New to CS3 is the ability to create captions from the photograph's metadata. Select Filename (leave Extension unchecked), Description (pulled from the information in the Caption field in Lightroom's metadata or the Description field in Bridge [see Chapter 6]), and Copyright by checking their respective checkboxes. Choose a less aggressive Font Size—say, 8 points—and 5 seconds in the Advance Every field for a quick run-through. Unless you really want to get under the viewer's skin, don't ever check Loop after Last Page. Every Transition is fine except for Dissolve. Avoid Random, too. In this case I have chosen Wipe Right, an homage to *Star Wars*.... Click Save (**Figure 15.6**).

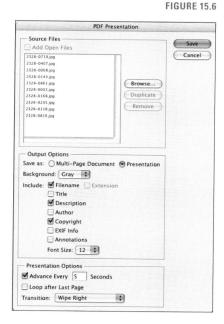

Name the file Nantucket.

STEP FOUR

The Save Adobe PDF dialog is the key to making the ten photographs into an emailable-sized document. Choose Smallest File Size from the Adobe PDF Preset menu. Leave Standard set at None and Compatibility at Acrobat 5 (PDF 1.4). Leave Optimize for Fast Web Preview checked and check View PDF After Saving so you can check the work (**Figure 15.7**).

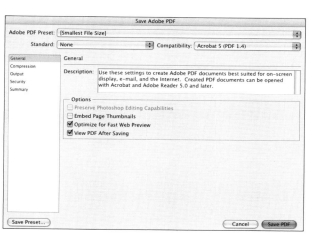

FIGURE 15.7

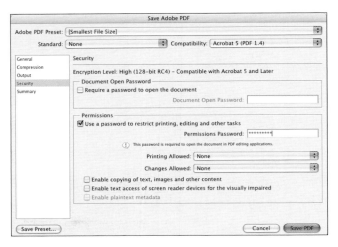

FIGURE 15.8

STEP FIVE

Click Security in the Options pane. A password may be set to even view the document by checking Require a password to open the document. More useful to photographers is the Permissions section. Check Use a password to restrict printing, editing and other tasks. Enter the password (**Figure 15.8**). After Save PDF is clicked, a password confirmation dialog appears. Leave Printing Allowed and Changes Allowed set to None. It's good to note that there are PDF readers that will bypass this security. Click Save PDF.

The PDF I made for this project is included in the sample files folder.

Acrobat or Adobe Reader

The file plays as soon as it is completed. When the final photograph appears, click Escape (Esc) to return to Acrobat's or Adobe Reader's document view. The pages are shown in the thumbnail strip on the left of the window. Click any of them to see them full-sized. Note the word (SECURED) in the title bar. This tells the viewer the file is restricted (**Figure 15.9**).

FIGURE 15.9

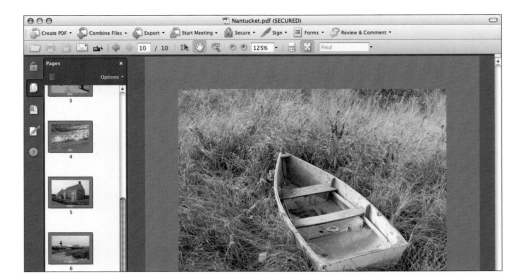

Going further

Want even more versatility for your PDF presentations? Go to www.russell-brown.com. Click on the tips and techniques link. Download the free Dr. Brown's Services 1.7 Easy Installer. At this writing it's still in the beta testing stages. Check out Dr. Brown's Caption Maker (**Figure 15.10**).

Russell is Adobe's Senior Creative Director and author of *The Photoshop Show*. His site is rich with tips and techniques. You owe yourself a visit.

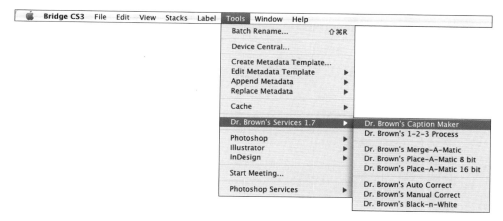

FIGURE 15.10

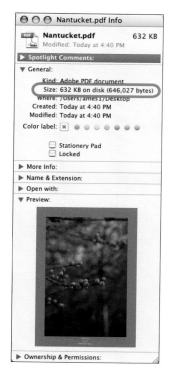

FIGURE 15.11

Send

The ten-photograph self-running captioned presentation weighs in at a tiny 632 kilobytes—not even three-quarters of a megabyte (**Figure 15.11**). Sweet.

You'll want to tell the recipient of these presentations to double-click to launch it in the default PDF reader on their computer. Also tell them to press the Escape (Esc) key at anytime to stop it.

That's it in a nutshell. This little known feature is a huge timesaver from the creative side, and a great convenience for the viewer who doesn't have to scroll through seemingly infinite JPEGs.

CHAPTER 16

Custom Contact Prints

THERE IS ABSOLUTELY NO DOUBT that we live in the digital world. Information, music, movies, and photographs flick from one side of the globe to the other in moments. Our lives often center around our computers and our cell phones. There's a secret. As much as we love our digital lives, there is an innate desire to hold our photographs in our hands as paper prints, to hang them on our walls, to decorate our lives with non-backlit low-tech ink on paper. It's not a stretch that the process of choosing the image that becomes part of the art of our lives includes wanting to see a proof on paper before choosing the "one."

My clients love having proofs on paper when they are making the final choice from an emailed PDF presentation or off of the Internet. The days of handing over an 8 x 10 with between a dozen and thirty-six images mashed together are over.

Larger *is* better!

The Template

Custom contact prints begin with a template for the images themselves. I like to print on 13 x 19-inch Super B (Super A3) sized paper. Depending on the finished print, I use either a luster, glossy, or fine art paper for the contact sheet.

Background pattern

Create a pattern for the background.

FIGURE 16.1

FIGURE 16.2

STEP ONE

Press Command (PC: Ctrl) + N to open the New Document dialog. Choose Web from the Presets menu. Make the file 4 pixels by 4 pixels. The rest of the settings are fine. Click OK.

STEP TWO

Click the Navigator tab. Drag the slider all the way to the left. It reads 3200%. This size is new to CS3 (**Figure 16.1**).

STEP THREE

Press M for the Rectangular Marquee tool. Click the Style menu, then choose Fixed Size. Enter 2 px in the Width field and 4 px in the Height field. Feather is 0. Click on the left edge of the document window. Marching ants outline the left half of the document (**Figure 16.2**).

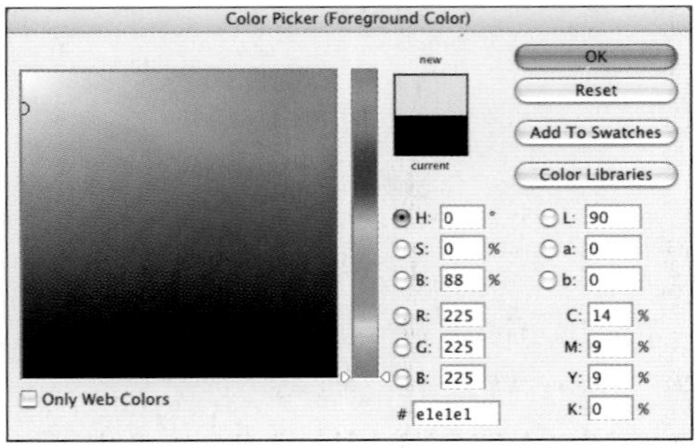

FIGURE 16.3

STEP FOUR

Double-click on the foreground color swatch to open the Color Picker. Enter 225 in the R, G, and B fields. Click OK (**Figure 16.3**).

STEP FIVE

Press Option (PC: Alt) + Delete (PC: Backspace) to fill the selection with the foreground color. Press Command (PC: Ctrl) + D to Deselect.

STEP SIX

Press Command (PC: Ctrl) + A to select the entire document. Choose Edit > Define Pattern…. Name it Contact Background. Click OK.

STEP SEVEN

Close the document without saving it.

Template building

STEP ONE

Open Photoshop. Press Command (PC: Ctrl) + N to create a new document. Name it 12 x 18 Template. Choose Photo as the Preset and choose 8 x 10. Set the Width to 12 inches, the Height to 18 inches, the Resolution to 240, Color Mode to RGB 8 bit, and the Background color to White. Click OK.

STEP TWO

Make a new layer by pressing Command (PC: Ctrl) + Shift + N to open the New Layer dialog. Name the layer Background Pattern. Click OK.

STEP THREE

Choose Edit > Fill.... Select Pattern in the Use menu. Click the Pattern drop-down menu, then choose Contact Background (**Figure 16.4**).

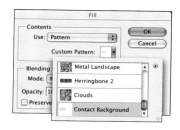

FIGURE 16.4

Click OK. Zoom in to 100% by pressing Command (PC: Ctrl) + Shift + 0. The Background Pattern layer is filled with very closely spaced vertical stripes (**Figure 16.5**).

STEP FOUR

Hit M to get the Rectangular Marquee tool. Click Fixed Size. Enter 10.7 in for the Width and 15.7 in for the Height. It's important to include the "in" to tell the Marquee tool you mean inches. Zoom to fit on screen view by pressing Command (PC: Ctrl) + 0.

STEP FIVE

Make a new layer named Alignment Guide. Click once inside the Photoshop file. A rectangle of marching ants appears.

FIGURE 16.5

STEP SIX

Open the Edit > Stroke... dialog box. Set the Width to 3 px, the Color to Black, and the Location to Inside. The Blending Mode is Normal at 100% Opacity. Preserve Transparency is unchecked. Click OK. An off-center box outlined in black appears.

STEP SEVEN

Press V to choose the Move tool. Command-click (PC: Ctrl-click) the Background Pattern layer to select it in addition to the Alignment Guide layer (**Figure 16.6**).

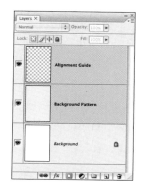

FIGURE 16.6

Click the Align Horizontal Centers button in the Move tool's Options bar. Then click the Align Vertical Centers button (**Figure 16.7**).

The Alignment Guide layer is centered in the image. Click the Alignment Guide layer in the Layers palette to make it the only active layer.

FIGURE 16.7

STEP EIGHT
Tap M for the Rectangular Marquee tool. Change the Style to Fixed Ratio. Enter 1 in both Width and Height. Choose View > Show Smart Guides.

STEP NINE
Zoom in to 100% view. Click on the left outer edge of the alignment guide then drag down to the edge of the document drawing a square selection (**Figure 16.8**).

STEP TEN
Click inside the selection. Drag it to the top of the document. Press Command (PC: Ctrl) + R to show the rulers. Drag a guide from the top ruler down until it aligns with the bottom of the selection (**Figure 16.9**). Deselect.

STEP ELEVEN
Choose the Move tool (V). Shift-drag the alignment guide up until its top outer edge meets the guide (**Figure 16.10**).

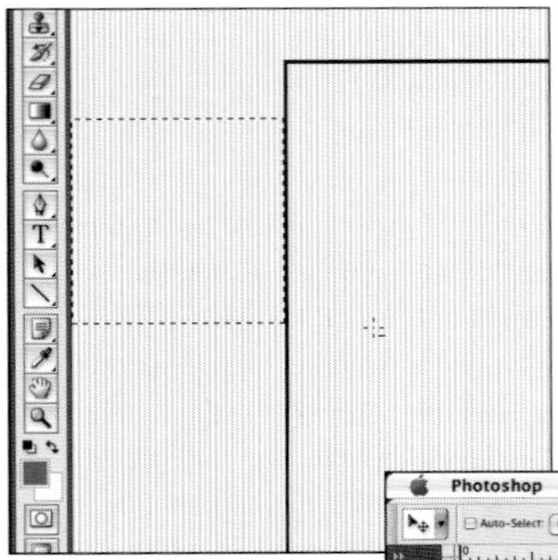

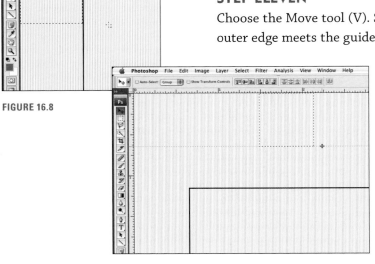

FIGURE 16.8

FIGURE 16.9

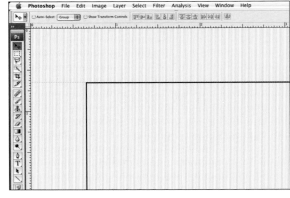

FIGURE 16.10

STEP TWELVE

Click the Background Pattern layer to activate it. Press Command (PC: Ctrl) + T to open Free Transform. Pull a guide from the top ruler down through the reference point (**Figure 16.11**).

Make it yours

STEP ONE

Press D to choose the default colors, setting black as the foreground color. Choose the Type tool (T). Pick your favorite typeface. In this case, I'm using Gill Sans. Enter something like Photography by Your Name; on the next line, enter contact info—your website or email address—and then a copyright notice, followed by the year and your name. I used a smaller font for the second line.

Click the Commit checkmark in the Options bar. Use the Move tool to drag it so that it aligns to the right of the center guide. The black type is aggressive. It is so dark against the light gray lines that the viewer's eye is going to be drawn to it (**Figure 16.12**).

Press Command (PC: Ctrl) + : to hide Photoshop's guides.

STEP TWO

Command-click (PC: Ctrl-click) the type layer's thumbnail to load the type as a selection. Highlight the Background Pattern layer. Press Command (PC: Ctrl) + J to make the selection into its own layer. Name the new layer Identity. Hide the type layer. Not much shows.

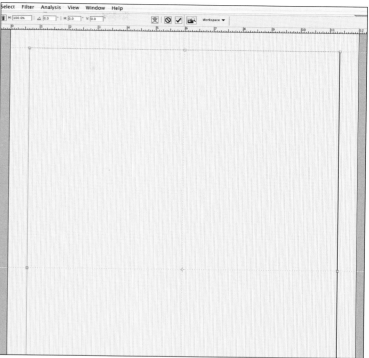

FIGURE 16.11

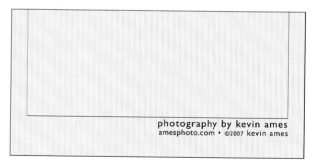

photography by kevin ames
amesphoto.com • ©2007 kevin ames

FIGURE 16.12

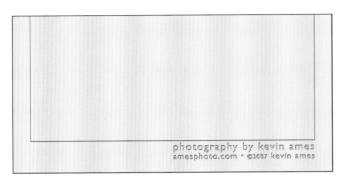

FIGURE 16.13

STEP THREE

Click the f/x icon at the bottom of the Layers palette. Choose Inner Shadow. Make the Opacity 100%. Click Save Style... so these settings are saved as a Style preset in the Styles palette. Using Styles saves a lot of time. Name it Contact Sheet Type Style. Click OK. That's much better (**Figure 16.13**).

STEP FOUR

Hide the Alignment Guide layer. Copy the visible layers to a new layer. (Hint: It's Command [PC: Ctrl] + Option [PC: Alt] + Shift + E.) Name the new layer Template. Save the file as 12 x 18 Template Master.psd.

STEP FIVE

Right-click the type layer and choose Delete Layer. Delete the Identity and Background Pattern layers. Highlight the Template layer then press Command (PC: Ctrl) + E to merge it into the Background layer (**Figure 16.14**). Save the file as 12 x 18 Template.psd.

FIGURE 16.14

SAVE THE STYLES

If Photoshop crashes, the new style just made will be lost. The fast way to make it semi-permanent is to quit Photoshop then restart. The best way is to click over the Styles palette, click its flyout menu, and choose Save Styles.... Put it in a separate folder named Photoshop Presets. I keep mine in the Applications folder on my Mac. Windows users might want to put it in the My Documents folder.

The contact sheet

The venerable Contact Sheet II has missed getting a makeover yet again in Photoshop CS3. It's interface is a bit clunky and it works just fine.

Download the files for this project from amesphoto.com/learning. The book code is DPN8414.

Setup

STEP ONE

Open Bridge, then click on the folder 2363-Steve and Kayla. Move the Thumbnail slider until the photographs are arranged in three rows and three columns (**Figure 16.15**). The size of the Preview / Metadata panel may have to be moved to get the content area to the right size to make this happen.

Arrange the thumbnails in the order they will appear on the proof sheet. Click a thumbnail and drag it into position until a vertical light blue line appears. Release the mouse.

STEP TWO

Deselect all of the thumbnails by pressing Command (PC: Ctrl) + Shift + A (or choosing Edit > Deselect All). Any of the Photoshop tools chosen in Bridge work on selected images only. Or when all of the thumbnails are selected, the chosen tool will work with all of them. No surprise there. Interestingly, though, when none of the thumbnails are selected, Photoshop's tools will still work on all of the thumbnails displayed in the content area. Choose Tools > Photoshop > Contact Sheet II.

FIGURE 16.15

STEP THREE

Set up the Contact Sheet II dialog. Select Inches for Units, enter 10.7 for Width, 15.7 for Height, 240 for Resolution, and select RGB Color for Mode. Uncheck Flatten All Layers. For the Thumbnails section, select Across First from the Place menu, check Use Auto-Spacing, enter 3 for Columns and 3 for Rows, and then check Rotate For Best Fit, assuring that all of the images on the sheet will be the same size. It's a proof sheet. When a horizontal image

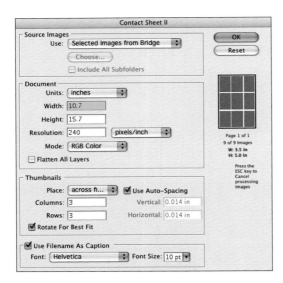

FIGURE 16.16

shows up in a vertical layout, clients happily rotate the page. Check Use Filename As Caption and leave the Font at Helvetica. Set the Font Size to 10. The preview shows how many pages will be created, the number of images selected, their size (in this case, 3½ x 5 inches), and a thumbnail of the layout. Click OK (**Figure 16.16**). Photoshop builds the contact sheet.

Customizing

Contact Sheet II offers an astonishing number of choices of fonts—three, I think. Not a really good showing when you consider that Adobe also sells hundreds of fonts. Oh well. They are easily changed.

STEP ONE

Click on the Layers tab in the Layers / Channels / Paths palette and drag it out onto the workspace. Make it tall by pulling down on the resize handle in the bottom right corner. Your thumbnail sizes are displayed smaller than the ones here. I chose large thumbnails from the palette options to make them bigger in the *Notebook*. Click on the top layer. It's a type layer. Now hold down the Command (PC: Ctrl) key and click on each of the remaining type layers to select them (**Figure 16.17**).

STEP TWO

Tap T for the Type tool. Click in the Font menu then choose the typeface you prefer. I'll use Gill Sans since that's the font I used in the template. All of the filenames change from Helvetica to Gill Sans (or the one you chose).

STEP THREE

Click on the Layer palette flyout menu (the three horizontal lines in the upper right corner). Choose New Group from Layers…. Name the group File-names. Click OK.

STEP FOUR

Click the top thumbnail layer to select it. Shift-click the bottom thumbnail layer in the stack to select all of them. Choose Merge Layers from the palette's flyout menu (**Figure 16.18**).

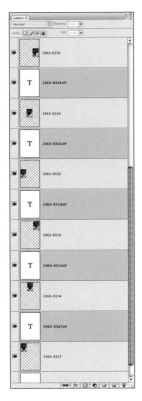

FIGURE 16.17

The layer stack now has a group named Filenames with all of the type layers in it, a layer of the proof sheet images with a filename, and the Background layer.

STEP FIVE

The contact sheet layer is highlighted. Command-click (PC: Ctrl-click) the Filenames group to highlight it, too. Click the Screen Mode button at the bottom of the toolbox. Choose Standard Screen Mode. The shortcut is to tap the F key until the open documents appear with headers. Press V for the Move tool. Click the thumbnail of the contact sheet in the Layers palette. Drag the highlighted layer onto the 12 x 18 Template.psd document, adding the Shift key before releasing the mouse. This centers the layers in the document.

STEP SIX

Close the ContactSheet-001 document without saving it. All the layers are in the template. Hit the F key twice to go to the Full Screen Mode with Menu Bar view. The contact sheet and filenames are off the top. Zoom in to 100%. Scroll to the top. Shift-click on one of the thumbnails, then drag down until the top edge of the sheet is just below the inside top line of the alignment guide. Hide the Alignment Guide layer.

The contact sheet is aligned on the template. It looks pretty flat (**Figure 16.19**). More customization is in order here, don't you think?

STEP SEVEN

Command-click (PC: Ctrl-click) the Filenames group to deselect it. Click the f/x icon at the bottom of the Layers palette. Choose Drop Shadow. The Layer Style dialog opens. Set the Opacity to 40%. The Angle is 128°, Distance is 17 pixels, Spread is 0 pixels, and Size is 5 pixels (**Figure 16.20**).

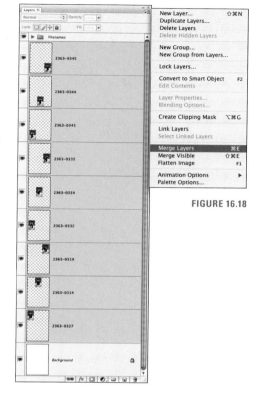

FIGURE 16.18

FIGURE 16.19

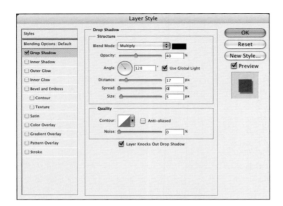

FIGURE 16.20

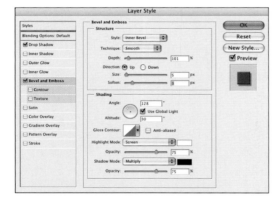

FIGURE 16.21

FIGURE 16.22

STEP EIGHT

Click the words Bevel and Emboss in the Styles section at the left of the dialog. Set the Style to Inner Bevel, Technique to Smooth, Depth to 101, Direction to Up, Size to 5 pixels, and Soften to 3 pixels. In the Shading section, check Use Global Light. The Angle will be 128°. The Altitude is 30°. Leave the rest of the settings at their defaults (**Figure 16.21**).

STEP NINE

This Style is going to get used for every proof sheet made from now on, so it really doesn't make sense to create it each time a contact sheet is made. Click New Style.... Name it Contact Sheet Images. The new style is available in the Styles palette. Click Save Style.... Okay.

The customized contact sheet is on the custom template and it's ready to print. Or is it?

There is one more thing...

Wouldn't the clients like their contact sheets personalized? Of course! Who doesn't love to see their name in print?

STEP ONE

Click the Background layer to select it. Choose the Type tool (T). Starting at the lower left edge of the contact sheet, enter Steve Moore & Kayla Taylor (return) Smartykat Entertainment. Click the Commit checkbox. Use the Move tool to align the type with your information on the template.

STEP TWO

Command-click (PC: Ctrl-click) the type layer's thumbnail, turning the type into a selection. Highlight the Background layer again. Press Command (PC: Ctrl) + J to put the selection onto its own layer. Hide the type layer. Name the new layer Steve and Kayla.

STEP THREE

Click the Styles palette. Choose Contact Sheet Type Style from the icons (**Figure 16.22**). (It will be at the bottom. Hover the cursor over an icon to see its name.) Click OK.

STEP FOUR

When you are making custom proof sheets for clients or friends, save the file in the project folder named with the words Working Files (2363-Steve and Kayla Working Files, for example). Then it's always there when you want it. Save the template in the Photoshop Presets folder.

There you have it (**Figure 16.23**). A gussied-up contact sheet, bigger than its predecessors and ready to make a great impression on family, friends, or clients!

FIGURE 16.23

PART FOUR

Photoshop:
From Review to Completion

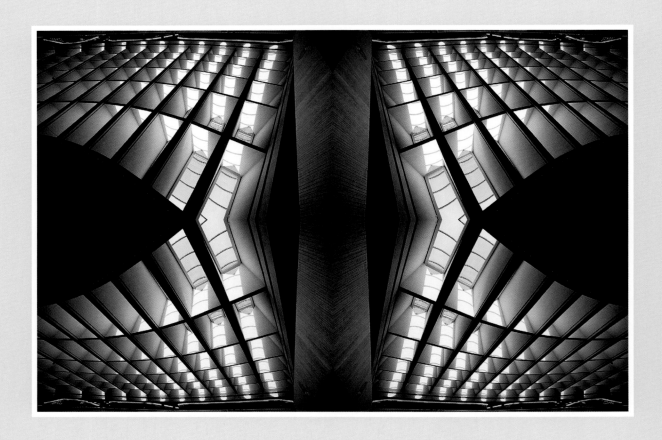

The digital photograph is born in the camera and raised in Photoshop…

CHAPTER 17

Cloud Goddess

IN THE FIRST SECTION of the *Notebook*, the Cloud Goddess came into being by tessellating a cloud formation. It is a cool photograph all by itself. Then I got to thinking, "What else could it become?"

What if the Cloud Goddess was rising over the ocean? That would be powerful. What if the Cloud Goddess had a face? What if a real goddess was in the photograph, too?

What if I stop with the "what-ifs" and get on with the steps?

"It's the Water"

Atlanta is landlocked. There isn't anything that resembles an ocean within a nearly four-hour drive. Atlanta does have rainstorms—big, fat, soak-you-to-the-skin-before-you-can-take-three-steps rainstorms. The base image of the ocean was shot out the front door of my studio with a telephoto lens focused on heavy rain falling on the pavement of the parking lot. The files for this chapter are at amesphoto.com/learning. The book code is DPN8414.

Ocean creation

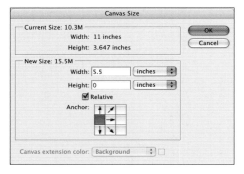

FIGURE 17.1

STEP ONE

Open Rain.tif in Photoshop. Right-click to the right of the Background layer's name and choose Convert to Smart Object from the contextual menu. The new Smart Object is named Layer 0. Rename it Left Side. Right-click again, then select New Smart Object via Copy. Rename it Right Side. Open the Canvas Size dialog by pressing Command (PC: Ctrl) + Option (PC: Alt) + C, or choosing Image > Canvas Size... from Photoshop's menu. Enter 5.5 inches in the Width field and check the Relative checkbox. Click the middle left box in the Anchor diagram. The Canvas extension color is grayed out because the result will be transparency. Click OK (**Figure 17.1**).

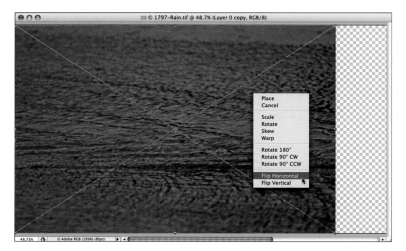

FIGURE 17.2

STEP TWO

Press Command (Control) + T to open Free Transform. Right-click inside the bounding box to invoke the contextual menu. Choose Flip Horizontal (**Figure 17.2**). Click the Commit checkmark in the Options bar or press Enter (on the number pad).

STEP THREE

Choose View > Show > Smart Guides. Highlight Right Side by clicking on the image thumbnail. Press V to select the Move tool. Hold down the Shift key and drag Right Side to the right until a vertical magenta Smart Guide appears, showing that the right edge of Left Side and the left edge of Right Side are aligned. The horizontal Smart Guide shows that the two layers are aligned in their vertical centers. The Shift key constrains the move horizontally (**Figure 17.3**).

STEP FOUR

Copy the two Smart Objects onto a regular layer by holding down Command (PC: Ctrl) + Option (PC: Alt) + Shift, then pressing E. Name the new layer Ocean, then save the file as Ocean.psd. Saving the file with the Left Side and Right Side Smart Object layers intact makes them available in case changes come to mind later (**Figure 17.4**). And, believe me, they always do when the source files are gone and have to be created again to make the new version. Think of this as change insurance.

Sky meets water

STEP ONE

Open Cloud Goddess.psd (or use the one you made in Chapter 5). Select Image > Canvas Size. Add 1.75 inches to the bottom of the image by choosing the top center anchor box and entering 1.75 in the Height field. Click OK.

STEP TWO

Click and hold the Screen Mode icon at the very bottom of the toolbox. Select Standard Screen Mode. It's the one where the document header shows. Highlight the file Ocean.psd. Select the Move tool and drag the Ocean layer onto Cloud Goddess.psd, adding the Shift key before releasing the mouse. Ocean is in the middle of the Cloud Goddess image. Shift-drag Ocean down until its top edge aligns at the bottom of the Cloud Goddess image. Release the mouse when the Smart Guides appear (**Figure 17.5**).

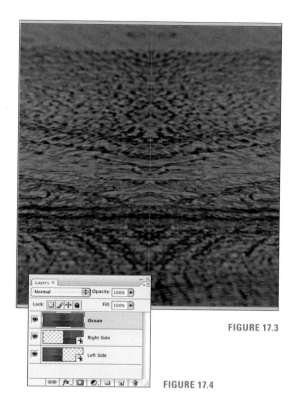

FIGURE 17.3

FIGURE 17.4

FIGURE 17.5

STEP THREE

Press Command (PC: Ctrl) + T to call up Free Transform. Move the reference point straight up from the center of the transform bounding box to the top center handle. The reference point tells Free Transform to move everything toward it or, in the case of rotation, around it (**Figure 17.6**).

Shift-drag the bottom center handle straight up to the bottom edge of the image. The Shift key allows the handle to only move vertically. Press Enter or click the Commit checkbox in the Options bar.

FIGURE 17.6

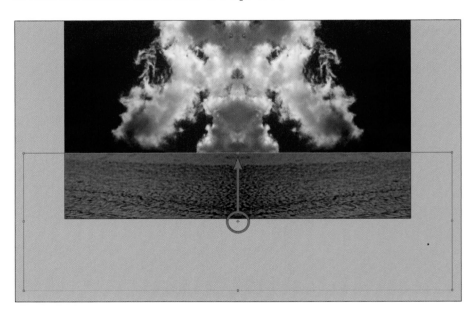

Blue sky, blue ocean

Things are looking good...except the water is not as blue as I think it ought to be. Remember this isn't really an ocean. It's a photograph of hard rain hitting a parking lot.

STEP ONE

Duplicate the Ocean layer by pressing Command (PC: Ctrl) + J. Rename the layer Ocean Blue. Hide Ocean. This is a backup because Step Two will use an adjustment that is not undoable once the file has been saved and closed (**Figure 17.7**).

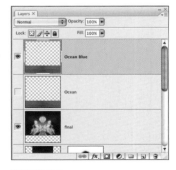

FIGURE 17.7

Command-click (PC: Ctrl-click) Ocean Blue's layer thumbnail to make a selection of the water. Press L to select the Lasso tool. Hold down the Shift key. Draw a selection around the sky in the upper left area of the Cloud Goddess. Include some of the lighter blue as well (**Figure 17.8**).

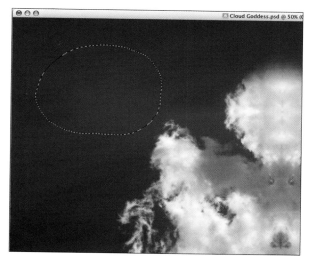

FIGURE 17.8

STEP TWO

Choose Image > Adjustments > Match Color. Set up the Image Statistics section of the Match Color dialog box like this: Set the Source drop-down menu to Cloud Goddess; the Layer is Final. Check both the Use Selection in Source to Calculate Colors and the Use Selection in Target to Calculate Adjustment boxes. Move the Luminance slider to 118. Click OK (**Figure 17.9**).

STEP THREE

The water is way too sky-blue. Select Edit > Fade Match Color. The keyboard shortcut for this one is Command (PC: Ctrl) + Shift + F. Set the Opacity to 60%. Click Ok. Cha-ching! Ocean Blue's ocean is blue (**Figure 17.10**). Cool. Deselect by pressing Command (PC: Ctrl) + D.

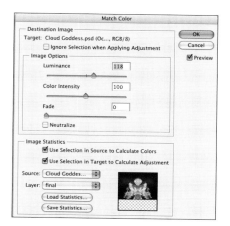

FIGURE 17.9

FIGURE 17.10

Face Time

The clouds want a face to empower them as the true goddesses that they are.

STEP ONE

Open the photograph of actress Tiffany Dupont named Tiff.tif. Select the Move tool. Drag the Background layer of Face.tif onto Cloud Goddess.psd. It appears at the top of the layer stack. Rename it Tiff.

STEP TWO

Change the blending mode of Face to Overlay. Position the face in the center of the Cloud Goddess's head (**Figure 17.11**).

FIGURE 17.11

STEP THREE

Add a layer mask to the Tiff layer. Select the Brush tool. Set its Opacity to 100%, its Hardness to 0%, and make it about 90 pixels in size. Paint black on the layer mask to conceal everything except the face and the hair that would fall behind the shoulders of the cloud. Blend the cut-off top of Tiffany's hair into the head of the clouds. Press the \ (backslash) key to show the Quick Mask for the layer mask. Paint in any holes that might not have been initially apparent (**Figure 17.12**).

STEP FOUR

Shift-click Tiff's layer mask to disable it temporarily. The borders of Tiffany's photograph appear. The layer mask's Quick Mask covers the border, assuring an even blending of the face with the clouds (**Figure 17.13**).

STEP FIVE

The layer mask work is complete. Tap the \ key to return to the regular viewing mode. Shift-click the layer mask on Tiff to enable it.

FIGURE 17.12

FIGURE 17.13

Masking layer masks

I love her face in the clouds and her hair looks too dark. Wouldn't it be nice to be able to add a layer mask to a layer mask? It would indeed. Here's how.

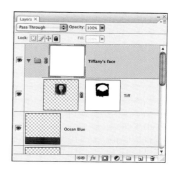

FIGURE 17.14

STEP ONE

Highlight the layer Tiff. From the Layer palette's flyout menu, choose New Group from Layer.... Name the group Tiffany's Face. Click OK. The Tiff layer is inside the Tiffany's Face group.

STEP TWO

Add a layer mask to the group by clicking the Add Layer Mask icon at the bottom of the Layers palette (**Figure 17.14**).

STEP THREE

Set the foreground color to black. Choose the Brush tool. Set it to 50% Opacity by pressing 5 on the keyboard. Using a single stroke, brush around her hair. Lift the brush and stroke over the outer edges of her hair. Each time the brush lifts and strokes again, another 50% of black is added to the layer mask to blend the hair into the sky. Shift-click the group's layer mask to see the before image. Shift-click it again for the after image (**Figure 17.15**).

FIGURE 17.15

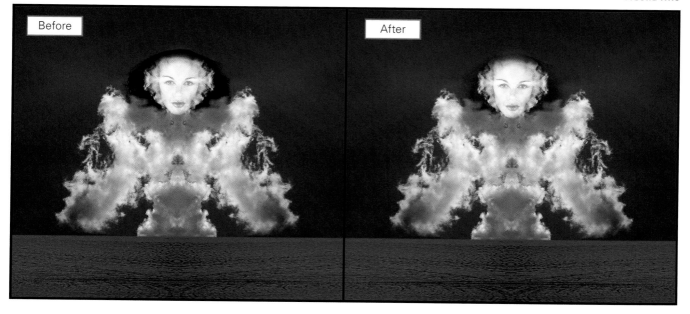

A Real Goddess

The Cloud Goddess has a face and the ocean is the right color. I think that having a real goddess rising out of the water is just the element to finish the photograph.

STEP ONE
Click the triangle to the right of the Tiffany's Face group to close it. Click the group once to highlight it.

FIGURE 17.16

STEP TWO
Open the file Rising Goddess.psd in Photoshop. This photograph of Tiffany is already on a transparent layer for your compositing convenience. Select the Move tool (V) then drag the Rising Goddess layer onto the file Cloud Goddess. It appears above the group Tiffany's Face in the layer stack. Notice that the Rising Goddess layer retains its name. Close Rising Goddess.psd.

STEP THREE
Convert Rising Goddess into a Smart Object.

STEP FOUR
Open Free Transform by pressing Command (PC: Ctrl) + T. Click the Constrain Proportions link between the W and the H in the Options bar. Click and drag the upper right-hand control handle inwards until the reading in either W or H is 61%. Click the Commit checkbox. Use the Move tool to position Tiffany as shown in **Figure 17.16**.

STEP FIVE
Make Ocean Blue active. Select the Elliptical Marquee tool. Draw a selection of the water around Tiffany's feet. Click Refine Edge… in the Options bar. Click the middle icon at the bottom of the dialog to show the selection against a black mask. Drag the Feather slider to the right until it has a soft edge (**Figure 17.17**).

FIGURE 17.17

Click the last icon to see the mask that will create the feather. Be sure that the center area is white. When the Feather slider is moved to the far right, the interior of the selection will have gray in it. If you see gray, move Feather back to the left. Feathering has always had a mask. Now we can see it (**Figure 17.18**). Thank you Adobe!

FIGURE 17.18

My choice for the feather is 23 pixels. Yours may be a bit different. That's fine. Set the rest of the sliders to 0 and click OK (**Figure 17.19**).

STEP SIX

Press Command (PC: Ctrl) + J to copy the selection to its own layer. Name it Foot cover. Drag Foot cover to the top of the layer stack above the Rising Goddess layer.

Not much of an improvement because Tiffany is cut off below the ankles (**Figure 17.20**). That's not truly attractive. It is easy to fix.

STEP SEVEN

Click on the Rising Goddess layer, then choose the Move tool (V). Hold down the Shift key and tap the up arrow about eight times until her ankles almost clear the water. (Adding the Shift key when using the arrows will move a layer ten pixels. Release the Shift key and tap an arrow key to move the layer one pixel at a time.)

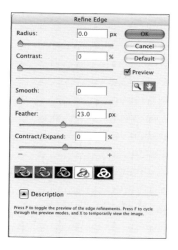

FIGURE 17.19

STEP EIGHT

Add a layer mask on Foot cover. Press Command (PC: Ctrl) + Option (PC: Alt) + 0 to view the actual pixels (100%). Press G to pick the Gradient tool. Tap D to set the default colors, then X to exchange them so white is the foreground color. Choose Foreground to Background from the Gradient tool's menu in the Options bar. (It's the icon in the upper left corner of the menu.) Click just above Tiffany's knees, add the Shift key, then drag down to about the midpoint of the top of her foot (**Figure 17.21**). A gradient is added to the layer mask revealing some more of her feet.

FIGURE 17.20

FIGURE 17.21

Clouds to clouds

Play is the most valuable time a photographer spends. It doesn't matter if the play is behind the camera or in front of the monitor. It's all about "What if?" The original Cloud Goddess photograph was made half a dozen years ago. Frankly, the way her feet blend into the water has always felt unfinished somehow. It finally hit me that maybe some steam rising around Tiffany's feet might be an answer. And steam is a form of a cloud, isn't it? Perfect!

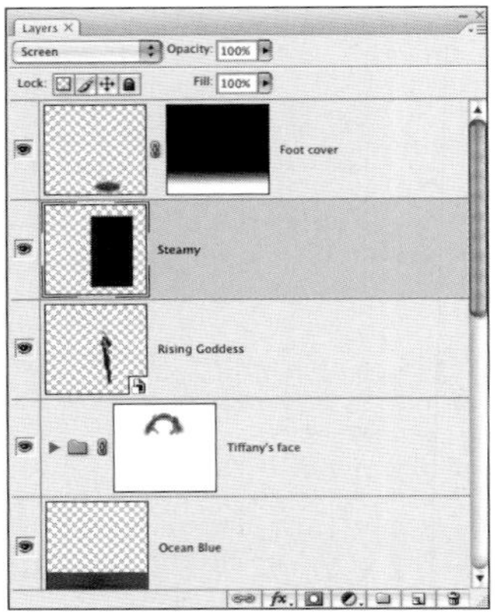

Steamy

FIGURE 17.22

STEP ONE

Highlight the layer Rising Goddess. Make a new layer named Steamy. Change Steamy's blending mode to Screen. Use the Rectangular Marquee tool. Draw a box around Tiffany. Press D for the default colors, making black the foreground color. Hold down the Option (PC: Alt) key and press Delete (PC: Backspace). Nothing happens on the screen. Look at the layers stack. Steamy's thumbnail is filled with black. The screen blending mode makes black invisible (**Figure 17.22**).

STEP TWO

Choose Filters > Render > Clouds... (appropriate, don't you think?). The hole at Tiffany's feet is the Foot cover layer. Click OK (**Figure 17.23**).

STEP THREE

Press Command (PC: Ctrl) + J to duplicate Steamy, rename it Steamy 2 and, finally, hide it by clicking Steamy 2's eyeball. (The official name is the Eye icon, according to those in charge of monikers inside Adobe.)

STEP FOUR

Add a layer mask to Steamy. Painting with black at 100% Opacity, brush away everything a bit above Tiffany's knees and then creatively remove the areas that don't feel like they belong (**Figure 17.24**). (Look. How can we be precise? This is playing!)

FIGURE 17.23

Remember to use the \ (backslash) key and to Shift-click the layer mask icon to see that the edges, and everything else you don't want, are covered in red.

STEP FIVE

Use a 10% Opacity brush to paint with black to bring back some of Tiffany's legs, from upper calf to just above the knee. When you love it, convert Steamy into a Smart Object.

STEP SIX

Choose Filter > Blur > Motion Blur.... Set the Angle to –79° and the Distance to 13 pixels. Press P or click the Preview checkbox on and off to view the effect (**Figure 17.25**).

STEP SEVEN

Drag Steamy 2 above Foot cover. Option-click (PC: Alt-click) Steamy 2's Eye icon. (It is nice to have another name besides eyeball, come to think of it.) All of the other layers are hidden. Find some clouds that would work well around the feet. Don't worry, it's almost impossible to mess this up. Besides, if you don't love the effect, go back and play with it until you do. Use the Lasso tool to select a good group of clouds. Feather the selection the same amount as before, around 23 pixels. The selection makes Photoshop forget that the other eyeballs are hidden. Click the Eye icons for all of the layers from Final to the top.

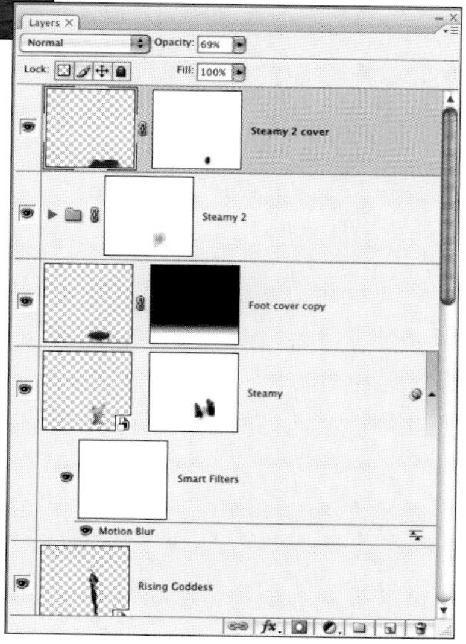

STEP EIGHT

Click the Add Layer Mask icon to hide all of Steamy 2 with the exception of the selection. Use the Move tool (V) to reposition Steamy 2 below Tiffany's feet. Put Steamy 2 into a group named Steamy 2, add a layer mask, and blend it into the water. Play with all the techniques in this chapter (like for the Foot cover layer, for example) to make the image look exactly how you like it. My layer stack wound up looking like **Figure 17.26**.

FIGURE 17.24

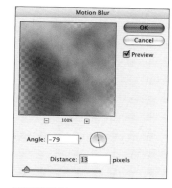

FIGURE 17.25

FIGURE 17.26

Here's mine (**Figure 17.27**). Email me yours.

There you have it. An ocean is created from rain falling on pavement. A Goddess floats above the water, while her face appears mystically in the clouds. It goes to show what happens when the "what-ifs" start happening along with a sense of fun and, of course, play.

FIGURE 17.27

CHAPTER 18

Black and White

I HAVE HAD A DARKROOM MOST OF MY LIFE. Growing up, the bathroom had an enlarger in it. To a child, it was an enigmatic appliance to be contemplated while thinking deep thoughts. I built one in the garage during high school. My house saw the spare bedroom windows covered in aluminum foil, not to keep out the heat—to keep out the light. When I moved into my studio, the darkroom was one of the first priorities (**Figure 18.1**). It was rough, completely utilitarian. That was okay. It was a darkroom! The sinks were made of 2 x 10s with plywood bottoms covered in fiberglass. The processing line could do eighteen rolls of 35mm black-and-white film at once. I could make prints up to 20 x 24 inches with either one of the two 4 x 5 enlargers: a Bessler and an Omega. Heaven!

FIGURE 18.1

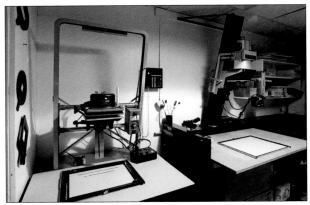

FIGURE 18.2

Now the darkroom is gone. For the first time in memory, I no longer have one. And frankly, I don't miss it. The smells—fixer, stop bath, sepia toner (rotten eggs)—the stains on my fingertips from chemicals, the stains on shirts, and only the ability to make black-and-white prints are nothing to lose sleep over. Nostalgia? Not even!

I am writing this in the darkroom. I still call it that because that's what it will always be to me. I am sitting about where the Omega enlarger was (**Figure 18.2**).

Behind me, the sinks and the wall they fronted are gone, replaced with printers that output prints twenty-four inches wide—in black and white or full color!

Darkroom Ring Arounds

That said, some techniques that evolved in the darkroom shed useful light on the new processes available in Photoshop. One of them is the ring around.

The traditional darkroom ring around started with a "normal" print. Then a series of prints, varying in exposure and contrast, would be made. The result was usually a total of nine prints: three prints in three rows with the "normal" one right in the middle of the middle row. Producing a nine-print ring-around test was a lot of painstaking, time-consuming work. Especially considering that the prints had to dry before judging which one was the best.

Channel Mixer Ring Arounds

Converting a color photograph into a great black-and-white image presents an intriguing challenge in Photoshop. Including Channel Mixer (my converter of choice), there are at least a half dozen methods for converting color to black and white in Photoshop alone. This doesn't include great plug-ins like nik software's Color EFX Pro.

This section of the *Notebook* helps you find the best settings for Channel Mixer to make that truly great black-and-white conversion and test print by automating the production of a ring around with an action, a script, and good old long-in-the-tooth, venerable Contact Sheet II.

Download the project folder for Chapter 18 from amesphoto.com/learning. The book code is DPN8414.

The R&R Trolley Car Bar

The Trolley Car Bar is a twenty-barstool tavern in Boise, Idaho (**Figure 18.3**). It sits in a quiet neighborhood not a mile from the picturesque Union Pacific Depot overlooking downtown and a short walk from where I used to live. Opened in 1934, it is the longest continuously operating bar in the city.

The exploration of black-and-white conversion begins by writing an action that creates Channel Mixer layers for each value in the Preset drop-down menu. The action is included in the downloads (if you already know how to write complicated actions, or so you can check your work).

FIGURE 18.3

The ring around action

STEP ONE

Open Trolley.tif in Photoshop CS3. Click the Layer Comps palette icon in the dock of palettes that have been collapsed to icons. (Hey, it's not me. That's what Adobe calls it. Sheesh.) Click the tab, then drag it away from the icon dock (**Figure 18.4**).

STEP TWO

Click on the Actions icon in the icon dock (**Figure 18.5**). Click the Actions palette's New Set icon (fourth from the left) at the bottom of the Actions palette. Name the set Black & White Conversions. Click OK. Click the New Action icon (just to the right of the New Set icon). Type Channel Mixer Ring Around in the field and click Record. The red Record icon appears.

FIGURE 18.4

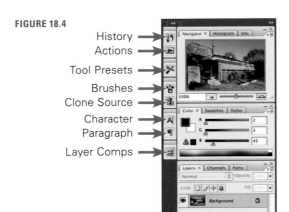

History
Actions
Tool Presets
Brushes
Clone Source
Character
Paragraph
Layer Comps

Flyout menu

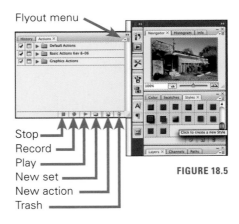

Stop
Record
Play
New set
New action
Trash

FIGURE 18.5

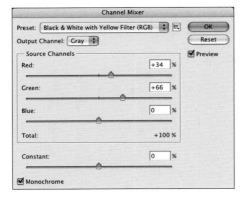

FIGURE 18.6

STEP THREE

Choose Channel Mixer from the New Adjustment Layer icon at the bottom of the Layers palette. A new feature in Channel Mixer is the Preset menu and Edit Preset icon at the top. Click the Preset menu and choose the bottom preset: Black & White with Yellow Filter (RGB). As a point of interest, the settings for a yellow photographic filter are +34% Red, +66% Green, and 0% Blue. The Total reading (also new to Channel Mixer) reads +100%. This saves us from the possibility of making mistakes in totaling the RGB value. For most uses, the Total wants to equal +100%. Click OK (**Figure 18.6**).

STEP FOUR

Double-click the words Channel Mixer in the layers stack. Rename the layer Yellow Filter Preset. Click the new Layer Comp icon in the Layer Comps palette. Name the new layer comp Yellow (**Figure 18.7**). Click OK. Click the Eye icon to hide the Yellow layer.

STEP FIVE

Make a new Channel Mixer adjustment layer. Choose the preset Black & White with Red Filter (RGB). Click OK. Name the layer Red Filter Preset. Make a new layer comp named Red. Click OK. Hide the Red layer. The photograph of the trolley is once again in color. I've spun down each of the triangles in the Actions palette to show the progress so far (**Figure 18.8**), as well as the states of the layer stack (**Figure 18.9**) and Layer Comps palette (**Figure 18.10**).

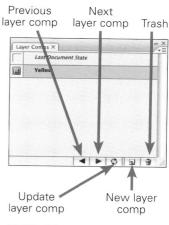

FIGURE 18.7

FIGURE 18.8

FIGURE 18.9

FIGURE 18.10

STEP SIX

Repeat Step Five for each of the remaining presets, saving a new layer comp for each new Channel Mixer layer. Remember to hide the last Channel Mixer layer before creating the next one. The trolley wants to be in full color before the next Channel Mixer layer is made.

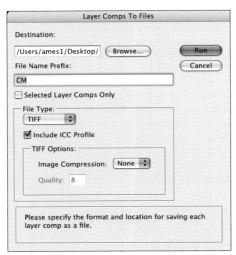

FIGURE 18.11

STEP SEVEN

Hide the last Channel Mixer layer (Infrared Filter Preset). Make a new layer comp of the full-color trolley, naming it Color.

STEP EIGHT

Go to Photoshop's menu bar, then choose File > Scripts > Layer Comps To Files…. Set the Destination to a folder on the desktop named Ring Around. This folder will be created when you click Run. Enter CM (for Channel Mixer) into the File Name Prefix field and uncheck Selected Layer Comps Only. Click Run (**Figure 18.11**).

STEP NINE

Choose File > Browse, and switch applications from Photoshop to Bridge.

STEP TEN

Click the square Stop icon. (It turns green when the cursor hovers over it. I know—green means "go" everywhere else, just not in Adobe-land.) The rest of the action is shown in **Figure 18.12**. **Figure 18.13** shows the finished layer stack, and the Layer Comps palette can be seen in **Figure 18.14**.

ACTIONS ARE PICKY

If the folder created in Step Eight is moved or deleted, or if the action is loaded onto a different machine—even if the Ring Around folder is in the same place on the new computer—the action will crash at this point. The fix is simple. On the same machine, make sure the folder on the desktop is named exactly as it appears in the action. Loading the action onto a new computer requires that the script be re-recorded. So if you choose to load the action that you downloaded from amesphoto.com/learning, here's how to do it: Open a color file in Photoshop. Run the action Channel Mixer Ring Around. The error message will appear. Click OK. Scroll down the action. When you get to Scripts, double-click Scripts. Photoshop will open the Layer Comps To Files dialog. Click Browse and set the new destination folder. Click Run. The script will execute and the folder will have the ring around files in it.

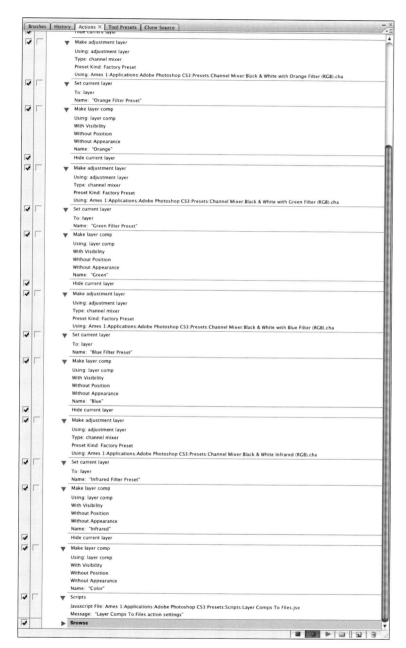

FIGURE 18.12

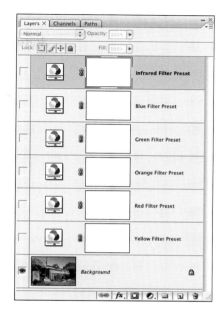

FIGURE 18.13

FIGURE 18.14

SAVE ACTIONS

The action is complete. At this point, if Photoshop crashes it's gone, Daddy, gone...forever. There are two ways to save it. The first is good only as long as Photoshop's preferences don't become corrupt: simply quit and restart Photoshop. The second—and best—is to choose Save Actions from the Actions flyout menu. The default location is in the Adobe Photoshop CS3 Folder > Presets > Actions in either the Applications (Mac) or Programs (Windows) folder. This is fine until there's an upgrade, and the old app folder gets trashed along with all your presets. I save, and back up, all my custom settings in a separate folder called Photoshop Presets.

FIGURE 18.15

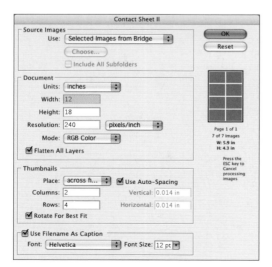

FIGURE 18.16

STEP ELEVEN

In Bridge, navigate to the Ring Around folder on the desktop. There are the seven versions complete with the names from the layer comps, all ready to be printed to see which one is right for the Trolley Car Bar's portrait (**Figure 18.15**).

The ring around print

STEP ONE

Choose Tools > Photoshop > Contact Sheet II from Bridge's menu. I prefer a test print that is large enough to see...so I am using 13 x 19-inch paper. In the Document section, set 12 as the Width and 18 as the Height. The Thumbnails get 2 in Columns and 4 in Rows. Leave Use Auto-Spacing checked. Pick your font from the massive number of choices, choose the font size, then click OK (**Figure 18.16**). Photoshop takes the seven images in the Ring Around folder and lays out the contact sheet.

STEP TWO

Press Command (PC: Ctrl) + P in Photoshop to open the updated Print with Preview dialog. There are a couple of changes. First, the preview reflects the printer profile on the print. In this example, Photoshop manages the color using a custom profile for an Epson 4800. It also warns to be sure to turn off color management in the printer driver (**Figure 18.17**). Nice touch! Click Print.

EXTRA ACTIONS

In addition to the one you made in the previous steps, there are three extra actions in the Black & White Conversions set.

Channel Mixer Clear Layer Comps > Layers

Playing this action clears the layer comps and the layers added to the master file by the Channel Mixer Ring Around action.

Black & White Ring Around
Black & White Clear Layer Comps > Layers

There is a ring around action for the new Black and White adjustment layer section of this chapter. The last action clears the Layer Comps palette and extra layers added to the master file by the Black & White Ring Around action. See the "Actions Are Picky" sidebar for instructions in setting up the Layer Comps to Files... folder for this action.

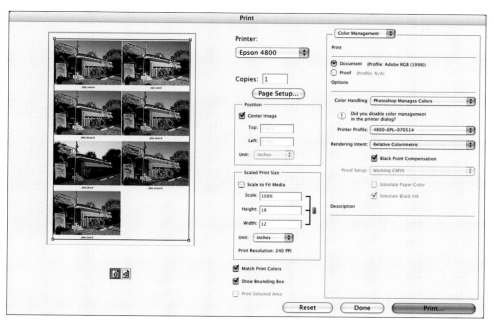

FIGURE 18.17

FIGURE 18.18

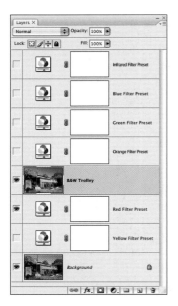

FIGURE 18.19

Evaluate the result

Which one works best? Red is the most dramatic for the awning and the sky. This version has the trolley close to jumping off the page. There is a problem: the sign is lost. Look at the color version. The sign has red letters that lighten significantly when viewed through a red filter.

The sign with the best contrast is the Infrared version. The trolley's siding is flat.

Green is the best overall choice. A print using that mix is a good compromise. Compromise was a fact of life with shooting film and printing in the darkroom. Fortunately, those days are behind us.

It seems that a combination of the sign and reader board from the Infrared version with the overall view from the Red is the answer (**Figure 18.18**).

STEP THREE

The file with the Channel Mixer layers is still open in Photoshop. Click the Eye icon on the Red Filter Preset layer to show it. Click its thumbnail to highlight it. Hold down the entire left-hand side of the keyboard—actually the Command (PC: Ctrl) + Option (PC: Alt) + Shift keys—then press E. This copies the visible layers to a new one. Name the layer B&W Trolley (**Figure 18.19**).

STEP FOUR

Hide the B&W Trolley and Red Filter Preset layers. Show, then highlight Infrared Filter Preset. Copy the visible layers to a new layer. Rename it B&W Signs. Hide the Infrared Filter Preset layer.

STEP FIVE

Show the B&W Trolley layer. Draw a path around the trolley sign and the reader board with my shadow on it. Double-click Work Path in the Paths palette. Save it as Path 1.

STEP SIX

Command-click (PC: Ctrl-click) the path to turn it into a selection. If you are used to feathering selections, the command has moved to Select > Modify >

Feather…. Press M for the Marquee tool. The new way to modify selections is found in the control bar of any of the selections tools. Click Refine Edge… and a brand new powerful dialog box opens. Double-click the Quick Mask icon—second from the left at the bottom, just above Description, which, by the way, when spun down shows what each option in the dialog box does. Nice! Click the Selected Areas button and set the Opacity to 100% (**Figure 18.20**). Click OK. Drag the Feather slider to the right to 7.0 pixels. Slide Contract/Expand to –8 (**Figure 18.21**). Tap the P key to see the effect of the combination of settings. The Contract adjustment has pulled the feathered selection inside both the sign and reader board. Click OK.

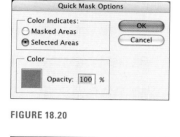

FIGURE 18.20

STEP SEVEN

The B&W Signs layer is active. Click the New Layer Mask icon at the bottom of the Layers palette. Lower the layer's Opacity to 80%. Copy the result to a new layer named Final (**Figure 18.22**).

STEP EIGHT

Save the file as Trolley BW.psd. Flatten it and save it as Trolley BW.tif. PSD files are the working files that contain all the layers that created the final. Save them in case you or more likely your client changes her or his mind. The TIF file is for output and delivery to the client (**Figure 18.23**).

FIGURE 18.21

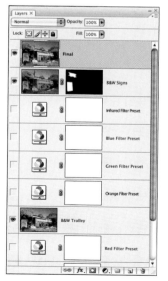

FIGURE 18.22

FIGURE 18.23

High-fashion black and white

Flashback to the sixties, seventies, and eighties when high-fashion photography meant edgy, high-contrast black-and-white prints were very en vogue. The skin tones were almost blown out to stark white. The images had mystical shadows. Black hair sported the most amazing detail. Eyes simply glowed. Lips popped off the page. And it all happened before computers—let alone Photoshop CS3! How *was* this magic done?

On film…

Overexposure was part of the secret potion back in the day. Photographers added from 1⅓ to 2 stops of light to the diffused value (see Chapter 4), so everything became brighter. To compensate, makeup artists made eyebrows, eyelids, mascara, cheekbones, and lips significantly darker so they would record as a normal tone in the final photograph. The film was shot with a red filter over the lens to brighten the skin. In the darkroom, it was over-developed, then printed on a #5 or #6 high-contrast paper. Blemishes and skin texture disappeared into milky white highlights. Eyes danced as if backlit, and textures normally hidden in shadows glowed. The result was theatrical and dramatic, and it was magical.

And digital capture

Fast-forward to the new millennium where overexposure still works really well on film—if you can still get black-and-white film processed exactly the way you did in the darkroom. It's not so hot when capturing digitally. There is no mercy from an overexposed JPEG. RAW files, on the other hand, carry so much data in the brightest f/stop of exposure that they are the perfect candidate for this technique. No overexposure required, at least not in the camera.

The styling of model Christina for this photograph was by L. J. Adams-Wellin; both are represented by Elite Model Management, Atlanta (404-872-7444).

STEP ONE
Open Christina.tif in Photoshop CS3 (**Figure 18.24**). The first job is converting the color photograph to black and white. Play the Channel Mixer Ring Around action you made in the last project. If there are photographs in the Ring Around folder, you might want to move them to the Trash (Mac) or the Recycle Bin (Windows) before running the action.

FIGURE 18.24

STEP TWO

Open the folder Ring Around in Bridge. Press Command (PC: Ctrl) + F6 to set Bridge's workspace to Vertical Filmstrip. Uncheck Favorites, Folders and Filters in the Window menu. Save this new workspace by choosing Window > Workspace > Save Workspace…. I named mine Vertical Filmstrip with Big Preview and assigned Command (PC: Ctrl) + F12 as the keyboard shortcut (**Figure 18.25**).

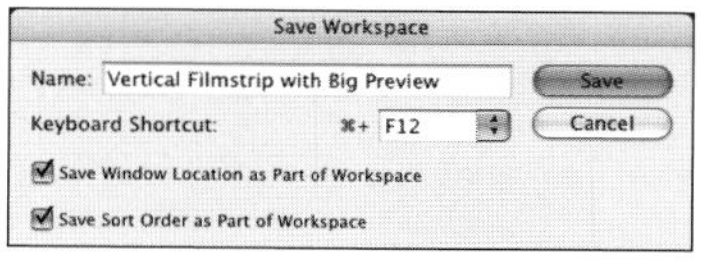

FIGURE 18.25

STEP THREE

Click _0000_Yellow.tif in the Filmstrip on the right. Hold down the Shift key and click the last black-and-white thumbnail to select the rest of them. They appear side by side in two rows in the Preview pane. Clearly, the Blue and Infrared aren't in the running. Command-click (PC: Ctrl-click) each of them in the Filmstrip to deselect and remove them from the preview (**Figure 18.26**).

FIGURE 18.26

STEP FOUR

The skin tones on Green are darker, so Command-click (PC: Ctrl-click) it to remove it from contention for the top spot. To my eye, Yellow is too dark, while Red is too bright. This makes Orange just right. Click Orange's thumbnail to make it the pick. Click the right-most dot under the thumbnail to

FIGURE 18.27

FIGURE 18.28

rate it five stars. Double-click the thumbnail to open the image in Photoshop CS3 (**Figure 18.27**).

STEP FIVE

The Layer Comps to Files… script does not flatten the image, so all of the layers from the original conversion to black and white are still there. Remove them by choosing Delete Hidden Layers from the Layer palette's flyout menu.

STEP SIX

Add a new Curves adjustment layer. Click OK without changing any of the settings. Rename the layer +⅓ stop. Choose the Move tool (V) and type 25 to lower the Opacity of the layer to 25%, which will approximate an increase in exposure of about ⅓ f/stop (see the sidebar "F/Stops and Blending Modes"). Change the blending mode of the layer to Screen. Christina gets brighter visually by close to a third of an f/stop (**Figure 18.28**).

F/STOPS AND BLENDING MODES

Exposure or brightness control in Photoshop doesn't relate directly to f/stops. The visual result, not the technical one, is really the goal. Two blending modes are used in raising or lowering brightness: Screen and Multiply. Screen brightens and Multiply darkens the image. Since Curves is used to control brightness and contrast, I use them for this technique. Any of the "exposure" adjustment layers—Levels, Curves, Color Balance, and Brightness/Contrast—will work. Visually, about 25% opacity delivers a ⅓ f/stop change *up* when the blending mode is Screen and *down* when it's Multiply. Duplicating layers seems to make a better result than increasing or decreasing opacity. Three Curves layers set to Screen at 25% opacity seem to brighten an image visually about one f/stop, while three of them in the Multiply blending mode darken the result by a stop.

WHY THIRDS?

Exposing film to light and then developing it causes density (highlights) to build up logarithmically. The more light, the higher the density of silver on the negative. An increase in exposure of ⅓ f/stop increases the density measured on the film by .1. So a density of .4, measured on the film with a densitometer, represents an exposure increase of 1⅓ f/stops.

ISO (or sensor sensitivity) is also rated in ⅓ f/stop increments, as are shutter speeds and apertures in higher-end DSLR cameras. Electronically controlled settings allow this ⅓ f/stop precision in shutters and apertures that were physically impossible with their mechanical predecessors.

FIGURE 18.29

STEP SEVEN

Press Command (PC: Ctrl) + J to duplicate the +⅓ stop layer. Duplicate the result twice more for a total of four layers—or +1⅓ stops. Christina's skin is now a glowing highlight. The background and her hair have opened up, as well.

This step represents overexposing black-and-white film by 1⅓ stops. Back then, one of the steps in making the print in the darkroom was to selectively add extra light to her hair and the background to darken them. That process was known as "burning." The technique in Photoshop is accomplished using a selection and a layer mask.

STEP EIGHT

Highlight the Background layer. Choose Select > Color Range. Click on Christina's forehead. Click the + eyedropper and sample just above her navel. Move the Fuzziness slider to 58. Click OK (**Figure 18.29**).

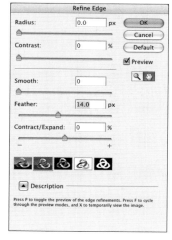

FIGURE 18.30

STEP NINE

Tap M for the Marquee tool. Either one is fine, as is any selection tool for that matter. I use the Marquee tool because it is the first one in the toolbox. The Refine Edge... button appears in the control bar when a selection tool is active. Click it to open the dialog. Click the Quick Mask icon. Set 14 pixels in Feather. The other controls are set to 0 (**Figure 18.30**). Click OK.

The feathering will leave a believable transition from Christina's skin to the background (**Figure 18.31**).

STEP TEN

Click the first +⅓ stop layer, then Shift-click the top one to highlight them all in the layer stack. Choose New Group from Layers... from the Layer palette's flyout menu (**Figure 18.32**). Name the new group +1⅓ stops.

FIGURE 18.31

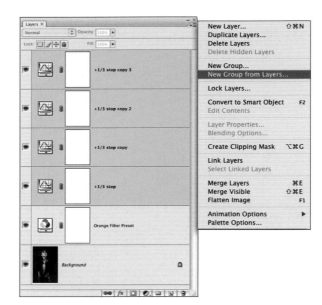

FIGURE 18.32

STEP ELEVEN

Click the Add Layer Mask icon. Instant drama!

The thought might arise in the ever-inquiring mind of a creative photographer: "What if the background would be better if it were not quite so dark?" Funny you would think that because I had the same thought!

STEP TWELVE

Duplicate the +1⅓ stop group by right-clicking and choosing Duplicate Group. Now Christina looks angelic or ghostly, depending on one's point of view. And it's probably too much of a good thing (**Figure 18.33**).

FIGURE 18.33

STEP THIRTEEN

Hide the +1⅓ stop group. Right-click the group +1⅓ stop copy's layer mask and choose Delete Layer Mask from the contextual menu. Tap D to set the default colors. Double-click the foreground color and enter R: 153, G: 153, and B: 153. Click OK. Click the Add Layer Mask icon. Press the Command (PC: Ctrl) key and click the layer mask on the +1⅓ stop group to load its selection. The goal is to fill the area around the selection with the gray foreground color. The current selection is set to fill on the inside. Press Command (PC: Ctrl) + Shift + I to inverse the selection. Hold down the Option (PC: Alt) key and press Delete (PC: Backspace) to fill the outside area with the foreground gray. There's more instant drama, just not so much.

STEP FOURTEEN

Delete all of the versions in the Layer Comps palette by clicking the first one (Yellow) and Shift-clicking the last (Color), and then clicking the Trash icon.

Compare the two to see which is your favorite by making a new layer comp named Not So Much Drama. Now hide the +1⅓ stop copy group and show the +1⅓ stop group. Make a new layer comp named Instant Drama. (Come on, have fun!) Click between them and choose the one you love (**Figure 18.34**).

FIGURE 18.34

Finishing touches

Both choices are good. I love the Instant Drama version. If you like Not So Much Drama, the following steps are the same.

I did not pre-visualize this photograph as a high-highlight black-and-white image, so the makeup artist did not overdo the eyes, brows, or lips. A few touches with the brush on the group's layer mask will take care of this.

STEP FIFTEEN

Highlight the group of your choice, then choose New Group from Layers… from the Layers palette's flyout menu. Name the new group Instant Drama—my favorite, in this case. Add a layer mask to the group. Nesting a group that already has a layer mask inside a new group allows multiple layer masks to work on the same layer.

STEP SIXTEEN

Choose a medium (50%) soft-edge brush, 7 pixels in size at 100% Opacity. That's the brush size that covers Christina's pupils. Press D to set the default colors. Set Black as the foreground color (press X) if it's not there already. Click the layer mask thumbnail to make it active. Brush over her pupils.

STEP SEVENTEEN

Set the brush to soft (0%) by holding down the Shift key and tapping the [(left bracket) key twice. (Shift + [softens the brush in increments of 25%. Shift +] hardens the brush's edge by 25% per keystroke.) Paint around the lower lid of each eye and then over the area of darkest eyeshadow on the upper lid. Change the brush to 50% Opacity (press 5 on the keyboard) and paint in the upper area of the eye socket up to the eyebrow on both eyes. There will be space on the right eye between the socket and eyebrow. Set the brush back to 100% Opacity (tap 0) and paint in the eyebrows. Use the same brush setting to paint over her lips.

FIGURE 18.35

STEP EIGHTEEN

Option-click (PC: Alt-click) the layer mask to see the results. If you see gaps in the brushwork—and it is likely—Option-click (PC: Alt-click) the color (this will be either black [100% Opacity] or gray [50% Opacity]) and paint in the holes. When you have finished, your result will look similar to **Figure 18.35**.

STEP NINETEEN

The edges of the paint on the layer mask are very distinct. The pupils look like hard-edged dots. Some softening is in order. Choose Filter > Blur > Gaussian Blur. Set the Radius to 1.9 pixels. The preview shows the softening effect. Click OK (**Figure 18.36**).

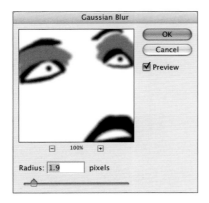

FIGURE 18.36

STEP TWENTY

Option-click (PC: Alt-click) the layer mask to return to the normal view. Press Command (PC: Ctrl) + Z to undo the blur and see what a difference this small amount of softening makes. Press Command (PC: Ctrl) + Z again to redo the blur.

High-fashion black and white that emulates the look of the latter decades of the twentieth century is pretty straightforward with Photoshop. Learning what was

FIGURE 18.37

done in the past reveals how to do it digitally. Oh, to see the effect in color, hide the Orange Filter Preset layer (**Figure 18.37**). Nice, isn't it?

Now photographers can have their original colors, brightened colors, and their black and whites all in the same place. Something that film could never do.

Black and White Differently

Kodachrome
They give us those nice, bright colors,
They give us the greens of summers,
Makes you think all the world's a sunny day.
I got a Nikon camera
I love to take a photograph.
So Mama don't take my Kodachrome away.

Paul Simon's song "Kodachrome" lives on long after Kodachrome film has gone. These lyrics were an anthem for a generation of photographers before digital capture. Simon even changed the lyrics nine years later during the concert in Central Park, admitting, "Everything looks better in black and white."

Photographers, no matter how much they love color, hold a warm spot in their hearts for striking black-and-white images. Digital photographers really have it all, compared to the days when the photograph was dictated by the film in the camera. Today, high bit-depth RGB captures are simply the best for whatever creative inspiration strikes—especially making stunning black-and-white prints. All of the black-and-white contrast filter combinations used in the "good old days" of film—and more—are built right into the digital color image.

Honoring this desire, Photoshop has at least half a dozen different ways to change color into black and white. Some are very good, and others, well, not so much. In Photoshop CS3, there's a new tool that is beyond "very good."

FIGURE 18.38

The Black and White adjustment layer

The Black and White adjustment can be called up in numerous ways: by selecting Image > Adjustments > Black & White…, by choosing Layers > New Adjustment Layer > Black & White, or by selecting it right from the Layers palette itself. That's where to find it. Here's how it works.

RGB and the complements

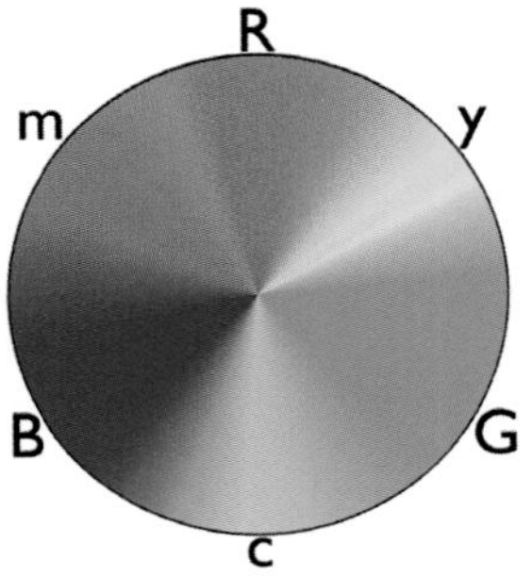

RGB color in Photoshop is mixed using varying values of red, green, and blue. The complementary colors are cyan, magenta, and yellow, respectively. On the color wheel, red, green, and blue are the primaries. Their complements are opposite them (**Figure 18.38**).

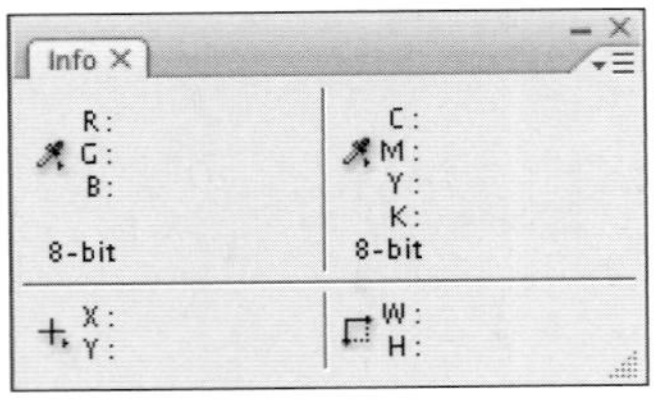

FIGURE 18.39

So red's complement is cyan, green's is magenta, and blue's is yellow. Remember it this way: RGB CMY, or look at the Info Palette. The complement for each RGB color is listed in the CMYK column (**Figure 18.39**). Ignore the K (black).

Channel Mixer

At first glance, the Black and White adjustment looks like an amped-up Channel Mixer. The difference is that Channel Mixer blends the three primary color channels—red, green, and blue—to create an effect that emulates placing a color filter over the lens when shooting black-and-white film. For example, the effect of a yellow filter over the lens is created in Channel Mixer by using 34% of the Red channel and 66% of the Green channel, with no Blue at all.

Black and White

The Black and White adjustment differs by affecting only the color represented by each of its six sliders: Reds, Yellows, Greens, Cyans, Blues, and Magentas. The colors in the dialog are arranged around the color wheel, starting with Red then moving clockwise.

For example, the Yellows slider moves only the yellow values. It does not change either the Red or the Green slider, even though in Channel Mixer it would seem logical to think so. There is a lot of power in this approach, especially when it comes to fine-tuning an image.

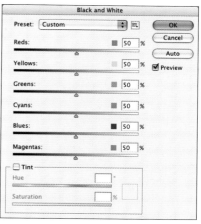

STEP ONE

Open Colorwheel.psd from the project folder for this chapter. Open the file in Photoshop CS3 and double-click the layer thumbnail icon for the Black and White adjustment layer. Enter 50 for all of the sliders. The result is middle gray (**Figure 40**).

STEP TWO

Click on the Yellows slider. Move it to the right and only the yellow values get brighter. All of the yellows go white by the time the slider reaches 300% (**Figure 18.41**).

FIGURE 18.40

STEP THREE

Move the Yellows slider to the left and they darken. Move it to the left until it reads –200%. The same tones are now black (**Figure 18.42**).

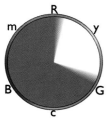

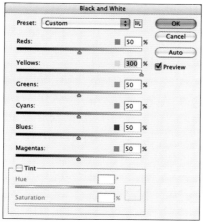

FIGURE 18.41

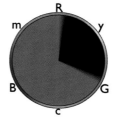

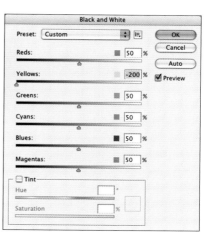

FIGURE 18.42

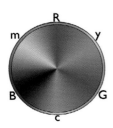

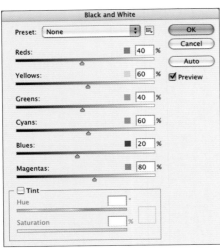

FIGURE 18.43

Presets

The Black and White dialog opens with None as the default Preset, where the RGB values total 100% and the CMY values add up to 200%. The color wheel for this conversion shows that Red and Green are equal values. Blue is darker. The outer ring is left in color to help illustrate what this adjustment layer does (**Figure 18.43**).

There are ten effects already in place in the Preset menu. Six of them mimic the effect of colored filters placed over the lens that photographers used to control contrast while shooting black-and-white film.

The Maximum Black preset has all of the sliders set at 0%. This produces a desaturated image taking the minimum values of Red, Green, and Blue for each pixel. Applying it to the color wheel returns black for all colors.

The Maximum White preset uses 100% as the value for all of the sliders, producing the brightest image using the maximum value for the Red, Green, and Blue of each pixel. The color wheel is white.

Custom presets can be saved by clicking the icon to the right of the Preset menu. This is most useful, for example, in preserving special settings for specific printers.

Black and White versus Channel Mixer

Compare the color wheels made using the Black and White adjustment's presets for Red Filter, Green Filter, and Blue Filter to the color wheels converted using Channel Mixer's presets for the same filters. The prefix BW is for the Black & White adjustment, while CM is for Channel Mixer (**Figure 18.44**).

There are significant differences in these conversions.

You can run the Black & White Ring Around action to see the effects of the presets for yourself. Be sure to read the sidebars in the "The ring around action" section above to know how to set this action up for your computer.

A word of caution

Each of the six colors in the Black and White adjustment has a range of –200% to +300%. Working at either extreme can cause unpleasant artifacts. The amount of control this tool provides is wonderful and scary at the same time.

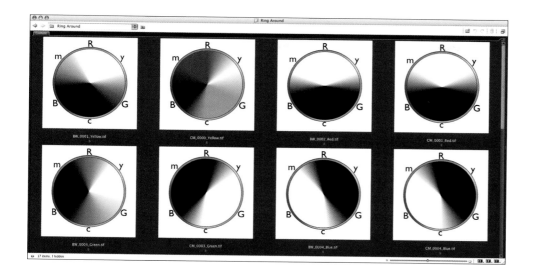

FIGURE 18.44

FIGURE 18.45

Pixels, especially brighter values, can be severely damaged with little effort. Always preview the effect at 100% enlargement and examine areas of contrast by scrolling the entire photograph, carefully checking (especially in the high-lights) for posterization. The artifacts look like stair steps or brushstrokes instead of continuous shades of gray into white (**Figure 18.45**).

FIGURE 18.46

Custom black-and-white conversions

STEP ONE

Open gazebo.tif in Photoshop CS3 (**Figure 18.46**). This early morning photograph of Lake Clara Meer in Atlanta's storied Piedmont Park is full of spring color. The water reflects and deepens the blues of the sky, which is dappled with scattered clouds. Click on the New Adjustment Layer icon (the half-black, half-white circle) at the bottom of the Layers palette. Choose Black & White.... The photograph instantly becomes a very nice black-and-white image automatically. If that were all the layer could do, this would be the end of the tutorial. It's that good. And, of course, there's more—lots more. Start by clicking Auto to see what the tool thinks will make a good conversion. Not bad!

STEP TWO

Six color sliders control the intensity of their hues. Click the Blues slider and move it to the left. The sky and the water get darker. It would be logical to think that adding value to the Yellows would also darken the Blues. Go ahead and move the Yellows slider to the right. What happens? Yep, the trees lighten while the sky and water don't change; the key to this tool is that each slider increases or decreases the brightness of only its color.

STEP THREE

Hold done the Option (PC: Alt) key. The Cancel button changes to Reset. Click on it. The sliders are repositioned to the settings the tool chose originally for the image. Remembering which color slider changes what tone in a black-and-white image is hardly intuitive. There has to be a better way—and, of course, there is. Click in the dark area of the sky above the trees to the left of the gazebo and between the clouds. The color swatch to the right of the Blues slider is bordered and the numbers in the entry field are highlighted. Darken the sky by dragging the cursor (it's now a scrubby slider) until the Blues reading says –71 (**Figure 18.47**). Toggle the Preview checkbox off and on by tapping the P key to see the before and after versions.

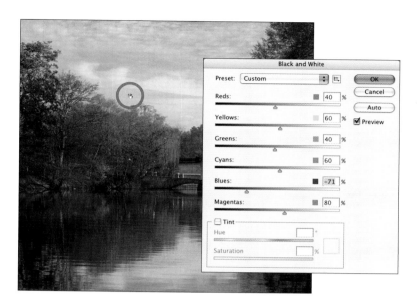

FIGURE 18.47

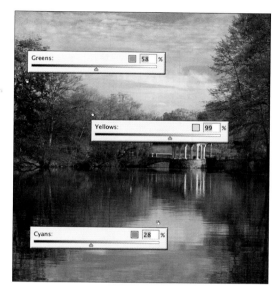

FIGURE 18.48

STEP FOUR

The trees are too dark. Click in the trees to the left of the gazebo. A scrubby slider appears, the Yellows color is bordered, and the number in the entry field becomes highlighted. Drag to the right until the field displays 99% to lighten the areas. Click and drag over the areas in the image that have scrubby sliders to lighten the Greens (58%) and to darken the Cyans (28%) (**Figure 18.48**). Click OK.

STEP FIVE

The trees still want to be a bit lighter. Hide the Black & White layer. There is a lot of warm, early morning light in the leaves and hitting the brick on the gazebo. Warm light is orange. In Photoshop, pure orange is Red: 255 and Green: 128. The Black and White tool doesn't think like this. Remember: Each slider controls only its color. Warm light is a combination of yellow and red, like mixing paint rather than mixing RGB numbers. Show the Black & White layer, then double-click it to open its dialog. Move the Reds slider to the right until it reads 60%. Much better (**Figure 18.49**).

FIGURE 18.49

Color Tints

A good black-and-white conversion is not complete unless it leaves options open for toning the final product. That's where the tool's Tint section shines, simulating traditional darkroom toning without fuss, stain, or smell!

STEP SIX

The vision I had for this scene was a turn-of-the-century (20th century, that is) sepia look. Just as there are many ways to convert color to black and white in Photoshop, there are several ways to tone images, as well. The best part of the Black and White adjustment is that toning is built right in. Click the Tint checkbox. Set the Hue to 39° and the Saturation to 10% (**Figure 18.50**).

Click the Preset icon (it's just left of the OK button). Choose Save Preset..., then name it Sepia. Next time you create a Black and White layer, it will be waiting right there in the Preset menu.

STEP SEVEN

There is just one more thing.... The conversion leaves me a little flat. It wants to radiate some intensity here. Show the Info palette (Window > Info). Create a new Curves adjustment layer. Choose the fine grid by either holding down the Option (PC: Alt) key and clicking in the grid, or clicking the Display Curves Options button and then clicking the fine grid icon. Starting at the lower left corner of the grid, count two boxes to the right and then two up. Command-click (PC: Ctrl-click) to set a point that will protect the shadow values. Hold down the mouse button while moving the cursor over the columns that are in bright sunlight. When the dot on the curve gets to its highest point, hold down the Shift key, release the mouse button, then click to place a color sampler on that point. Read the RGB numbers in the Info palette. My numbers show R: 234, G: 222, and B: 196. They are a little dark for the highlight in a print. Hold down the Command (PC: Ctrl) key and click on top of the sampler in the column.

FIGURE 18.50

Before curves

After curves

FIGURE 18.51

A black dot appears on the Curve. Press the up arrow key until the Red reads around 245. There is still detail in the column and the image has a lot more snap. Click Ok. Hide and show the Curves layer to see what a difference this makes. If it is too much of a change, lower the opacity. Now it's time to make test prints and see which one works best for your taste (**Figure 18.51**).

Kodachrome (may it rest in peace) was all about bright, saturated color. Black and white is all about the contrasting tones, and the highlights and shadows contained in the photograph. We want to see deep rich blacks and sparklingly bright whites with detailed shades in between. The Black and White adjustment layer is a welcome new tool for creating stunning prints without any wasted water washing them in the darkroom (**Figure 18.52**).

FIGURE 18.52

CHAPTER 19

Enchanting Enhancements

THERE ARE SOME BOOKS on photographing and retouching women, one of which I wrote. This chapter looks at simple enhancements that are easy to master, offering subtle fixes to eyes and teeth, as well as body slimming. I use some of them every time I work on a portrait, editorial, or fashion photograph.

Taller and Slimmer

Yep. It's true. That camera makes you look fat.

Translating a beautiful woman—or anyone else, for that matter, who lives in the four dimensions of height, width, depth, and time—into millions of pixels representing only width and height makes even the most svelte figure appear heavier than it seems in life. Really! This part of the *Notebook* shows how to make a girl taller and, of course, a bit slimmer (**Figure 19.1**). Now if it would only work for us in real life....

FIGURE 19.1

The camera does add weight. Photoshop offers tools like Liquify that require quite a lot of work for a tuck or two here or there. Use this quick fix to easily reconfigure those two dimensions to offset the camera's perversity.

Download the files for this project from amesphoto.com/learning. The book code is DPN8414.

Body work

STEP ONE

Use Bridge to navigate to the folder for this chapter. Open LeAnn. tif. Make a duplicate of the Background layer by pressing Command (PC: Ctrl) + J. Name the layer Stretch.

STEP TWO

Next, increase the canvas size by pressing Command (PC: Ctrl) + Option (Alt) + C. Click the Relative box. The middle box in the center row of the Anchor section is chosen by default. Enter 3 inches in the Height field. Select White for the Canvas extension color (**Figure 19.2**). Click OK. The canvas grows by 1½ inches on the top and bottom.

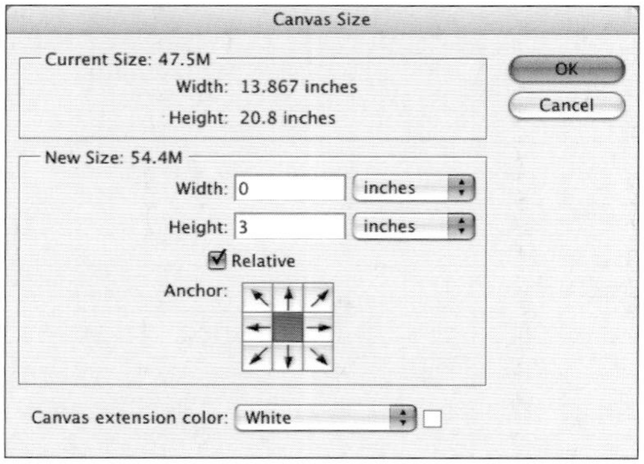

STEP THREE

Press Command (PC: Ctrl) + T to enter Free Transform. Enter 110% in the Height field. Highlight the Width box and hit the down arrow three times to set it at 97%. Click the Commit checkmark or press Enter (**Figure 19.3**).

FIGURE 19.2

Play with the height and width numbers when you are working on your photographs. It's a good idea not to go taller than 115% or slimmer than 90%. It should be believable, after all.

Changing heads

LeAnn now looks taller and slimmer. There's a new problem. Her face is distorted. As a result of being stretched to 110%, her face is way too long from her hairline to her chin. That's fine for the body and not so good for her face. It's time to bring her real head back into the picture.

STEP FOUR

Choose the Lasso tool (L). Draw a selection around LeAnn's head that goes around her hair and neck. Continue it all the way to the edges of the frame and to the top, as well (**Figure 19.4**).

STEP FIVE

Highlight the Background layer. Make the selection into it's own layer by pressing Command (PC: Ctrl) + J. Rename the new layer Original Head. Drag it to the top of the layer stack (**Figure 19.5**). LeAnn's head is now normal, though a little out of position.

FIGURE 19.3

FIGURE 19.4

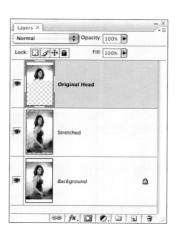

FIGURE 19.5

FIGURE 19.6

FIGURE 19.7

STEP SIX

Get the Move tool (V). Change Original Head's blending mode to Difference by pressing Option (PC: Alt) + Shift + E. (The blending mode shortcuts for layers only work when the Move tool is active. Otherwise, they will change the blending mode of the active painting tool. And, yes, knowing these shortcuts means I don't have a life.) Drag LeAnn's head down until the chin lines match. Press Option (PC: Alt) + Shift + N to set the blending mode back to Normal (**Figure 19.6**).

STEP SEVEN

Add a new layer mask by clicking the Add Layer Mask icon at the bottom of the Layers palette. Make the foreground color black by tapping D on the keyboard. Choose a completely soft, 50-pixel brush set to 100% Opacity and Flow. Paint on the layer mask from LeAnn's collar bone, up her neck and into her hair, to blend her original head with her taller, slimmer, no-longer-camera-enlarged self. Hide and reveal her original head and look for places in the image where the hair or background does not blend. Paint over them with black on the layer mask (**Figure 19.7**).

Before and after

STEP EIGHT

Hide the Background layer. Copy the two visible layers to a new layer by pressing Command (PC: Ctrl) + Option (PC: Alt) + Shift + E. Rename the resulting layer Taller & Slimmer. Hide the Stretch and Original Head layers.

The keyboard shortcut in this step is super-quick when compared to choosing Merge Visible from the Layers palette's flyout menu while holding down the Option (PC: Alt) key. Either way, you still have to use the keyboard. Be efficient; leave your mouse alone whenever you can.

FIGURE 19.8

FIGURE 19.9

STEP NINE

Get the Crop tool (C) and draw a crop around the photograph eliminating the white and transparent areas. Click the Hide button, then the Commit checkmark (**Figure 19.8**). Hiding instead of deleting the pixels with the Crop tool is part of editing photographs non-destructively. Get the original pixels back by choosing Image > Reveal All.

STEP TEN

Show the Background layer. Hide and reveal Taller & Slimmer to see the results of this technique (**Figure 19.9**).

I always save the working layers to a PSD file in case changes are requested later. You just never know when she might decide she wants to look even taller or slimmer. A girl has the right to change her mind, you know.

FIGURE 19.10

FIGURE 19.11

The Eyes Have It!

It has been said that the "eyes are the window of the soul." It is so true, especially since the eyes, and not their whites, are what draw us into a person's portrait. And yet how many times have we seen magazines with eyes overpowered, surrounded by the glaring paper white of the publication itself? Eye whites aren't white, they're light gray. (Sometimes they have a little red, too, depending on the amount of partying the night before.) This section of the *Notebook* shows how to enhance a subject's eyes to draw in the viewer's (**Figure 19.10**).

Contrast

We humans love our contrast. We are drawn to it uncontrollably. So it's understandable why eyes and teeth in photographs are often made to appear unnaturally bright, even though it's just, well, wrong! The fact is that neither teeth nor eye whites are windows to the soul. The contrasts that matter are within the eye itself.

The layers

STEP ONE
Double-click Cara.tif's thumbnail in Bridge to open it in Photoshop. Let's set up the necessary layers for this technique. Make a new Curves adjustment layer by clicking the half-black/half-white circle at the bottom of the Layers palette. Choose Curves... from the menu. When the Curves dialog opens, click OK. A Curves adjustment layer appears in the layer stack. It has a Reveal All (white) layer mask. Press Command (PC: Ctrl) + I to invert the layer mask to black (Hide All). Change the blending mode to Multiply, then rename the layer Pupils (**Figure 19.11**). The Multiply blending mode darkens the image.

Hold down the Option (PC: Alt) key before clicking on the Add Layer Mask icon to make the new layer mask a Hide All mask (one that's filled with black).

STEP TWO

Hold down the Option (PC: Alt) key, click in the blue space of the Pupils layer, and drag it above itself to make a copy of the Curves adjustment layer. (Option-dragging [PC: Alt-dragging] selected layers, layer masks, or layer styles duplicates them within the layer stack.) Rename the new layer Irises and change the blending mode to Screen (**Figure 19.12**).

FIGURE 19.12

Darken the pupils

STEP THREE

Click the Pupils layer to make it active. Press B to get the Brush tool. Make the brush 30 pixels in diameter by pressing the open, or left, bracket key ([) to make the brush smaller, or the close, or right, bracket key (]) to enlarge it. Hold down the Shift key and press] twice to make the Hardness 50%. Press D to set the default colors, with white as the foreground color. Press 0 (zero) to set the brush to 100% Opacity. Press Command (PC: Ctrl) + Option (PC: Alt) + 0, then Command (PC: Ctrl) + = to zoom in to 200%. Center the brush in Cara's right eye and click (**Figure 19.13**). If you are using a Wacom tablet, wiggle the brush in a circular motion. Repeat on Cara's left eye.

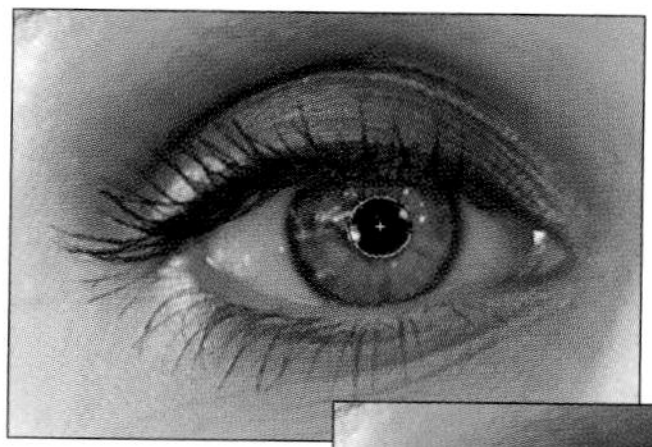

FIGURE 19.13

STEP FOUR

Type 5 to set the brush to 50% Opacity. Make the brush 3 pixels by tapping the [key seven times. Hold down the Shift key and hit the [key another four times to make the brush soft (0% Hardness). Carefully, with one stroke, trace the dark line around each of Cara's irises. The line gets darker as you go around it (**Figure 19.14**).

FIGURE 19.14

STEP FIVE

Hold down the Option (PC: Alt) key and click on the Pupils layer mask. The screen goes black except for white dots over the pupils and lines around the outside of the iris. Look at the edges, especially for the pupils. They are hard-edged. There are no hard edges on people (I'm talking physically here, not about some of *those* personalities), so these lines want to be softened, which will also blend the enhancement and make it look more natural. Choose Filter > Blur > Gaussian Blur... from the Filters menu. Enter 3.1 in the Radius field and click OK (**Figure 19.15**).

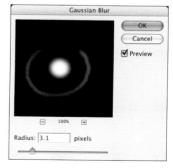

FIGURE 19.15

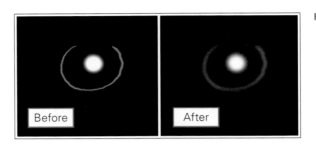

FIGURE 19.16

Option-click (PC: Alt-click) the layer mask icon to return to the normal view. See the difference by pressing Command (PC: Ctrl) + Z to undo the blur, then again to reapply it (**Figure 19.16**).

Lighten the irises

STEP SIX

Highlight the Irises layer. Press 0 to set the brush Opacity to 100%. Paint over the *specular highlights* (a.k.a. catchlights) in Cara's irises (**Figure 19.17**). Chapter 4 has more on specularity.

FIGURE 19.17

Set the brush to 50% Opacity by pressing 5. Paint over each of her irises without lifting the mouse button (or stylus). Finally, draw a line along the upper edge of the lower eyelid, from tear duct all the way to where the lid ends (**Figure 19.18**).

STEP SEVEN

Soften up the iris-brightening by Option-clicking (PC: Alt-clicking) the layer mask on Irises and pressing Command (PC: Ctrl) + F to repeat the blur performed on the Pupils layer mask. Option-click (PC: Alt-click) the mask again to return to the normal view. Press Command (PC: Ctrl) + 0 to return to the fit-in-window view. The last filter used in Photoshop can be reapplied by pressing Command (PC: Ctrl) + F.

FIGURE 19.18

STEP EIGHT

Now Cara's eyes look like they belong to one of the huskies in the Iditarod sled race in Alaska. Not to worry. Press V to choose the Move tool and then press 5 to reduce the Opacity of Irises to 50%. Now highlight Pupils and

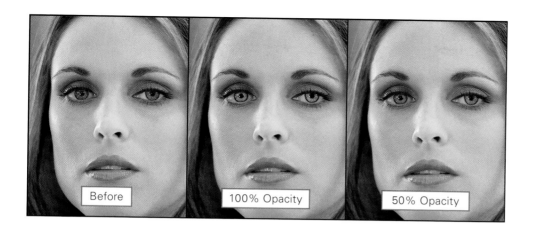

FIGURE 19.19

Before   100% Opacity   50% Opacity

press 5 again. Click and roll your cursor over the Eye icons of the two adjustment layers to see the Before image. Do it again to see the After enhancement effect. The opacity of the Irises and Pupils layers may be adjusted to taste after making a test print. The opacities do not have to be equal (**Figure 19.19**).

Lighten the nostrils

Cara's eyes look great. Remember that contrast thing we humans do? Well, there is just one more thing. Just as our eyes are drawn to bright areas, they also seek out dark spots on light tones. Are you noticing her left nostril like I am? It is a large dark spot pulling my eye away from her eyes, so....

STEP NINE

Click on Irises to highlight the layer. Hold down the entire left hand side of the keyboard—really, it's the Command (PC: Ctrl) + Option (PC: Alt) + Shift keys—and press the E key. The visible layers are copied onto a new layer. (If you are using a version previous to CS2, use the same modifiers and press N, then the E key.) Rename the layer Final.

STEP TEN

Pick the Healing brush from the toolbox and set the brush size to 20 and the Hardness to 100%. Sample from a clear area of the skin on her left cheek and heal over the entire nostril in one stroke. And *oh boy* is it freak show city!

FIGURE 19.20

Hold down the Command (PC: Ctrl) + Shift keys and press F. The Fade Healing Brush dialog box opens. Enter 25 and click OK. Everything is all better now. Whew.

Compare the nostril before lowering the contrast to the new version (**Figure 19.20**). It is a subtle change. All of these small enhancements add up to a large difference in the final print. The important point is to make them undetectable.

The Edit > Fade command in this step is available with all of the painting tools. It only works on the last stroke applied. It also works with filters.

Finally, hide the Pupils and Irises layers so only the Background and Final layers are showing. Hide and reveal Final by clicking its Eye icon to see the effects of the enhancements.

Cara's eyes have that spark and twinkle that pull the viewer right into them. Mission accomplished! And no eye whites have been altered, harmed, or made to look unreal during the course of this work (**Figure 19.21**).

Extreme Makeovers

Cosmetic dentistry and surgery have been all the rage on television. Makeovers aren't only for TV or in surgical suites. They are more of the subtle work that takes a photograph to a higher level. The best part: they are easy to do in Photoshop, and without scalpels, bandages, blood, or bruises.

Mindy is a friend of mine who wanted me to make her portrait. After the photo session, she told me that she really wished her teeth were even and that her nose was symmetrical. I thought about it and asked her if I could do an extreme makeover, Photoshop-style (**Figure 19.22**).

FIGURE 19.21

Paths

Believe it or not, the Pen tool creates editable selections. Beyond question, it is the most powerful selection tool in all of Photoshop. I encourage you to learn it well. Once you master this somewhat tricky tool, you're on your way to Photoshop nirvana (slightly different from grunge-rock favorite Nirvana). If you want the practice, draw individual paths around her two left (as you look at them) teeth. Save the paths as Front Tooth 1 and Side Tooth 1. Otherwise, use the Front Tooth and Side Tooth paths that I have already drawn for you.

FIGURE 19.22

STEP ONE

Open Mindy.tif in Photoshop. (It's in the files you downloaded earlier.) Press Command (PC: Ctrl) + Option (PC: Alt) + 0 to zoom into 100%. Then press Command (PC: Ctrl) + + to reach a 200% view. Duplicate the Background layer by pressing Command (PC: Ctrl) + J. Name the new layer Retouch.

Seeing feathers

How much does Select > Modify > Feather actually feather a selection anyway? This burning question is resolved simply and visually. Read on....

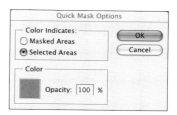

FIGURE 19.23

STEP TWO

Double-click the Quick Mask icon in the toolbox. Click the Selected Areas button for the color indication and set the Opacity to 100% (**Figure 19.23**). Click on the Paths tab. Hold down the Command (PC: Ctrl) key and click on Front Tooth to load it as a selection.

STEP THREE

The selection around Mindy's front tooth is solid red and has a sharp edge. As mentioned earlier, there are no hard edges on people so the selection wants to be softened to match the edges of the teeth it's between. Choose Blur > Gaussian Blur. Enter 1.1 pixels in the Radius field. Click OK. The edge of the selection in red closely matches the edge of the neighboring tooth (**Figure 19.24**). Press Q to exit Quick Mask. The radius amount in pixels of Gaussian Blur applied to a Quick Mask gives the same result when it's entered in the Feather dialog box; choose Select > Feather or use the keyboard shortcut, Command (PC: Ctrl) + Option (PC: Alt) + D. (If you are using

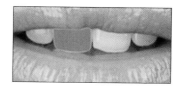

FIGURE 19.24

a Mac and the Dock pops up, refer to the "Note for Mac Users" sidebar in Chapter 1 for the fix.)

Another way to get to this is to have any selection tool active and click the Refine Edges... button in the Options bar. The Quick Mask icon is second from the left. Double-click it to set the Quick Mask options.

A new front tooth

STEP FOUR

Press Command (PC: Ctrl) + J to jump the selection of the tooth to a new layer. Name the layer Front Tooth. Choose the Move tool (V) and drag the tooth over to Mindy's right front tooth. Flip the tooth by pressing Command (PC: Ctrl) + T to enter Free Transform. Control-click (PC: right-click) the tooth and choose Flip Horizontal. The tooth is now oriented correctly. It wants a slight counter-clockwise rotation. Drag the Reference Point from its default center position to the upper left edge of the tooth (**Figure 19.25**).

Move your cursor just outside of the lower right corner of the bounding box. When the Rotation cursor (a curved, double-headed arrow) appears, drag up until the Angle window in the Options bar reads –2.4°. Click the Commit checkmark in the Options bar, or hit Enter.

Free Transform rotates an image around the reference point. It can be positioned anywhere in the image.

STEP FIVE

The reflections on the new tooth are a mirror image of the other front tooth. They are a giveaway of the duplication and flip. Also, the tooth is outside of Mindy's lip. Ouch! Click the Add Layer Mask icon. Get a 9-pixel brush at 50% Hardness and 100% Opacity. Set the foreground color to black. Paint on the layer mask over the top of the tooth to reveal the original tooth below. Continue until the edge over her lip and the mirrored reflections are gone (**Figure 19.26**). The front teeth are now perfectly symmetrical.

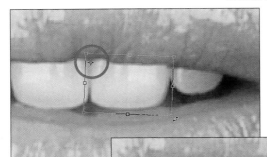

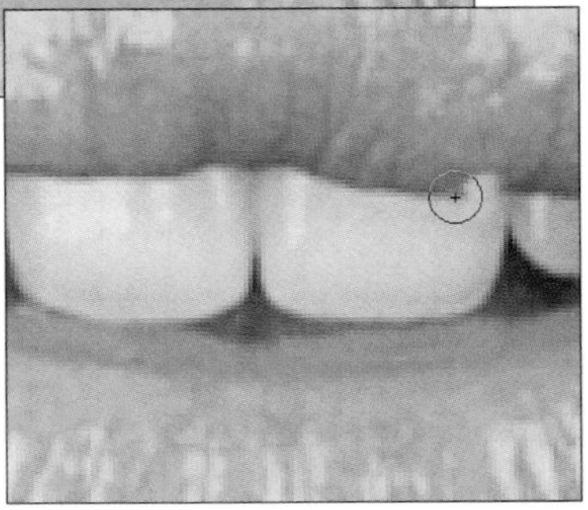

FIGURE 19.25

FIGURE 19.26

Digital bonding

This is another way to build up a tooth, using the Clone Stamp and the Healing brush within a selection. Think of it as a bit of digital tooth bonding.

STEP SIX

Click the Paths tab. Command-click (PC: Ctrl-click) the path named Side Tooth to make it into a selection. Press Q to show the Quick Mask. Press Command (PC: Ctrl) + F to apply the Gaussian Blur filter. (This keyboard shortcut applies the last filter used.) Choose the Move tool (V). Press Command (PC: Ctrl) + Shift + T. This is the Transform Again shortcut. Drag the Quick Mask to the left until it is in position over the side tooth on the right.

STEP SEVEN

Click the Retouch layer to select it. Hit S for the Clone Stamp tool. Set the brush size to 4 pixels, 100% Opacity, and 50% Hardness. Choose Current & Below in the Samples menu in the Options bar. Option-click (PC: Alt-click) on the enamel on the tooth and clone over the selection to build up the tooth. Don't worry if the tones don't match exactly. Choose the Healing brush (J). Make its options the same as for the Clone Stamp tool. Sample on Mindy's right front tooth, then heal over the edge of the cloned pixels to blend them with the rest of the side tooth. Cloning and healing the side tooth introduces variations of tone and texture. The shape of this tooth is not as perfect as the front teeth. It's important to have slight imperfections in this type of retouching to keep the believability high.

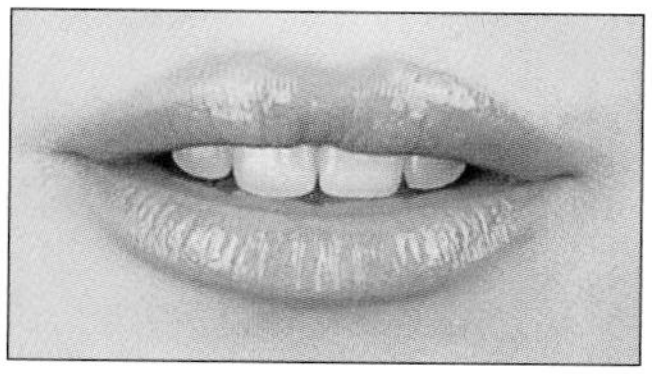

FIGURE 19.27

Press Command (PC: Ctrl) + D to deselect. Brilliant! Mindy's new smile is nice, too (**Figure 19.27**).

Rhinoplasty

Technically, rhinoplasty is smoothing out bumps along the ridge of the nose. It sounds more elegant than "nose job," and it helps some folks think I know a couple of big words. Whoever heard of a "nostril job" anyway? Besides, "nostril" has already been used as a heading in this chapter. Straightening out Mindy's crooked nostril is similar to fixing her front teeth.

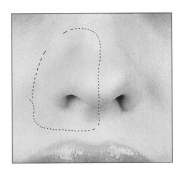

FIGURE 19.28

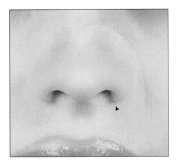

FIGURE 19.29

STEP EIGHT

Press the L key to select the Lasso tool. Draw a selection around Mindy's left nostril, cutting it in half then choosing more skin to its left (**Figure 19.28**). Press Command (PC: Ctrl) + J to make a new layer from the selection. Name it New Nostril. Press Command (PC: Ctrl) + T for Free Transform. Control-click (PC: right-click) inside the bounding box and choose Flip Horizontal. Press Enter to commit the transform.

STEP NINE

Choose the Move tool (V). Drag the New Nostril layer to the right until the edge down the middle of Mindy's nose disappears. The shadow under her nose will look like a butterfly (**Figure 19.29**).

Finally, add a layer mask and paint with a soft-edged black brush over the right edge of the skin to blend it smoothly into her face.

STEP TEN

Copy all of the layers to a new one by holding down Command (PC: Ctrl) + Option (PC: Alt) + Shift and pressing E. Rename the new layer Final. Hide all of the layers except the Background layer. Hide and show Final to see Mindy after and before her makeover (**Figure 19.30**).

After

Before

FIGURE 19.30

Digital cosmetic dentistry and surgery, like its real-life equivalents, must be done with a light touch. The enhancements in this chapter will make your already-excellent photographs even more appealing. No one will know that any work has been done at all.

I'll never tell.

Remember: What's done in this chapter stays in this chapter. Heh, heh.

CHAPTER 20

Lighting Without Lights

I CHECKED INTO A CHARMING LITTLE HOTEL while on assignment in San Diego recently. When I opened the door, the soft, diffused light streaming into the room through the windows was beautiful. There were flowers on the table in the alcove. I had to have a photograph of it. There was one tiny problem. No lights.

I could see detail in the curtains (**Figure 20.1**). When I looked at the side of the bed closest to me, there was detail there, too (**Figure 20.2**). The problem is contrast. While my brain put the highlight and shadow details into one image automatically, what I saw was beyond the ability of the camera to record it. Or was it?

FIGURE 20.1

FIGURE 20.2

No Lights. No Way?

Without lights to fill the shadows, the very bright outside light overpowers the room's interior. An exposure that captures detail in the curtains makes everything else seriously underexposed. An exposure that reveals the foreground blows out the windows, curtains, and most of the walls around them. Painting the two together with layer masks is an option, though not a very good one. The subtle shadows around the window and on the floor by the chair would be way too dark. There is a better way. It's called Merge to HDR. HDR means High Dynamic Range. It is Photoshop CS3's continued foray into the amazing world of 32-bit photography.

THE RULES OF SHOOTING FOR HDR

Here are the rules that must be followed in order for the merge to work.

1. Shoot a series of photographs in one-f/stop brackets over a six-stop range.

2. The camera must be on a sturdy tripod. Movement between exposures will cause the merge to fail.

3. The brackets must be made with the shutter. Changing the aperture subtly changes the size of the files relative to each other. This is a type of movement. Using the aperture for the bracket won't allow the merge to work.

4. Shoot RAW.

5. Set Camera Raw's Workflow Options to 16-bit.

I set up the camera on a tripod and composed the scene. I made a series of six photographs, increasing the exposure by one f/stop each time The aperture is f/8.0. The ISO is 160. The shutter speeds for the six shots are $\frac{1}{6}$, $\frac{1}{10}$, $\frac{1}{20}$, $\frac{1}{45}$, $\frac{1}{90}$, and $\frac{1}{180}$ (**Figure 20.3**).

Merging to HDR

Once the photography is finished, assembling a finished HDR file is straightforward and mostly automated. The six photographs used in this project are available on amesphoto.com/learning. The book code is DPN8414. They are original

FIGURE 20.3

RAW files and will take a while to download. Please use them only for the purposes of learning this tutorial.

STEP ONE

Select the six RAW files for the merge in Adobe Bridge CS3. (This also works in CS2.) Click on the first one in the series, hold down the Shift key, and click on the last one.

STEP TWO

Choose Merge to HDR from the Bridge menu bar: Tools > Photoshop > Merge to HDR (**Figure 20.4**). Photoshop opens each file in turn and then presents a dialog box. The Filmstrip on the left side shows the files that will build the

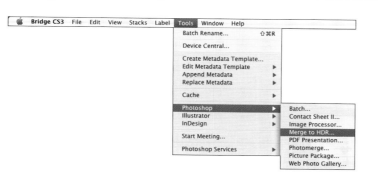

FIGURE 20.4

FIGURE 20.5

HDR file. The checkboxes allow you to exclude one or more from the merge. Uncheck one of the files and the dialog view refreshes to show how that change would affect the merge (**Figure 20.5**).

STEP THREE

The Set White Point Preview shows the brightness range you can see on the monitor. Move it to the right to reveal the highlight detail (**Figure 20.6**). Move it to the left to open up the shadows so that you can see the caster that holds up the bed, even though it is in deep shadows and the only light used was streaming in from the window (**Figure 20.7**). HDR files have so much information in them that to see it all you would need a monitor with a white nearly as bright as the sun.

This setting is a preview. Move the white point slider close to its original position. Select 16-bit from the Bit Depth menu and click OK.

FIGURE 20.6

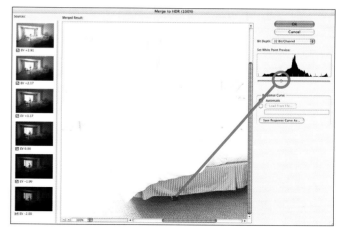

FIGURE 20.7

Converting the merged file

STEP FOUR

The HDR Conversion dialog opens. Choose Local Adaptation and click the triangle to reveal the Toning Curve and Histogram. The other choices do not allow the use of curves. The preview looks yucky (yucky is the technical term for really, *really* bad).

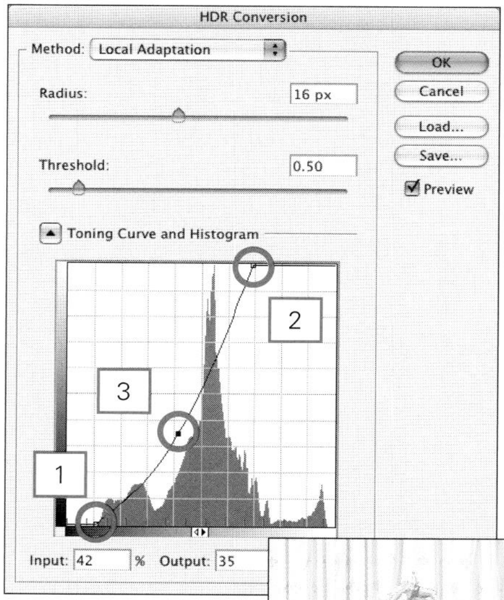

Click on the dot in the lower left corner of the curve (the #1 shown in **Figure 20.8**) and drag it to the right until it is almost touching the shadow pixels. When you release the mouse button, the preview picks up the shadows. Click on the dot in the upper right corner (#2) and drag it to the left about two and a half boxes to bring in the highlights. Finally, click on the line about three boxes up from the bottom (#3) and press the down arrow key four or five times to boost the contrast.

FIGURE 20.8

STEP FIVE

Zoom in to a 100% view by pressing Command (PC: Ctrl) + Option (PC: Alt) + 0. Close examination shows a halo effect in some areas—especially around the backlit flowers (**Figure 20.9**)—and jaggies along the lower edge of the table.

FIGURE 20.9

FIGURE 20.10

Move the Radius up to 18 pixels. Click the Threshold slider and drag it to the right. Release the mouse to refresh the preview. Move Threshold to 1.45. The halo disappears, as do the jaggies (**Figure 20.10**). Click OK and Photoshop converts the High Dynamic Range file to an editable 16-bit PSD.

Finishing touches

There is just one more thing. In the days of film, architectural photographs were made using view cameras. The backs could be pivoted so the film was parallel with the walls. This movement made the vertical lines parallel, too. Some of the higher-end digital cameras rival, or even exceed, the resolution of the large-format view cameras. Most do not offer the movements. DSLRs don't have them, either. This is a job for Photoshop's Lens Correction filter. Then adding a bit of warmth to the scene will wrap up the post-production on this photograph.

Perspective correction

STEP ONE
Duplicate the Background layer by pressing Command (PC: Ctrl) + J. Rename the layer Lens Correction.

STEP TWO
Open the Lens Correction dialog box (Filter > Distort > Lens Correction). Adjust the grid's Size to 50. Change its color to black by double-clicking on the Color patch to open the Color Picker dialog, and entering R: 0, G: 0, and B: 0. Click OK in the Color Picker. You can move the grid by clicking the Move Grid tool (M) and dragging it until it is over the line you want to be vertical (**Figure 20.11**).

STEP THREE
Click on the Vertical Perspective slider and drag it to the left until the window displays +13. You want to make the vertical edges of the two walls parallel to each other. By lining them up to the grid, you are assured that they are. When everything is aligned and in perspective, click OK.

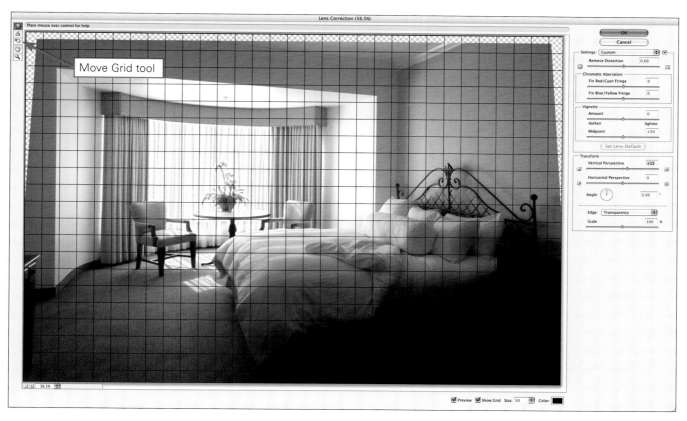

FIGURE 20.11

STEP FOUR

Hide the Background layer. Press C to get the Crop tool. Crop the photograph inside the edges of the walls that show as transparent. Crop out the side of the table on the left. Click the Commit checkmark in the Crop tool's Options bar (**Figure 20.12**).

FIGURE 20.12

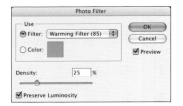

FIGURE 20.13

Warm up

STEP FIVE

The curtains are too blue and the room looks a little bit cold. That was not what I remember feeling. Warm it up some using a Photo Filter layer from the contextual menu you get by clicking on the New Adjustment Layer icon at the bottom of the Layers palette. The default setting of a number 85 Warming Filter at a 25% Density with Preserve Luminosity checked is perfect (**Figure 20.13**). Click OK.

Wrap up

STEP SIX

Finally, highlight Lens Correction. Choose the Healing Brush (J). Select Current Layer from the Sample menu. Hold down Option (PC: Alt) and click to the left of the sprinkler head that's just in front of the valence. Brush over the head to remove it.

That's much better (**Figure 20.14**). Now the photograph has the feeling I remember when I walked into the room that first time. The important lesson is that if you can't take lights with you, be sure you have your tripod and Adobe Photoshop CS3.

FIGURE 20.14

Digital Interiors

One of the keys to successful interiors is doing everything possible at the scene so it's easy to assemble later in Photoshop. I always use a tripod when I shoot interiors. The tripod locks down the camera position. It eliminates the variable of camera movement, improves composition, and allows me to make multiple exposures of the scene in perfect registration with each other. Once the camera is set, I take a light reading and shoot a test into my laptop. (See Chapter 3.) The result is a room with a view—a very bright view (**Figure 20.15**).

FIGURE 20.15

In-camera fixes for use in Photoshop

The first thing I do when I first see a shot appear on the laptop is decide what I can fix in the scene itself. The second is to determine the areas best handled in Photoshop. All that's left is to shoot the necessary components. The reflection in the print over the sofa is an example of the latter.

The print is covered with glass that makes it act like a mirror. The trick is to show the mirror what I want it to show the camera—in this case, black. I have my assistant, Cameron Krone, hold a 48 x 48-inch Chimera panel covered with

FIGURE 20.16

black fabric up against the right side of the print. I still see a reflection. He angles the black panel toward the center of the print until the reflection disappears, then I capture the photograph (**Figure 20.16**).

Reflected black

STEP ONE
Click on the folder you downloaded (earlier in this chapter) in Bridge. Double-click the thumbnail 2276-145.psd to open it in Photoshop CS3.

STEP TWO
Select File > Place in Photoshop. Use the Place dialog box to navigate to the downloaded folder. Highlight 2276-147.CR2 and click Place. The Camera Raw dialog box appears. Click Open. The RAW file opens in Free Transform. Click the Commit checkmark. Cameron appears holding the black-covered panel. The layer stack shows a new Smart Object layer named 2276-147. Placing the RAW file assures that the image is the same size. The Smart Object, indicated by the icon at the bottom right of the thumbnail, contains a copy of the original RAW file (**Figure 20.17**).

FIGURE 20.17

Aligning layers

Hide and reveal the Smart Object. You may notice that the room jumped a little bit. That's because the tripod got bumped and it moved ever so slightly, so the images aren't quite perfectly aligned.

STEP THREE

Change the blending mode of the Smart Object layer 2276-147 to Difference. Select the Move tool (V). Nudge the layers into alignment by pressing the down arrow twice and the left arrow once. When the white outline almost disappears, the two layers' pixels are aligned. Cameron looks like a ghost because he doesn't exist in the Background layer (**Figure 20.18**). Change the layer's blending mode back to Normal.

FIGURE 20.18

Eliminating the reflection

STEP FOUR

Use the Pen tool (P) to draw a path inside the frame and around the white matte of the print. Double-click the work path in the Paths palette and save it as Path 1. Hold down the Command (PC: Ctrl) key and click Path 1 (or the supplied path, named Print) to make it into a selection. Press Command (PC: Ctrl) + Option (PC: Alt) + D and feather the selection .3 pixels. Click the Add Layer Mask icon at the bottom of the Layers palette. Cameron and the reflection disappear.

STEP FIVE

The print is dark because the black panel that killed the reflection also took light away. Command-click (PC: Ctrl-click) the layer mask icon to make it into a selection. Click the layer thumbnail icon to select it. Copy the selection to a new layer by pressing Command (PC: Ctrl) + J. Rename the layer Brighten Print. Change the blending mode to Screen (**Figure 20.19**). That's better. Now for the way-too-bright balcony.

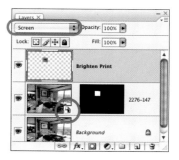

FIGURE 20.19

Taming balcony brightness

STEP ONE

Choose File > Place, and this time select the file 2276-145.CR2. The file opens in Camera Raw. Move the Temperature slider to 4250, the Exposure slider to –2.30, and the Brightness slider to 33 (**Figure 20.20**). Click OK. Click the Commit checkmark to finish placing the file as a Smart Object layer named 2276-145.

FIGURE 20.20

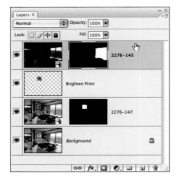

FIGURE 20.21

STEP TWO

Draw a path inside the frame holding the glass in the balcony doors. Double-click Work Path in the Paths palette and click OK to name it Path 2. Command-click (PC: Ctrl-click) on Path 2 (or the supplied path, named Doors) to load it as a selection. Feather the selection .3 pixels. Add a layer mask to the layer by clicking the Add Layer Mask icon (**Figure 20.21**). The room returns to normal illumination and the exterior buildings are a lot less bright.

Lamp lightening

The exposure required to make the room look right made the lamp dark, even though it was on. It's time to make it shine.

STEP ONE

Highlight the Background layer. Press I to choose the Eyedropper tool. Sample the color at the center of the lampshade. Click the Color palette. Choose the HSB Sliders option from the palette's flyout menu. Drag the B (Brightness) slider to the right to a value of around 86 (**Figure 20.22**). The foreground color in the toolbox is brighter than the shade.

STEP TWO

Make a new layer and name it Lamp Shade Light. Choose the Elliptical Marquee tool. Start in the center of the lampshade and draw down toward its bottom. Now hold down the Option (PC: Alt) key to make the selection grow from the shade's center. Continue dragging until the selection almost reaches the top and bottom of the shade. This selection will make the lamp light shine through (**Figure 20.23**).

STEP THREE

Hold down the Option (PC: Alt) key and hit Delete (PC: Backspace) to fill the selection with the foreground color. Deselect (Command [PC: Ctrl] + D).

STEP FOUR

Change Lamp Shade Light's blending mode to Screen. Choose Filter > Blur > Gaussian Blur. Drag the Radius slider to the right until the glow looks like it fits, somewhere around 16 pixels. The lamp is glowing nicely now.

So far, the work shows no reflection in the framed picture, darker buildings outside, and a lamp that glows (**Figure 20.24**).

FIGURE 20.22

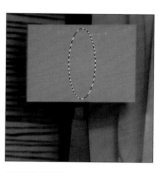

FIGURE 20.23

FIGURE 20.24

This interior looks so much better. Notice how your eye is starting to be drawn back into the room in this version with the darker exterior and lit lamp. It's the little things that make a big difference! And wait...there's more!

Now it's time to brighten the too-faint light on the curtains above the lamp, tame the too-bright sky, and straighten the non-parallel verticals.

Spill light enlightened

The disconnect at this point in the interior's post-production is that the lamp shade is bright, while the light on the curtains and ceiling above the lamp is barely visible.

STEP FIVE

Draw a path along the top of the lampshade and up along the line of the light from the lamp. Make it curve around the ceiling and back to the other edge of the shade to complete the path. Save the path as Lamp Light (or use the supplied path, Lamp Light).

STEP SIX

FIGURE 20.25

Make a new layer named Lamp Light. Make Screen its blending mode. Command-click (PC: Ctrl-click) on the path named Lamp Light to make it into a selection. Use the Eyedropper tool (I) to choose the orange-ish light on the curtains (**Figure 20.25**).

Choose the Color palette (Window > Color) from Photoshop's menu. Choose HSB Sliders from the palette's flyout menu. Move the B slider until it reads 76 in the Color palette. Fill the selection with the foreground layer. Deselect. Blur the layer using Gaussian Blur at a radius of 8.9 pixels.

STEP SEVEN

This is a good start, though it's a tad bright. Add a layer mask to Lamp Light. Press D to set the default color, then press G for the Gradient tool. Select the foreground-to-background gradation from the tool's Options bar. Start at the top of the shade and drag up to the edge of the ledge above the curtain. The light falls off as the distance increases from the lamp, as it would in real life. Finally, lower Lamp Light's Opacity to 40%. Look at the result (**Figure 20.26**). That's one happening (and totally believable) effect!

This interior has come a long way, and there is still a little further to go with it.

FIGURE 20.26

Hot summer days

One of the drawbacks about shooting in Hot'Lanta is the summer. Not only does Atlanta live up to its high-temperature nickname; it is the poster child of humidity, haze, and smog for cities living east of the Mississippi. The skies of the season seem extraordinarily bright and colorless when photographed. Not a pretty sight at all!

The human eye always looks to the brightest area in a scene. In this case, it's still drawn away from the room itself by the bright sky to the balcony doors on the right. That gets and holds our attention. It's time to deal!

FIGURE 20.27

FIGURE 20.28

Masking the windows

STEP ONE

Draw a path around the building outside, up the frame of the glass door, then along the valence, and back down the brick wall. Make another path around the other side of the door. Save it as a path named Sky.

STEP TWO

Highlight the Lamp Light layer. Copy all of the visible layers to a new layer above Lamp Light by holding down Command (PC: Ctrl) + Option (PC: Alt) + Shift + E. Name the new layer Interior.

STEP THREE

Command-click (PC: Ctrl-click) on the Sky path to load it as a selection. Feather it .3 pixels. Press Option (PC: Alt) and click the Add Layer Mask icon to add a mask that shows black where the blown-out sky is. Black conceals what's on the layer; in this case, the blown-out sky is hidden. Option-click (PC: Alt-click) the Eye icon to hide all of the other layers. The sky portion of the windows is transparent (**Figure 20.27**).

Option-click (PC: Alt-click) the Eye icon again to show the hidden layers.

A new sky

STEP FOUR

Once again, highlight the Lamp Light layer. Bring in the sky by choosing File > Place in Photoshop CS3. Go to the download folder and highlight 2272-026.CR2. Click Choose. The RAW file opens in Camera Raw. For now, leave the adjustments as they are. Click Open. The sky opens in Photoshop in Free Transform. Click the Constrain Proportions link, then highlight the Width field and enter 35%. Click inside the bounding box and move the clouds until they fill the window. Click the Commit checkmark or press Enter (**Figure 20.28**). The sky is magically filled with darker clouds. The shot looks a lot better now.

Parallelism redux

By now you know how I feel about those skewed verticals. As with most things Photoshop, there's more than one way to do the job. Earlier I showed the Lens Correction filter. This time it's straight to Free Transform.

STEP ONE

Highlight the Interior layer. Hold down Command (PC: Ctrl) + Option (PC: Alt) + Shift + E to copy all of the visible layers to a new layer. Name it Final. Press Command (PC: Ctrl) + R to show the rulers, then Command (PC: Ctrl) + ; to show the guides. Click inside the vertical ruler on the left of the image and drag a guide to the dark wood that goes up to the ceiling at the right of the print. Drag another line out to the top right edge of the frame toward the middle of the glass doors, then draw a third line to the top left of the dark wood at the edge of the table in the foreground at left (**Figure 20.29**).

FIGURE 20.29

STEP TWO

Press Command (PC: Ctrl) + T for Free Transform. Hold down the Control key and click (PC: right-click) inside the image and choose Distort from the contextual menu. Click on the lower right-hand corner and begin dragging to the right while holding down the Shift key. Continue dragging until the glass door support appears centered through the guide. Adding the Shift key constrains the distortion horizontally. Click on the lower left corner, add the Shift key, and drag to the left until the wooden frame is parallel to the guide. Adjust the right corner until the door frame is parallel to its guide. Finally, click the Commit checkmark to apply the transformation.

The reflection on the print is gone, the lighting is balanced, the once blown-out sky has dramatic clouds with patches of blue, and the verticals are parallel (**Figure 20.30**). Our work here is done.

FIGURE 20.30

CHAPTER 21

Interior Nuances

A LOT OF WORK goes into preparing a room for photography. A room that looks great to the eye often doesn't work at all when viewed through the camera. In this chapter, the *Notebook* looks at photographing another interior and the nuances involved, first for the camera and later on in Photoshop.

For the Camera

Club room entertainment center

The room looks inviting and well appointed to people actually in it. That isn't how the camera sees it. The camera has no visceral experience, no feelings about what's going on when it enters the room. It's not distracted by conversation, music, video, or the antics of those in the room. It records the reality of what is, through a monocular and often unkind point of view (**Figure 21.1**).

FIGURE 21.1

Tripods for interiors

Always use a tripod when photographing interior spaces. Three good things happen. The first is that the camera position is locked down so the angle of view never changes. To see why this is important, shoot ten frames, putting the camera down between each shot. You'll see that as repeatable, steady camera supports, humans are great creatives. Second, the tripod holds the camera steady so small apertures and their required long shutter speeds can be used to have more of the scene in focus in front of and behind the actual point of focus. (This is called depth-of-field.) Finally, using a tripod improves photographic composition by actually placing the camera exactly where it has to be to make the best photograph.

I shoot interiors with the camera tethered to an Intel Core 2 Duo laptop running either Lightroom or Bridge into an external hard drive (Chapter 3). The Grid or Content view shows me the evolution of the photograph. Each time an element in the room is moved, another exposure is made. After each one, I study it on the laptop's screen, zooming in with the Loupe tool to check focus critically.

Photo furniture arranging

Clients are often surprised by the amount of furniture rearrangement a photograph requires. This club room in a condominium conversion is a great example. First, the sofa had to be pulled toward the camera to create a foreground element (**Figure 21.2**).

Next, the sofa is pushed to the left to fill the composition.

The new position made the cushions look huge, so they were removed for the photograph. The coffee table also came toward the camera, then to the left. Looking at the scene from any other angle, the room was awkward and wrong. It looked great from the camera (**Figure 21.3**).

When making photographs, the only angle that counts is the camera's.

Once the composition is satisfactory, the final exposures are made and copied back to the laptop from the external hard drive for a backup. I open the final image in either Lightroom's Develop module or Adobe Camera Raw 4 to check the focus, exposure, and color (Chapter 13). I also look for problems I can fix on the set. This is almost always the best choice, rather than making repairs in Photoshop. The final photograph isn't final until the camera is moved.

No matter how intently I study the photograph on the screen sometimes, obvious things slip by.

FIGURE 21.2

FIGURE 21.3

In Photoshop

Interior refinements

This interior has five post-production modifications. Four that I knew about when I made the exposure and one I missed completely. Do you see the one I missed that would have been a super easy fix at the location?

- The bright window.

- The HVAC vent on the right wall.

- The vertical lines that get wider from the bottom to the top of the photograph.

- The blank television screen.

And the one I did not see...

- The burned-out bulb in the entertainment center's alcove to the right and behind the coffee table. Arrghhh!

Begin the projects for this chapter by downloading the files from amesphoto. com/learning. The book code is DPN8414.

Navigate to the folder in Bridge, highlight the thumbnail for 2276-083.CR2, and press Command (PC: Ctrl) + R to open it in Camera Raw. The settings are included in the accompanying XMP file and are shown in **Figure 21.4**.

Place the RAW file into the new Photoshop document by either clicking on the Workflow Options hyperlink at the bottom of the Camera Raw dialog box and checking Open in Photoshop as Smart Objects, or if you see Open Image displayed, hold down the Shift key to change it to Open Object and then click it.

The sample file containing the paths for this exercise is at the native resolution of my camera, 4992 x 3328 pixels. If you would prefer to work with the supplied paths, open the file 2276-083.psd instead. The RAW file for the next step has been placed. There are also the final layers for you to reference.

FIGURE 21.4

Window light

The light coming through the curtains is distractingly bright. I'll begin this enhancement by making it darker.

STEP ONE

Right-click on the layer 2276-083 then choose New Smart Object via Copy. Name the layer Window Light.

STEP TWO

Press S to select the Color Sampler tool. Click on a bright area on the curtain to place a sample point. Hold down the Option (PC: Alt) key then click the Recovery slider. Drag it to the right until the colors in the curtains over the window disappear. Lower the Exposure to -1.20, the Brightness to 50, and then move Clarity up to 68. The window has a bluish colorcast. Move the Temperature slider to the left until it reads 4800. The sampler readouts in the example are R: 229, G: 222, B: 219. The color of the light through the curtains is a warm tone, similar to those in the room. Click OK.

STEP THREE

Draw a path around the sheer curtains. Click the Paths tab to show the Paths palette. Double-click the Work Path and name it Window in the Save Path dialog box. Click OK.

The Pen tool is Photoshop's most powerful selection tool. If you haven't gotten comfortable with this formidable and editable selection tool yet, the paths are already in the PSD version provided in the downloads for this chapter.

FIGURE 21.5

STEP FOUR

Command-click (PC: Ctrl-click) the path named Window. It is loaded as a selection. Feather the selection (Command [PC: Ctrl] + Option [PC: Alt] + D) .7 pixels. Click the Layers tab. Click on the Add Layer Mask icon at the bottom of the Layers palette. The window is darker and warmer. There is a little bit of blue on the window sill, a hint to the viewer that the great outdoors lies beyond (**Figure 21.5**).

Vent removal

HVAC vents are very important to properly ventilate a room. Photographically, they are an eyesore. This one has to go away. Fortunately, architectural interiors are allowed a certain amount of artistic license.

STEP ONE

Copy the two visible Smart Object layers to a new layer by holding down the Command (PC: Ctrl) + Option (PC: Alt) + Shift keys, then tapping E. Name the new layer Retouch.

STEP TWO

Make a new layer above that one by clicking the Add New Layer icon at the bottom of the Layers palette. Name the layer Vent Cover.

The keyboard shortcut is Command (PC: Ctrl) + Shift + N. It opens the New Layer dialog box with the name field highlighted for adding a new name. Adding the Option (PC: Alt) key to the shortcut will bypass the New Layer dialog box.

FIGURE 21.6

STEP THREE

Draw a selection on the wall to the right of the vent with the Rectangular Marquee tool (**Figure 21.6**).

FIGURE 21.7

STEP FOUR

From the Edit menu, choose Define Pattern.... Name the pattern Vent Cover, then click OK (**Figure 21.7**). Press Command (PC: Ctrl) + D to deselect.

STEP FIVE

Draw a path around the vent from under the painting to the edges of both sides and around the sofa. Save the path as Vent Cover.

The path Vent Cover is also available in the Paths palette if you'd rather not draw your own.

STEP SIX

Command-click (PC: Ctrl-click) on the path Vent Cover to make it into a selection. Choose Select > Modify > Feather.... Feather the selection .7 pixels. (Yes, the Feather command has moved in Photoshop CS3. The shortcut is still Command [PC: Ctrl] + Option [PC: Alt] + D. Mac users: If this brings up the Dock, see page 15.)

STEP SEVEN

Choose Edit > Fill. Pick Pattern from the Use menu. Now choose Vent Cover from the Custom Pattern menu. Choose Large List from the Custom Pattern flyout menu to display a thumbnail and the pattern's name (**Figure 21.8**).

STEP EIGHT

Fill the selection with the pattern at 100% Opacity. The vent is covered up with a step-and-repeat pattern. It doesn't look so good right now. Hang in there 'cause, of course, there's more (**Figure 21.9**).

STEP NINE

Deselect. Click the Lock Transparent Pixels icon at the top of the Layers palette. Select the Healing brush from the toolbox. Heal the seams created where the pattern sections met. Finally, sample some of the light areas on the adjacent wall to the right of the vent and heal them into the pixels covering the vent to give it that "faux" look. Work at 100% view when retouching. That shows all of the pixels in the file. Check carefully that there are no repeating patterns in the healing. That is a tell that Photoshop has been in play on the photograph.

Heal the seams almost all the way to the edge of the shadow cast by the painting's frame (**Figure 21.10**).

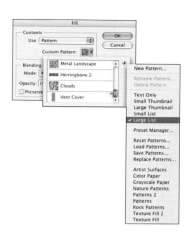

FIGURE 21.8

FIGURE 21.9

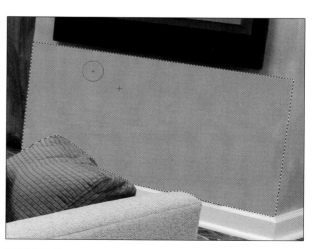

FIGURE 21.10

FIGURE 21.11

STEP TEN

Add a layer mask to Vent Cover. Choose the Brush tool. Set it to 0% Hardness, 20 pixels, and 100% Opacity. Press D to set the default colors, then press X to make the foreground color black. Paint on the layer mask under the painting to bring back the shadow (**Figure 21.11**).

If you reveal part of the vent, press X to exchange the colors then paint over the vent to cover it back up.

Dark alcove

The alcove light under the lower right corner of the television screen is burned out. Unfortunately, I didn't notice it at the time I made this photograph. If I had, it would have been simple to shoot the exposure, then take a bulb from one of the other alcoves and replace the burned-out one. It could have been so much easier to shoot a second photograph with the formerly dark alcove lit, and then painted it into the original scene in Photoshop. I should have been seeing more deeply at the time.

Would'a, could'a, should'a. The fact remains I didn't see it so here's how to solve it in post-production.

The solution lies in knowing as much as possible about the tools in Photoshop. Knowing they are there and what they can do is a great resource, even if you aren't a master of every one of them. Has anyone mastered them all? If the answer is "yes," do they have a life?

Perspective

The real problem is perspective. The camera angle makes the alcove under the television's left side larger than the one that has a burned-out bulb. Cloning or making a copy and then moving from the left one to the right will look wrong. Free Transform is an option. There is a better one in Photoshop's Filters menu.

STEP ONE

Highlight the Retouch layer. Press Command (PC: Ctrl) + Shift + N to open the New Layer dialog. Name the layer Alcove.

STEP TWO

From the Filter menu choose Vanishing Point, or press Command (PC: Ctrl) + Option (PC: Alt) + V to open the Vanishing Point preview/dialog box. Zoom in to View Actual Pixels (100% magnification) by pressing Command (PC: Ctrl) + + until the View menu in the lower left corner reads 100%. Hold down the Spacebar to scroll inside of the filter the same way you do in Photoshop. Move to the alcove under the lower left corner of the television. The Create Plane tool (C) is selected by default. Click on the upper left-hand corner of molding around the alcove. Move the cursor to the upper right-hand corner. Hold down the X key to zoom in temporarily while placing the cursor on the corner. Click to set the second point of the plane. Move to the lower right corner. Click to place the third point. Finally, move the cursor to the lower left corner and click to complete the plane (**Figure 21.12**).

FIGURE 21.12

Hold down the X key to zoom in for precise point placement. Release it to return to the selected magnification.

STEP THREE

Select the Edit Plane tool (V). Click on the center handle at the top of the alcove grid. Drag it out. Repeat this for the left side and bottom. Finally, drag the right side handle out until it covers the dark alcove (**Figure 21.13**).

FIGURE 21.13

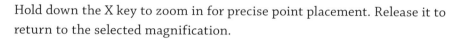

FIGURE 21.14

STEP FOUR

Click the Marquee tool (M) then draw a selection around the edges of the molding around the lighted alcove. The selection is drawn in the perspective of the alcove in the photograph (**Figure 21.14**). The left side is taller than the right.

STEP FIVE

Hold down the Option (PC: Alt) key. Click inside the selection and drag toward the dark alcove. A copy of the lighted one moves inside the selection, sizing down in perspective. Align the edges over the dark alcove. Release the mouse button. The lighted alcove now covers the dark one. Click OK (**Figure 21.15**).

The in-perspective smaller copy of the lighted alcove is placed on the layer Alcove.

The lighted alcove copied in perspective in Vanishing Point overlaps the coffee table.

FIGURE 21.15

STEP SIX

Hide the layer Alcove. Draw a path around the dark alcove down to, and then around, the edges of the table that cover part of it. Click the Paths tab. Name the Work Path Alcove.

The path has already been drawn for you to use if you prefer not to make your own.

VANISHING POINT IN PERSPECTIVE

The Vanishing Point filter was new to Photoshop CS2, and it was improved in CS3. Its job is to do the "impossible"—retouching in perspective. The filter works based on a perspective grid you draw. Blue grids are good working ones. Yellow grids are marginal, and red ones are not useful for accurate work in perspective. Cloning, healing, selecting, copying selections, and moving them in perspective are just some of the features available in Vanishing Point (**Figure 21.16**).

The Vanishing Point toolbox

- Edit Plane tool (V)
- Create Plane tool (C)
- Marquee tool (M)
- Stamp tool (C)
- Brush tool (B)
- Transform tool (T)
- Eyedropper tool (I)
- Measure tool (R)
- Hand tool (H)
- Zoom tool (Z)

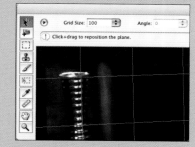

FIGURE 21.16

Each tool's function, and tips on how to use it, displays in the info bar below the flyout menu's disclosure triangle.

Vanishing Point will also do all of its work to a transparent layer located just above the layer being edited in the layer stack. Make the layer active to take advantage of this most useful feature.

Vanishing Point keeps objects in perspective around corners, too. Take the time to explore this amazing tool.

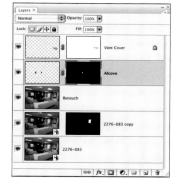

FIGURE 21.17

STEP SEVEN

Show the Alcove layer by clicking its Eye icon. Make the path named Alcove into a selection by Command-clicking (PC: Ctrl-clicking) its thumbnail in the Paths palette. Feather the selection .3 pixels. Remember, Feather has moved. It's in the Modify menu, under Select. Finally, click the Layers tab, then click the Add Layer Mask button at the bottom of the Layers palette. The table covers the lit alcove instead of vice versa (**Figure 21.17**).

The layer mask hides the parts of the layer covering the table edges. The dark alcove now shines in its new light, completing this part of the post-production (**Figure 21.18**).

FIGURE 21.18

Diverging verticals

Anytime the camera is not dead level, vertical lines in the photograph will either converge or diverge, depending on whether the camera is pointed down or up, respectively. This drives artists who draw or paint, as well as architects, nuts. They *know* that the vertical lines of a square or rectangle are parallel and draw or render them appropriately. And as you have become aware through the course of reading the *Notebook*, it's one of my pet peeves as well. The problem is that the camera is happily oblivious to the obvious—geometrically speaking, of course.

Stand in the middle of a set of train tracks (not while a train is coming). The farther away they go, the closer together they get until they merge at the vanishing point.

Look up at a four-story or taller building. The top looks narrower than the base. It isn't really. What you see in both situations is perspective. Were the building tall enough, its sides would merge at the vanishing point (like the railroad tracks). No problem. Except that in the extreme, the diverging verticals make a building or a room look like something's wrong.

Lens Correction redux

STEP ONE

Click the layer thumbnail of Vent Cover to activate it. Now hold down the Command (PC: Ctrl) + Option (PC: Alt) + Shift keys and tap E. This keyboard shortcut copies the visible layer to a new layer. Rename the layer Vertical Lines.

STEP TWO

Vertical Lines is now the active layer. Before making any corrections, I like to be sure the camera was level in the first place. Press Command (PC: Ctrl) + R to show the rulers. Press Command (PC: Ctrl) + T to enter Free Transform. The reference point is shown in the exact center of the image. Choose the Move tool (V)—although any tool will work—click on the vertical ruler at the left edge of the document window, then drag a guide out until it snaps to the center of the reference point. Tap the Escape (Esc) key to close Free Transform without applying it.

The guide shows the center of the image. Verticals running through the center of a photograph made with a level camera will follow the guide exactly. The edge of the alcove to the left of the guide is very close to the center. It is close enough to being the photograph's true vertical. This is good to know (**Figure 21.19**).

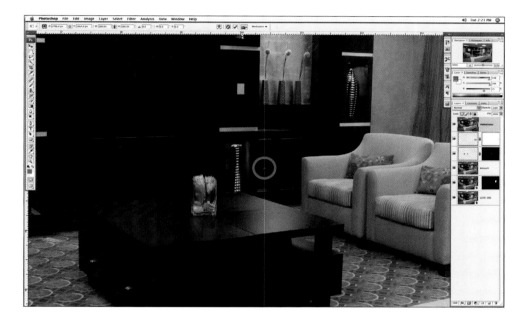

FIGURE 21.19

Note: If the "true" vertical isn't close to being parallel with the guide, make that the first correction in the Lens Correction Filter shown in the next step. Choose the Straighten tool (A). Draw a line along the vertical nearest the center line. The filter will rotate the preview.

STEP THREE

Select Filter > Distort > Lens Correction. The default color of the grid is gray. It's a little hard to see against the dark wood. Double-click the color swatch at the bottom right of the dialog box. The Color Picker dialog opens. Set R: 0, G: 255, B: 0 and then click OK. The grid turns an almost overpowering green. Set 72 as the size of the grid. That's better. Enlarge the view to 100% by choosing either View Actual Pixels or 100% from the preview size menu at the bottom left of the dialog. Tap M to activate the filter's Move Grid tool.

Click and drag the grid until one of the verticals lines up with the left edge of the alcove. It doesn't quite line up. Press A for the Straighten tool. Draw a line from the top of the alcove's vertical to the bottom. Release the mouse. The preview rotates .73°. Not much at all and, okay, I'm picky. I admit it.

Choose the Fit in Window view. Use the Move Grid tool to realign the grid with the alcove's left edge.

STEP FOUR

Move the Vertical Perspective slider to the right. The preview rotates along a horizontal axis. This movement is almost exactly what tilting the back of a view camera does. Move the slider until the entry field reads +27. The left edge of the entertainment center and the vertical of the wall to the right of the painting (above where the vent was) are now almost parallel to the grid. The center line is still aligned with the grid (**Figure 21.20**).

As when tilting the view camera's back, the top of the image shrinks. There is a fix inside Lens Distortion for the effect. I prefer to use Free Transform to finish the task.

FIGURE 21.20

STEP FIVE

Zoom back to the Fit in Window view (Command [PC: Ctrl] + 0). Drag a guide out from the left side, then line it up with the left edge of the entertainment center. The top is still not quite parallel.

STEP SIX

Enter Free Transform. Right-click in the image and select Distort from the contextual menu. Drag the upper left handle of the bounding box to the left until the left edge of the entertainment center is parallel with the guide.

STEP SEVEN

Right-click inside the photograph again and choose Scale from the menu. Click the middle handle on the left edge of the bounding box. Drag it to the right until the overlap is gone. Scroll to the right. Do the same thing with the center handle on the right side of the bounding box. Finally, drag the top center handle up until the image below is covered (**Figure 21.21**).

FIGURE 21.21

FIGURE 21.22

STEP EIGHT

Hide the guide by pressing Command (PC: Ctrl) + ;. Now hide and reveal the Vertical Lines layer to see what a great difference parallel verticals make (**Figure 21.22**).

Television, Photoshop-style

Entertainment centers have televisions. TV screens with nothing on them are black holes of emptiness that unfailingly draw the eye...especially in photographs. This section is about adding television content using Photoshop's Smart Objects, the Type tool, some layer styles, and Free Transform. Creating a custom television image is a bit of work that gives you control over the screen and helps avoid potentially uncomfortable legal issues to boot!

Making content

STEP ONE

With Vertical Lines highlighted in the layer stack, click the Go to Bridge icon and double-click the thumbnail of the Massai girl (1814-3692.tif) to open her photograph in Photoshop. Choose the Move tool (V) and drag it onto the club room document. It appears in the layer stack above Vertical Lines. Rename the layer TV Screen. Choose Group into New Smart Object from the Layers palette's flyout menu.

STEP TWO

Press Command (PC: Ctrl) + T to call up Free Transform for the TV Screen layer. Drag the reference point from the center to the upper left corner handle. Click inside the image, then drag it until the corner with the reference point is over the upper left corner of the television screen. Release the mouse. Hold down the Option (PC: Alt) key and drag the lower right handle to the lower right corner of the screen. This move sets the initial position of the image in the screen (**Figure 21.23**).

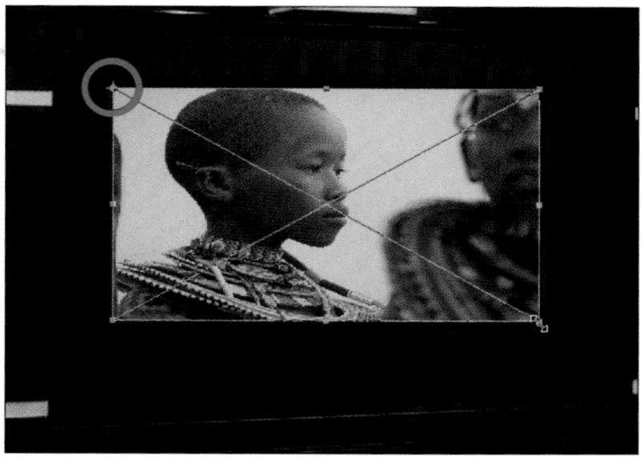

STEP THREE

Zoom in to a 100% view (actual pixels) with the shortcut Command (PC: Ctrl) + Option (PC: Alt) + 0. Click the Warp icon in the Free Transform Options bar. It's just left of the Cancel Transform icon (**Figure 21.24**).

Click and drag each corner of the photograph to the corresponding corner of the screen. Finally, drag the handles from each corner until they intersect the edges of the bounding box. The warp function tucks the image into the screen exactly.

When the direction handles line up with the lines of the warp box, the edges of the image are aligned with those of the screen (**Figure 21.25**). Click the Commit checkmark to accept the changes.

Network news

The photograph in the screen is nice. Adding a couple of newsy graphics will seal the believability deal.

STEP ONE

Double-click the foreground color to open the Color Picker. Enter R: 255, G: 255, and B: 0. Click OK.

Yellow becomes the foreground color. Choose the Type tool (T). Select Helvetica Regular as the font and 24-point for the size. Click inside the photograph and type Live. Click the Commit checkmark. Press Command (PC: Ctrl) + T for Free Transform. Drag the reference point over the lower

FIGURE 21.23

FIGURE 21.24

FIGURE 21.25

FIGURE 21.26

left corner formed by the letter L. Click inside the bounding box and drag it until the reference point is on the top edge of the screen. Hover the cursor outside the bounding box's lower right handle. It turns into the Rotate cursor. Click and drag the cursor until the baseline of the word Live aligns with the edge of the screen (**Figure 21.26**).

STEP TWO

In the Transform Options bar, click the Constrain Proportions link and enter 60% in the W field. Click the Commit Transform checkmark.

STEP THREE

Dress up the slug by double-clicking the text layer to open the Layer Style dialog box. Click the words Drop Shadow. The Drop Shadow section of the dialog is displayed. The Blend Mode is Multiply at 75% Opacity. Set the angle to 124°, then click the Use Global Light checkbox. Set the Distance to 5, the Spread to 0, and the Size to 5.

FIGURE 21.27

Click the word Stroke. Double-click the Color box to open the Color Picker. Set R: 0, G: 0, B: 255 as the color. Enter 2 into the Size field. Set the Position to Outside, the Blend Mode to Normal, and the Opacity to 100%. Click OK to close the dialog and apply the changes. Finally, drag the type into the screen as shown in **Figure 21.27**.

STEP FOUR

Choose the Polygonal Lasso tool (L + Shift + L). Draw a selection similar to the one in **Figure 21.28**.

STEP FIVE

Create a new layer named Location Slug. Choose a dark blue from the Swatches palette. I used R: 0, G: 0, B: 255. Press Option (PC: Alt) + Delete (PC: Backspace) to fill the selection with blue. Click the Add Layer Mask icon at the bottom of the Layers palette. Choose the Linear Gradient tool by pressing G and clicking the first gradient in the Options bar. Set white as the foreground color. Click the top edge of the selection and drag straight down, half again more than the height of the selection (**Figure 21.29**).

The layer mask makes the bottom of the slug partially transparent.

FIGURE 21.28

STEP SIX

Choose the Type tool (T). Set the tool's color to white and the font size to 8 points. Enter Amboseli, Kenya. Click the Commit checkmark. Use the Move tool (V) to drag the type toward the left edge of the slug (**Figure 21.30**).

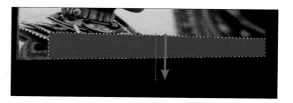

FIGURE 21.29

STEP SEVEN

Make a new layer named Final. Copy the visible layers to it by holding down the Option (PC: Alt) key, then choosing Merge Visible from the Layers palette's flyout menu. Hide all of the layers except the Background and Final layers. Hide and then show Final to see the before and after images of this project. Save your work.

That's it. The club room's photography and post-production is finished and the entertainment center is, well, entertaining (**Figure 21.31**).

FIGURE 21.30

FIGURE 21.31

Index

Soundtrack

Photography and music go together. I can't imagine shooting to silence. On set, art directors, clients, models, assistants, wardrobe stylists, and makeup artists all participate in creating the playlist for the mood of the day. Everyone constantly shares her or his favorite new artist, song, or album they've brought on their iPod.

Book writing, too, has a rhythm, melody, and harmony. Over the years, a lot of artists have provided the music that shaped the shoots portrayed in this book and, therefore, my writing, as well. Some are well known, some aren't. All have been inspirations. I thought I'd share....

The Blow, The Fray, Snow Patrol, The Raconteurs, Cat Power, Corinne Bailey Rae, Don Henley, Fatboy Slim, Silversun Pickups, Plain White T's, Peter Bjorn and John, My Chemical Romance, Modest Mouse, The Bravery, White Stripes, Satellite Party, Gnarls Barkley, The Ataris, Smashing Pumpkins, Nirvana, The Chevelles, Weezer, Foo Fighters, Blink 182, Nirvana, The Killers, Jimmy Buffett, John Phillips, Mason Williams, Sigur Rós, The Knack, The Beatles, Pink Floyd, Led Zeppelin, Franz Ferdinand, Elvis, Norah Jones, Three Doors Down, Train, The 5, 6, 7, & 8s, 311, Jimmy Eat World, R.E.M., U2, The Rolling Stones, Steppenwolf, Neil Diamond, Joan Jett, Placebo, Poe, The Police, Portishead, Morphine, Cocteau Twins, Bobby Vinton, Red Hot Chili Peppers, Rickie Lee Jones, Sister Hazel, Barenaked Ladies, Collective Soul, Guster, Billy Joel, Pearl Jam, Zwan, Yes, Styx, Queen, No Doubt, Cake, Cardigans, Garbage, Chicago, Chumbawamba, Alanis, Morissette, The Association, Coldplay, Counting Crows, Sheryl Crow, David Bowie, Dire Straits, Mark Knopfler, Donovan, The Hollies, The Guess Who, Dirty Vegas, Eminem, Jerry Vale, Cream, Fuel, Filter, Gorillaz, The Laura Glyda Band, The RZA, Heart, Hole, James, The James Gang, Vengaboys, Jane's Addiction, The Violent Femmes, John Mayer, Angie Aparo, The Lemonheads, Live, Massive Attack, Madonna, Simon and Garfunkel, Sinéad O'Connor, Natalie Imbruglia, Prodigy, Radiohead, Tal Bachman, Kayla Taylor, Stone Temple Pilots, The Thorns, Van Morrison, Wyclef Jean, Pink, Janis Joplin, and Warren Zevon, to name a few.

Let me know what you are listening to by posting an iMix to the iTunes Store then sending me a link by clicking the *tell a friend* link. My email address is kevin@amesphoto.com.

Colophon

The Digital Photographer's Notebook spanned Photoshop versions 7, CS, CS2, CS3 (Extended), Adobe Camera Raw (ACR) versions 1 through 4, Bridge and Bridge CS3, as well as Lightroom versions 1 and 1.1. These applications run on Apple Power Macintosh G4 Dual 1.42 GHz and G5 Dual 2.0, 2.7, and Quad 2.5 GHz computers with Apple 20- and 23-inch Cinema Displays. Color management is with X-Rite Eye One Photo for calibration monitors and print output. X-Rite (Gretag-Macbeth) Color Checker charts provided accurate color references. The actual writing was done using Microsoft Word running on various Macintosh PowerBook G4 laptops over the years, and it was completed on a MacBook Pro using a wireless keyboard and Mighty Mouse. The photographs were made with Kodak DCS 760 and SLR/n in the early years, then with Canon 1DS Mark II, 5D, and 20D cameras. Book production was carried out with Macintosh computers. Page layout was done using InDesign CS2. The text was composed in Univers ƒ, Geometric Med Black-Bitstream, Chaparral Pro, and European Pi ƒ. The book was printed on 60# Influence Matte paper on Man Roland presses at Courier Kendalville.

the digital photographer's notebook

A Pro's Guide to Adobe Photoshop CS3, Lightroom, and Bridge

IN THE WORLD OF DIGITAL PHOTOGRAPHY, inspiration can come at any time. Great images are created behind the camera and then refined at the computer. "Photographers live in the moment when shooting, and I believe we do the same when in front of the monitor," writes Kevin Ames, veteran photographer and Photoshop master. Building on his popular column in *Photoshop User* magazine, Kevin expands the scope of the original articles to include in-depth information about all aspects of digital photography.

With this book, you'll gain a focused and thorough under-standing of Adobe's suite of digital photography applications—Photoshop CS3 (including the Camera Raw plug-in), Lightroom, and Bridge. You'll learn which application is best for a given task and see how they come together to allow you to work efficiently—all while creating and delivering stunning photographs. Whether dealing with workflow, organization, or truly creative enhancements, Kevin candidly shares his personal image-making process from start to finish. In addition, there are clear and illuminating explanations of many issues relevant to the digital photographer, such as the profound differences between RAW and JPEG. Whether you've been shooting digital for years or you're just making the switch from film, *The Digital Photographer's Notebook* is an essential guide to managing your portfolio and creating head-turning photographs.

If you're serious about Photoshop and photography, this book will definitely make you "see the light"!

—Scott Kelby
Editor and Publisher, *Photoshop User* magazine

Peachpit Press
www.peachpit.com

Book Level: Intermediate/Advanced
Computer Book Shelf Category: Digital Photography
Cover Design: Aren Howell, **Cover Images:** Kevin Ames

US $39.99 CAN $45.99 UK £28.99
ISBN-13: 978-0-321-35841-7
ISBN-10: 0-321-35841-4

9 780321 358417

5 3 9 9 9